Definitive Guide
to LEGO® MINDSTORMS™,
Second Edition

DAVE BAUM

Apress™

Definitive Guide to LEGO® MINDSTORMS™, Second Edition

Copyright ©2003 by Dave Baum

ISBN (pbk): 1-59059-063-5

Printed and bound in the United States of America 2345678910

Trademarked names may appear in this book. Rather than use a trademark symbol with every occurrence of a trademarked name, we use the names only in an editorial fashion and to the benefit of the trademark owner, with no intention of infringement of the trademark.

Technical Reviewer: Rodd Zurcher

Editorial Directors: Dan Appleman, Gary Cornell, Jason Gilmore, Simon Hayes, Karen Watterson, John Zukowski

Managing Editor: Grace Wong

Copy Editor: Ami Knox

Compositor: Diana Van Winkle

Illustrators: Rodd Zurcher, Tony Jonick

Indexer: Ann Rogers

Cover Designer: Kurt Krames

Production Manager: Kari Brooks

Manufacturing Manager: Tom Debolski

Marketing Manager: Stephanie Rodriguez

Distributed to the book trade in the United States by Springer-Verlag New York, Inc., 175 Fifth Avenue, New York, NY, 10010 and outside the United States by Springer-Verlag GmbH & Co. KG, Tiergartenstr. 17, 69112 Heidelberg, Germany.

In the United States, phone 1-800-SPRINGER, email orders@springer-ny.com, or visit http://www.springer-ny.com. Outside the United States, fax +49 6221 345229, email orders@springer.de, or visit http://www.springer.de.

For information on translations, please contact Apress directly at 2560 Ninth Street, Suite 219, Berkeley, CA 94710. Phone 510-549-5930, fax: 510-549-5939, email info@apress.com, or visit http://www.apress.com.

The information in this book is distributed on an "as is" basis, without warranty. Although every precaution has been taken in the preparation of this work, neither the author nor Apress shall have any liability to any person or entity with respect to any loss or damage caused or alleged to be caused directly or indirectly by the information contained in this work.

The source code for this book is available to readers at http://www.apress.com in the Downloads section.

For Jessica and Jason

CONTENTS AT A GLANCE

CONTENTS

Part One
Fundamentals ... 1

Chapter 1
Getting Started ... 3

Chapter 2
The RCX . . . 17

Chapter 3
Introduction to NQC . . . 35

Chapter 4
Construction . . . 65

Part Two
Robots ... 91

Chapter 5
Tankbot ... 93

Chapter 6
Bumpbot ... 105

Chapter 7
Bugbot . . . 117

Chapter 8
Linebot . . . 143

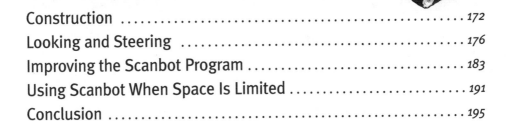

Chapter 9
Dumpbot ... 161

Chapter 10
Scanbot ... 171

Chapter 11
Tribot ... 197

Chapter 12
Onebot ... 205

Chapter 13
Steerbot ... 213

Chapter 14
Diffbot ... 233

Chapter 15
Brick Sorter . . . 247

Chapter 16
Vending Machine . . . 259

Chapter 17
Communication . . . 279

Chapter 18
Using the Datalog . . . 295

Chapter 19
Roboarm . . . 313

Part Three
Appendixes . . . 349

Appendix A:
MINDSTORMS Sets . . . 351

Appendix B:
Supplementary Parts . . . 359

Appendix C:
Programming Tools . . . 363

Appendix D:
NQC Quick Reference . . . 367

Appendix E:
Online Resources . . . 381

ABOUT THE AUTHOR

Dave Baum received a bachelor of science degree in mathematics and computer science from the Massachusetts Institute of Technology. When LEGO released the MINDSTORMS Robotics Invention System in 1998, Baum was able to combine two of his favorite interests: LEGO and computer programming. He developed Not Quite C (NQC), a powerful language for programming MINDSTORMS robots that has been widely accepted by advanced users, and then went on to write the best-selling *Definitive Guide to LEGO MINDSTORMS*. When not playing with LEGO, he is a Distinguished Member of the Technical Staff at Motorola Labs.

ACKNOWLEDGMENTS

The instructions for assembling robots are a critical part of this book. I explored a number of options before settling on using 3-D renderings. My initial concern about 3-D renderings was that creation of accurate 3-D models is a difficult and time-consuming business. Actually, the hard part was modeling the individual pieces. Once the pieces themselves were created, putting together an entire robot out of them was quite simple. I would like to thank Rodd Zurcher for creating all of the 3-D pieces, as well as taking care of most of the 3-D rendering process and serving as a sounding board for all of my ideas. Rodd also served as a technical reviewer for the second edition of the book. Rodd's attention to detail is what makes the renderings come alive, and I can honestly say that this book would not exist without his enormous contributions.

I would like to thank my wife, Cheryl, for being supportive and understanding throughout this project. Like most things, writing a book turned out to be a lot more work than I first assumed, but Cheryl never once complained about the significant amount of time I was spending on it.

Rodd's wife, Amy, was equally supportive. Thank you for putting up with the late-night calls and visits as Rodd and I sorted through the details of the book.

I would also like to thank Apress founders Gary Cornell and Dan Appleman for giving me the opportunity to create this book. Thank you for your encouragement and patience.

Dan's feedback during the early stages of writing helped establish the style for the entire book. Dan also led the technical review team for the first edition, which included Idan Beck and Eddie Herman. Their efforts ensured that I presented things appropriately to novices and experts alike.

Last, I'd like to thank my parents for buying LEGO sets for me in the first place.

PREFACE TO THE SECOND EDITION

MINDSTORMS users are a diverse group of people. Some are experienced LEGO builders who are ready to move up from the LEGO Technic sets, but don't know very much about programming. Others are professional software developers who have not touched a LEGO brick in years (or perhaps ever). I originally wrote *Definitive Guide to LEGO MINDSTORMS* as a kind of MINDSTORMS class. It uses a project-based approach to teach a lot of construction and programming techniques.

When Robotics Invention System (RIS) 2.0 was later released, I was reluctant to update the book. To be honest, the majority of the information in the first edition was still valid, and the topics presented were still relevant. However, after a while it became clear that RIS 2.0 provided a lot more power—especially in the realm of LEGO's programming language, RCX Code. Many programs that were difficult, or even impossible, to create with earlier versions of RCX could be easily accommodated with the 2.0 software. Improvements to RCX's firmware also enabled some new programming techniques when using NQC.

Once I decided to update the book, the big question was *how much* to update. I thought of numerous new projects and ideas that could be incorporated into a new book, but too much of that would make the book more of a sequel than an update. Instead, I decided to preserve most of the content of the book and keep my changes focused on the new programming capabilities introduced with RIS 2.0. As a result, most of the existing RCX Code programs have been rewritten, and several new RCX Code programs have been created. In addition, several of the NQC programs have been updated to take advantage of features in the RCX 2.0 firmware. Finally, it had been getting more and more difficult to obtain the special parts for Steerbot (which I discuss in Chapter 13), so I redesigned the robot to use parts from only the RIS set itself. While I was at it, I also decided to switch from using a bumper to using the light sensor for proximity detection.

Hopefully, owners of RIS 2.0 sets will find this book just as useful and instructive as earlier readers found the first edition to be.

PREFACE TO THE FIRST EDITION

The MINDSTORMS Robotics Invention System from LEGO is a new kind of toy. True to its heritage, it contains a generous assortment of LEGO pieces that snap, slide, and click into place with amazing simplicity. Nearly all of the pieces can interlock with one another, sometimes in rather unusual ways. What sets MINDSTORMS apart, however, is LEGO's programmable brick, the RCX. Sensors and motors can be attached to the RCX (again with LEGO's hallmark simplicity), and suddenly the RCX brings a LEGO model to life. It not only moves, but also senses and responds to its environment.

Robotics itself is nothing new. Industrial robots have been in use for years and are constantly getting more sophisticated. Likewise, hobbyists have been able to build their own robots for quite a while. Even so, creating robots (even simple ones) has been out of reach for most people. The problem was that constructing robots typically involved soldering, metalworking, and other skills, along with a healthy dose of computer programming. MINDSTORMS has changed all of that. No soldering is required, nor any welding, cutting, or gluing. Even programming has been made easier—a graphical interface allows commands to be "stacked" together almost as easily as LEGO bricks themselves.

MINDSTORMS is an exciting toy. With it, children can learn mechanical design, engineering, and computer programming while they are playing. MINDSTORMS has equal appeal to adults. As a result, MINDSTORMS robots are popping up everywhere—not just in classrooms and toys stores, but also at conventions, trade shows, and even around the office. This is a good thing. Somewhere along the way many adults forget how important it is to just play, and MINDSTORMS is a nice reminder.

Of course, MINDSTORMS only made the process of building a robot easier; designing robots is still a challenging blend of mechanical engineering and computer programming. This can leave many people a little overwhelmed and asking "What do I do now?" That is where this book comes in. Perhaps you're an expert LEGO builder but have never programmed a computer. Or perhaps you just finished writing The World's Most Complicated Computer Program, but you don't know the first thing about gear ratios. Either way you'll find material in this book to guide you through creating MINDSTORMS robots.

Part One covers all of the basics needed to create MINDSTORMS robots. Chapter 4 is especially valuable because it describes a variety of essential construction techniques. Since "hands-on" experience is the most effective form of learning, Part Two, which details how to construct robots, makes up the bulk of the book. In it, step-by-step instructions for building and creating an assortment of robots are provided. Each of the robots demonstrates some interesting construction and/or programming techniques. Together the chapters in this section can almost be considered a course in MINDSTORMS Robotics.

Many of the robots can be built using only the parts contained in the MINDSTORMS Robotics Invention System. However, in several cases some extra parts are required. Often, this is because the purpose of the robot is to demonstrate some feature that can only be achieved with such extra parts. A complete list of extra parts required, including which robots use which ones and where to obtain them, can be found in Appendix B.

You will also need some means of programming the robots. Two different options are presented in the book: RCX Code and NQC. RCX Code is the programming language supported by the official software included with the MINDSTORMS Robotics Invention System. NQC is a free, alternative development system. It is attractive for those who are more comfortable with a traditional approach to programming, require more power than RCX Code provides, or want to program their robots using something other than a computer running Windows. (NQC runs under a variety of operating systems including Windows, MacOS, and Linux.)

The most important thing is to have fun. MINDSTORMS is about playing. There will also be plenty of learning, because you learn through playing, but the key is to play. Experiment with the different robots and change them around. Take things apart and try building them a different way. Change the programming slightly and see what happens. Decorate your robot in your own personal style. Above all, have fun.

Part One
Fundamentals

Chapter 1
Getting Started

Welcome to *Definitive Guide to LEGO MINDSTORMS*. This book represents a journey through the exciting world of LEGO MINDSTORMS. We'll start slowly at first, introducing basic concepts and techniques, then proceed to constructing and programming a number of different robots. By the end of the book, you'll be well prepared to build your own robotic creations.

If you haven't yet played with your LEGO MINDSTORMS Robotics Invention System, you should take a few moments now to open it up, read through the first several pages of the *Constructopedia,* and take care of the mundane tasks such as installing batteries. In addition, if you are using a computer running Windows, you should install the RIS 2.0 software on your computer.

This chapter introduces the RCX (the brains inside a MINDSTORMS robot) and the programming environments featured in this book. A simple test program will be created, then downloaded and run on the RCX. This test program serves as a convenient way of controlling a motor for some of the examples in subsequent chapters.

This chapter assumes that the IR tower—included in the LEGO MINDSTORMS set—is already hooked up to your computer. When communicating, the IR transmitter and the RCX should face one another, about 6 inches apart. Communication can be adversely affected by direct sunlight or other bright lights. If communication between the IR transmitter and the RCX is unreliable, try adjusting the position of the RCX and shielding it from unwanted light.

ROBOTICS INVENTION SYSTEM

This book assumes that you are using the Robotics Invention System 2.0 set (RIS 2.0), which includes the RCX, two motors, three sensors, a USB-based IR tower, RIS 2.0 software, and about 700 assorted LEGO pieces. Most of the projects in the book can be built with the pieces included in the set, and the programs were designed to illustrate various features of the RIS 2.0 software. Earlier versions of the RIS set differ from 2.0 in several ways:

- **RIS software**—The RIS software has continually evolved, with each version bringing more power and features. Several of the projects in this book rely on features introduced with the RIS 2.0 software, so you will not be able to complete those projects if you are using an older version of the software. In addition, the 2.0 software has a completely different appearance, so even in the cases where the project could be completed using 1.0 or 1.5, the resulting program will look much different from the illustrations in the book. Fortunately, LEGO has made the RIS 2.0 software available as an upgrade (RIS 2.0 Upgrade Kit, #3805). If you are planning on using the RIS software, I strongly recommend purchasing this upgrade.

- **IR tower**—RIS 2.0 uses a USB-based IR tower, while the older sets feature an IR tower that connects to a serial port. From the standpoint of this book, it doesn't matter which kind of tower you use.

- **LEGO pieces**—Lego made several changes to the pieces included with RIS between the 1.0 and 1.5 versions. For 2.0, they simply added one piece to those already included with 1.5. The projects in this book generally stick to the pieces common to all three RIS sets.

- **RCX**—For RIS 2.0, the printed label on the RCX was changed from "1.0" to "2.0". Other than that cosmetic change, the RCX included in RIS 2.0 is identical to its RIS 1.5 predecessor. The RCX included in RIS 1.0 sets had an additional difference: it featured a connector for an optional external power supply.

- **Firmware**—The RCX has its own little operating system, which is known as *firmware*. RIS 2.0 includes updated firmware (referred to as the 2.0 firmware) that adds new features to the RCX. If you are using RIS 1.0 or RIS 1.5, then you can still obtain the 2.0 firmware and install it on your RCX (details on this are provided later in the chapter).

SOFTWARE

Programs for the RCX are created on a personal computer (called the *host computer*), then downloaded to the RCX. The RCX can then run these programs on its own without further intervention from the host computer. There are a number of different programming environments that can be used to create RCX programs.

The software included with the Robotics Invention System can be used to write programs in *RCX Code,* which is an easy-to-use, graphical programming environment. Although limited in functionality, RCX Code does provide a friendly, intuitive way for beginners to start programming the RCX.

Not Quite C (NQC) is a more traditional, text-based computer language that can also be used to program the RCX. Versions of NQC for Windows, MacOS, and Linux can be downloaded from the NQC web site: http://www.baumfamily.org/nqc. NQC takes a little longer to learn, but it provides more power and flexibility.

RCX Code and NQC are the two languages featured in this book. Sample code is usually provided for both languages, although in a few of the more complex cases only an NQC example is appropriate. Descriptions of some other programming environments can be found in Appendix C.

The next few sections will guide you through the installation and use of NQC. If you do not plan on using NQC at all, you can skip to the section titled "The START Program" later in this chapter.

When the RCX is powered up for the first time, a special piece of software called *firmware* must be downloaded to the RCX. This firmware provides a sort of operating system for running your own programs. RIS 2.0 includes an updated version of firmware that adds some new features to the RCX.

If the RCX's display looks like Figure 1-1, firmware has not yet been downloaded. Once it is loaded, the RCX will remember the firmware even when it is turned off. The easiest way to download the firmware to the RCX is to run the RIS software. However, if you do not wish to run the RIS software at all, then you can use NQC to manually download the firmware.

Figure 1-1.
Firmware-needed display

The firmware file can be obtained several ways. The exact name of the file depends on its version number. As of this writing, the current 2.0 firmware file is firm0328.lgo; however, it is conceivable that a newer firmware version will be available in future products.

If the RIS 2.0 software has been installed on your computer, then the firmware is located in a folder underneath the RIS 2.0 software. For example, if you install RIS 2.0 into its default location, then the firmware is at C:\Program Files\LEGO MINDSTORMS\RIS 2.0\script\firmware\firm0328.lgo.

Another option, for those without access to a computer that can run RIS 2.0, is to download the beta version of the RCX 2 Software Development Kit (SDK) from http://www.legomindstorms.com/sdk2beta. The downloaded file is a ZIP archive that contains, among other things, the needed firm0328.lgo file.

Once you have obtained the 2.0 firmware, you can use NQC to download it to the RCX. There are actually several different NQC programming tools, and each of them has different ways of downloading firmware. Details are provided in the "Using BricxCC," "Using MacNQC," and "Using NQC for Windows" sections later in this chapter.

NQC QUICK START

NQC is a textual computer language. Programs are written in an editor, then compiled and downloaded to the RCX. The NQC compiler is primarily available as a command line tool. This means that it must be invoked by typing the proper commands into a *command shell* (such as command.com or cmd.exe in Microsoft Windows). Integrated Development Environments (IDEs), which provide a program editor and a graphical user interface to the NQC compiler, exist on some platforms. Bricx Command Center (BricxCC) is one such IDE that runs under Microsoft Windows, and MacNQC is a Macintosh-based IDE (links for these, and several other IDEs, may be found on the NQC web site). IDEs make using NQC a bit easier and more friendly, and they are, in general, the preferred solution where available. One important point, however, is that all of these solutions use the exact same language to specify an NQC program. For example, a program written with BricxCC can also be used with the Linux version of the NQC compiler. Quick Start information is provided for three different versions of NQC: BricxCC, MacNQC, and NQC for Windows.

Using BricxCC

If you are planning on using a USB IR tower (such as the one included in RIS 2.0), then LEGO's driver for the tower must be installed before NQC can use it. The best way of getting the driver installed properly is to simply install and run the RIS 2.0 software and follow its instructions.

The latest version of BricxCC can be downloaded from http://hometown.aol.com/ johnbinder/bricxcc.htm. To install BricxCC, simply run the downloaded application. After installation, a **Bricx Command Center** folder will have been added within the **Start** menu's **Programs** folder.

When you launch BricxCC it will display a dialog box that allows you to specify how your IR tower is connected to your computer. If you are using a USB tower, then it will be connected as **USB1** (the other USB ports are only useful if you have multiple USB IR towers connected to the same computer). If you are using a serial IR tower, then you should select the name of the COM port the tower is connected to. You can also select **Automatic,** which tells BricxCC to search all available ports looking for the IR tower.

This startup form also allows you to specify which kind of programmable brick you are using. Select **RCX2** since that will allow your program to use all of the new features from the 2.0 firmware. If BricxCC has trouble communicating with the RCX, it will display an error and let you try again. If you click **Cancel,** BricxCC will still start, but those functions that require communication with the RCX (such as downloading a program) will be disabled.

If you get tired of seeing the startup form every time you start BricxCC, select **Edit ➤ Preferences,** and then click on the **Start Up** tab. You can then choose default values for BricxCC and specify what it should do on startup.

Once started, BricxCC will show two windows: the main window and a floating **templates** window. The **templates** window is a sort of cheat sheet for remembering the various NQC commands. For our present example we can ignore it.

If firmware has not been previously downloaded to the RCX, it should be downloaded now. Select menu item **Tools ➤ Download Firmware** and choose the firmware file to download. A progress bar will appear while the download is in progress (it will take a few minutes). Once this is completed, the RCX will be ready to use.

Select menu item **File ➤ New** in the main window to create a new NQC program. Inside the program's window enter the following text:

```
task main()
{
}
```

This is an extremely simple NQC program. It does nothing. That won't stop us from compiling and downloading it to the RCX, though. Select the menu item **Compile ➤ Download,** which will compile the program and download it to the RCX. (If BricxCC was not able to communicate with the RCX at startup, then **Download** will be disabled.) If any errors were encountered during compiling, you may click on the error messages to see the offending program line. If no errors were present, a sound from the RCX will confirm that the program was indeed downloaded.

That's all there is to editing, compiling, and downloading NQC programs with BricxCC. You can now skip to the section titled "The START Program."

Using MacNQC

The latest version of MacNQC is located at http://homepage.mac.com/rbate/MacNQC/. Refer to that web page for specific instructions on downloading and installing MacNQC. The instructions that follow are for version 3.0a4 of MacNQC, which is the latest version as of this writing.

If you are planning on using a USB IR tower with an operating system other than Mac OS X, then you will need to install a driver and some libraries from LEGO, collectively known as the GhostAPI. These can be downloaded from http://mindstorms.lego.com/mac. First run the **LEGO USB Tower 1.0 Installer** to install the driver. Second, copy the files named **GhostAPI**, **Port Rs232 Classic**, **Port USB Classic**, and **Protocol Session Classic** from the GhostAPI **Binary** folder into either your **Extensions** folder or the folder that contains the MacNQC application. You will then need to reboot your computer in order for the driver to be loaded.

When you first start MacNQC you will need to tell it how the IR tower is connected to your computer. This can be done from the **Communications** tab of the **Preferences** dialog box, which presents a list of any available serial ports and USB IR towers. If you are using a USB IR tower, make sure you plug it in before opening the **Preferences** dialog box. If you are running Mac OS X, then USB support works best when Classic is not running (otherwise Classic and OS X fight for control over the IR tower). Therefore you should make sure that Classic has been stopped (this can be done from the **System Preferences** dialog box).

You also need to tell MacNQC that you want to write programs for an RCX, and that you want all of the 2.0 features enabled. To do this, go to the **Compiler** table of the **Preferences** dialog box, and select **RCX 2** in the **Target** pop-up menu.

If you need to download firmware to the RCX, select **Download Firmware** from the **RCX** menu. You will be prompted to choose a firmware file, which will then be downloaded to the RCX (you should have already obtained the firmware—perhaps from http://www.legomindstorms.com/sdk2beta).

When you launch MacNQC, it will create an untitled window in which you can enter a new program. If this window has been closed for some reason, you can create a new program by selecting **New** from the **File** menu. Inside this window type the following text:

```
task main()
{
}
```

It isn't much of a program, but it will at least allow you to familiarize yourself with the process of creating an NQC program. To compile and download this program to the RCX, select **Compile and Download** from the **Program** menu. If you made a mistake typing in the program, one or more errors will be shown; otherwise, MacNQC will attempt to download the compiled program to the RCX. The RCX will play a sound to confirm that the program was successfully downloaded. If you do not hear the confirmation sound, then verify that the correct serial port or USB tower has been selected in the **Preferences** dialog box.

That's all there is to editing, compiling, and downloading NQC programs with MacNQC. You can now skip to the section titled "The START Program."

Using NQC for Windows

If you are planning on using a USB IR tower (such as the one included in RIS 2.0), then LEGO's driver for the tower must be installed before NQC can use it. The best way of getting the driver installed properly is to simply install and run the RIS 2.0 software and follow its instructions.

In order to use NQC under Windows, the NQC command (nqc.exe) must be put in a location where the command shell can find it. One solution is to create a single folder containing the NQC command and the programs you create. Download the latest version of NQC from the NQC web site and unzip the downloaded file using a utility program such as WinZip or PKZIP. The resulting folder will have a long name such as "nqc-win-2-2-r2". It is a good idea to move this folder to a convenient location and give it a shorter name. The remaining instructions assume that the folder has been named "nqc" and is located at the top of drive C.

The next step is to start a command shell. Under Windows 95, 98, and ME, select **Run** from the **Start** menu, type "command" (without the quotes), and press the <return> key. For Windows NT, 2000, and XP, type "cmd" instead of "command". This will create a window in which you may type commands. First we need to tell the command shell to work inside the NQC folder. The folder that the command shell is working in is called the *current directory*. Type the following command and hit the <return> key to instruct the command shell to use the NQC folder as the current directory:

```
cd c:\NQC
```

If you see an error message, then double-check the spelling and location of the NQC folder that was created on your hard disk.

By default, the NQC command assumes that a serial IR tower is being used and that it is connected to the first serial port, COM1. If a different serial port or a USB tower is used, then any NQC commands should start with an option of the form -Sport, where port is the name of a serial port or the word "usb". The examples that follow assume that a USB IR tower is being used, thus they all include the option -Susb.

If firmware has not been previously downloaded to the RCX, you will need to download it now. The NQC command has a special option for doing this, but you must tell it where to find the firmware file. The upcoming examples assume that the firmware file is named firm0328.lgo and has been copied to the same folder that NQC is being run from. The command to download firmware is:

```
nqc -Susb -firmware firm0328.lgo
```

The download will take several minutes to finish, but once it is completed, the RCX will be ready to use.

To create an NQC program we need to use a text editing program. Windows comes with a very simple editor called *Notepad*. Use the following command to create a program called trivial.nqc.

```
notepad trivial.nqc
```

Since trivial.nqc doesn't exist yet, Notepad will ask if you want to create the file; click **Yes** in the dialog box. In Notepad's window, type the following text:

```
task main()
{
}
```

After entering the text, select **File ➤ Save** in Notepad's menus. Then click on the command shell window and type the following command:

```
nqc -Trcx2 -Susb -d trivial.nqc
```

This will invoke the NQC compiler, instructing it to compile the program you just created, and download it to the RCX. The -Trcx2 option instructs NQC that you are using an RCX and want all of the 2.0 features enabled. If NQC prints any error messages, check the trivial.nqc program and make sure it reads exactly like the listing just shown. If you need to change the program, simply edit it in the Notepad window, then save the changes and compile again. To compile and download a different program, replace trivial.nqc with the other program's name.

As mentioned before, nqc.exe must be put in a place where the command shell can find it. Our current solution is to keep nqc.exe in the same folder as the programs we are writing (such as trivial.nqc). Another option is to copy nqc.exe to some other folder that is already in the *command path*. The command path is a list of directories that the command shell searches when looking for commands. You can display the command path by typing the following command:

```
PATH
```

This will print a list of directories separated by semicolons. For example, on my computer I see the following:

```
C:\WINDOWS;C:\WINDOWS\COMMAND
```

This means that two directories are searched: C:\WINDOWS and C:\WINDOWS\COMMAND. If I copy nqc.exe to either of these two directories, the command shell will be able to find it regardless of what the current directory is set to. Another option would be to add C:\NQC to the search path.

THE START PROGRAM

Our program will be quite simple; the goal is to start a motor running, then flip the motor's direction each time a touch sensor is pressed. Before writing the program, however, we need to hook up the touch sensor and motor to the RCX, as shown in Figure 1-2.

Figure 1-2.
Connecting the RCX

There is something odd about this picture—all of the wires have been cut! For such a simple illustration it would have been possible to show the actual wires, but as the number of motors and sensors increases, these wires become a rat's nest and it is impossible to tell which wire goes where. To make the illustrations clearer, each end of the wire is labeled with either a number or a letter indicating the input or output port on the RCX that the wire will be connected to. For example, the wire attached to the motor is labeled "A", indicating that it should connect to output A. (The labels on the ends attached to the RCX are somewhat redundant.)

Now we're ready to write the program. Don't worry if you don't understand it—explanations will follow later. For now, we are just concentrating on how to use the RCX itself. If you are using RCX Code, create and download the program shown in Figure 1-3.

Figure 1-3.
Getting Started program in RCX Code

If you are using NQC, compile and download the following program:

```
// start.nqc - a very simple program for the RCX
task main()
{
    SetSensor(SENSOR_1, SENSOR_TOUCH);
    On(OUT_A);

    while(true)
    {
        until(SENSOR_1 == 1);
        Toggle(OUT_A);
        until(SENSOR_1 == 0);
    }
}
```

Once the program is downloaded, you can start it by pressing the **Run** button. The LCD should show an animated rendition of a running person, and the motor should start spinning. If this is not happening, check the program and your connections.

If you look carefully, you should also see a small triangle in the LCD above output port A. There are two such indicators for each port, one for the forward direction and one for reverse. This allows you to easily determine which motors are currently running (and in which direction).

If you press the touch sensor, a small triangle will appear on the LCD display just below the sensor's connector. This triangle indicates that the sensor has been activated. Although these indicators are displayed regardless of the type of sensor being used, it is most meaningful with a touch sensor. Pressing the touch sensor will also cause our program to respond—specifically, it will reverse the motor's direction. You can continue to press the touch sensor; each time it will flip the motor's direction either from forward to reverse or from reverse to forward.

The program can be stopped by pressing the **Run** button. Stopping a program in this way will also automatically stop any motors that are running.

THE VIEW BUTTON

By default, the RCX normally displays the value of its internal clock, called the *watch*. Time is displayed in hours and minutes and is reset to oo.oo whenever the RCX is turned on. The RCX is also able to display the current reading from a sensor or the status of a motor. The **View** button is used to cycle through these various display modes. When a sensor or output port is being viewed, a small arrow appears on the LCD pointing to the port that is being monitored.

Pressing the **View** button once will switch from displaying the watch to displaying sensor 1. Assuming that the touch sensor is not currently being pressed, the display will read 0. Pressing the touch sensor will change the displayed value to 1.

Pressing **View** three more times will display the status of output A. Assuming that the motor isn't presently running, the status will be 0. If you run the program (hence starting the motor), the display will then show a value of 8. The RCX can run the motors at 8 different power levels, and the number 8 indicates that the output is at full power.

The **View** button can also be used in conjunction with the other buttons to control a motor. If the **View** button is held down and the display is presently showing an output's status, the **Run** button will turn the output on in the forward direction and the **Prgm** button will turn the output on in reverse. The output will remain on only while the **Run** or **Prgm** button is being held down.

Let's start at the default display mode by turning the RCX off, then back on. The display should be showing the watch (00.00), and the motor should be stopped. Press the **View** button four times, but do not release it on the fourth press. While still holding the **View** button down, try pressing the **Run** or **Prgm** buttons to activate the motor.

ATTACHING MOTORS

Wires are attached to the RCX using a special square connector. There are four ways that a wire may be attached to such a connector (the wire may come from the front, right, back, or left). For sensors, the orientation of the connector makes no difference whatsoever. For motors, it determines in which direction the motor spins (clockwise or counterclockwise) when the RCX activates the output in the forward direction.

In our example, the wire extends down from the RCX output port and sits within the groove along the top of the motor. In this orientation, the motor will spin clockwise when the output is activated in the forward direction. You can verify this by running the sample program again. If you have trouble telling which way the motor is spinning, attach a large wheel to it. Try changing the orientation of the connectors on the RCX or the motor and observe how it is possible to make the motor spin counterclockwise.

When building a robot, it is often helpful to change the orientation of the wires so that the output's forward direction corresponds to some obvious motion for the robot itself (moving a vehicle forward, raising an arm, etc.).

DEBUGGING

Sometimes a robot doesn't behave as expected. Isolating the cause of the problem and solving it is called *debugging*. Some common items to check during the process of debugging are presented here:

■ Verify that all motors and sensors are correctly wired to the RCX. For motors, not only must the wire attach to the correct output port, but the orientation of the wire at both ends must also be correct; otherwise, the motor's rotation may be reversed.

■ Use the **View** button to monitor a sensor's value as the program is being run. Verify that the actual sensor values match what the program expects to see. For example, when using a light sensor, be sure that the readings are consistent with any thresholds set in the program. When using touch sensors, verify that they are being pressed and released as expected; sometimes the sensors do not get pushed in firmly enough and will not have the expected value.

■ Use the **View, Run,** and **Prgm** buttons to manually activate each of the robot's motors. Verify that the motor turns in the correct direction and that any mechanisms driven by the motor are operating properly.

■ For RCX Code programs, verify that the correct sensor number is selected within the various program blocks. In some cases the RCX Code software will automatically pick the correct sensor, but sometimes it guesses wrong. When using touch sensors, it is also important to make sure that the code blocks have the correct icon for the button being either pressed or released.

■ Often, it is important to figure out if (or when) the RCX is executing certain parts of your program. Adding instructions that either play sounds or display a certain value can help you keep track of a program's progress as it is running.

MOVING ON

Now that you know how to write and download a program to the RCX, we can proceed to more interesting material. Before moving on, however, I'd like to leave you with a few pieces of advice.

All of the programs shown in the book may be downloaded from the Apress web site: http://www.apress.com. In many cases you will find it easier (and less error-prone) to use the downloaded programs, rather than reproducing them manually. On the other hand, you will probably learn a bit more if you enter the programs yourself.

The RCX tends to have a voracious appetite for batteries, so the use of rechargeable batteries is strongly recommended. In general, NiMH or rechargeable alkaline cells (such as Rayovac Renewal batteries) perform much better than NiCad rechargeables.

Another battery-saving measure is to run the robots on a smooth surface such as wood or tile, rather than on carpeting. Motors must work much harder to propel a vehicle across carpet, resulting in slow-moving robots that consume batteries rapidly.

The MINDSTORMS Robotics Invention System contains a large number of pieces, including many small ones with very special purposes. Finding the correct piece can become a tedious task and distract from the overall process of building and experimenting with a robot. Thus, I find it helpful to keep the pieces sorted and to store them in small, multicompartment plastic containers such as those used to store assorted hardware or fishing tackle.

Now, on to the next chapter, which explains what the RCX is and what it can do.

Chapter 2
The RCX

At the heart of every LEGO MINDSTORMS robot is the LEGO programmable brick—the RCX, shown in Figure 2-1. Various sensors and motors may be connected to the RCX, allowing it to perceive and interact with the world. There are several different ways to program the RCX, but they all share a set of common functions—namely those of the RCX itself. This chapter describes how the RCX works and what it can do.

Figure 2-1.
The RCX

THE HARDWARE

The RCX is actually a tiny computer based on a Hitachi H8 series microprocessor. This 8-bit CPU provides most of the control logic for the RCX including serial I/O, analog-to-digital conversion, and built-in timers. It even contains 16K of internal ROM, which is preprogrammed with some low-level operating system software.

The RCX also contains 32K of static RAM. Most of this memory is occupied by firmware (discussed later in this chapter) and various system parameters. However, 6K is reserved for "user memory"; this is where the programs you write for the RCX reside. Compared to a desktop computer, 6K sounds too small to be of any practical value. However, within the RCX, programs tend to be only hundreds of bytes long (rather than the millions of bytes for desktop applications); thus 6K is more than adequate.

The RCX also contains special circuitry to interface with the real world. An LCD and four pushbuttons are provided for user interaction. Special driver chips allow the RCX to control motors or other electric devices attached to the output ports, and the internal analog-to-digital converter (ADC) allows the RCX to read its three sensor ports.

The RCX uses infrared light (IR) to communicate with a desktop computer or another RCX. IR communication for the desktop computer is provided by an IR interface (included in the Robotics Invention System), which attaches to a USB port (an older version of the IR tower connects to a standard 9-pin serial port). Many laptop computers (and palmtop devices) already have their own IR port. All IR devices use infrared light for communication, but the protocols they use to communicate can differ widely. Most laptops and other computing devices use the IrDA protocol for communication, while the RCX uses a simpler proprietary protocol. Because of this, a laptop's IR port will not automatically be able to communicate with the RCX. Of course, anything is possible with the right amount of hacking, but as of this writing I know of no general-purpose solution to making a laptop IR port communicate with the RCX.

The RCX is powered by 6 AA batteries (and some older versions can also be powered by an optional AC adapter). How long the batteries last is highly dependent on how the RCX is being used. The biggest drain on the batteries comes from the motors that the RCX must power. When running, motors can consume considerable power, and this power increases when the motor is under great strain. Needless to say, heavy use of the RCX will result in lots of battery changes—using rechargeable batteries is a good idea (I prefer NiMH batteries, but rechargeable alkaline cells will also work well). The firmware and any programs that have been downloaded are remembered even when the RCX is turned off. If the batteries are removed for any significant amount of time, however, this memory will be erased. When you need to change batteries, make sure the RCX is turned off, then quickly remove the old batteries and insert new batteries. As long as you work reasonably fast, the memory will be retained and you will not need to reload the firmware.

FIRMWARE

The RCX has its own operating system, which is split into two parts. The first part is stored in ROM and is always present. The second part is stored in RAM and must be downloaded to the RCX the first time the RCX is turned on. This second part is often called the RCX *firmware*, although technically both parts can be considered firmware. This operating system performs all of the mundane functions such as keeping track of time, controlling the motor outputs, and monitoring the sensors.

 Firmware *is a generic term for software that is built into a device. The term is intended to convey the fact that such software is something in between hardware and the common notion of software.*

When a program is written for the RCX, it does not contain native code for the CPU. Instead, it consists of special bytecodes that are interpreted by the firmware. This is similar to the way Java programs are stored as Java bytecodes that may be then interpreted by a Java Virtual Machine. Using bytecodes, rather than native machine code, allows the RCX to maintain a safe and reliable execution environment for programs. Although it is possible to write and load custom firmware that would completely take over the RCX hardware, RCX programming is often done within the confines of the standard firmware (hereafter referred to as simply the firmware).

Although it is possible to alter the RCX's capabilities with custom firmware, this book assumes that the standard 2.0 firmware is being used. Hence, when the RCX is stated to provide certain functions, what is really meant is that the "RCX with 2.0 firmware" provides those functions.

TASKS AND SUBROUTINES

An RCX program may contain up to ten tasks. Each task is a sequence of bytecodes, which is simply a list of instructions to be followed. Tasks are either active or inactive. When the task is active, the RCX executes the instructions listed for the task. When a task becomes inactive, the RCX no longer executes its instructions. When a program is started, its first task is made active, and any other tasks are inactive. Stopping a program is equivalent to making all of its tasks inactive.

Multiple tasks may be active at the same time, and in this case the RCX switches back and forth between the active tasks, executing a little bit of each one, so as to make it appear that all of the active tasks are running at the same time. This is known as *concurrent execution,* which has both advantages and disadvantages. The advantage is that for functions that are relatively independent, placing them in separate tasks often makes their instructions much simpler. The disadvantage is that if the separate functions need to interact with each other, concurrent execution can lead to some very subtle bugs (see Chapter 7 for an example of this).

A program may also define up to eight subroutines, which are also sequences of instructions to be executed. The difference between a task and a subroutine is that tasks all run concurrently with one another. Subroutines do not run by themselves; they must be called from a task. When called, the subroutine is executed, but the task that called it must wait for the subroutine to complete before continuing with its own instructions. Any task may call any subroutine, but a subroutine may not call itself or another subroutine. Such restrictions limit the usefulness of subroutines in many applications.

OUTPUT PORTS

The RCX has three output ports (A, B, and C), each of which can be in one of three modes: *on*, *off*, or *floating*. The *on* mode is just what it sounds like—any motor attached to the output will be running. In the *off* mode, the RCX turns off the output and the motor will be forced to stop. The *floating* mode is somewhat unusual. In this mode, the RCX is no longer powering the output, but a motor is still allowed to spin freely. In some cases, this will have a much different effect than the off mode. In terms of a car, the off mode is like applying the brakes, while the floating mode is more like coasting in neutral.

Each output also has a direction associated with it: either *forward* or *reverse*. This direction only has effect when the output is on, but the setting is remembered and can even be modified while the output is turned off (or floating). As mentioned previously, the actual direction of a motor's rotation (clockwise or counterclockwise) depends upon how the wires are attached between it and the RCX.

The *power level* of an output may also be adjusted to one of eight settings. Like the direction setting, the power level only has an effect when the output is turned on, but it is remembered and may be altered when the output is turned off. The RCX is primarily a digital device, and digital devices like things to be either on or off, and not "half on" or "three-quarters on." Hence the RCX needs some way to create these intermediate power levels from a digital signal.

One way of doing this is with Pulse Width Modulation (PWM). Instead of turning a signal on and leaving it on, PWM rapidly switches back and forth between on and off, as shown in Figure 2-2. The amount of time that is spent "on" is called a pulse, and the duration of this pulse is called its *width*. The percentage of time that the signal is "on" is called its *duty-cycle*. When using PWM, intermediate levels of power are created by varying the pulse width to generate the appropriate duty cycle.

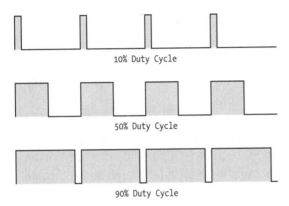

10% Duty Cycle

50% Duty Cycle

90% Duty Cycle

Figure 2-2.
Pulse Width Modulation

In the case of the RCX, the pulses are sent every 8ms. At the lowest power level, the pulse is 1ms long; thus power is supplied only $1/8$ of the time (duty cycle = 12.5%). Higher power levels result in longer pulses, until at the highest power level the pulse actually takes the entire 8ms; in this case power is supplied continuously.

One of the problems with PWM is that instead of continuously supplying partial power, it will instead supply full power part of the time. In many cases this subtle difference has little overall effect. The LEGO MINDSTORMS motor, however, is an exception. These motors were designed to be very power efficient, and they have an internal flywheel that acts as a sort of energy storage tank. The flywheel is most effective when the motor has very little physical resistance (called *load*). Starting the motor consumes a lot of energy since the flywheel must also be spun up to speed. Once running, however, a lightly loaded motor (perhaps a motor that is turning a gear that isn't connected to anything else) can maintain its speed with very little external power. In this case, PWM does not affect the motor very much since the short pulses keep the flywheel spinning, and the flywheel itself keeps the motor spinning when the pulses stop. Under a heavy load (propelling a vehicle across a carpeted surface), the flywheel is less effective, and changing power levels will have a more noticeable effect on speed.

SENSORS

The RCX has three sensor ports, each of which can accommodate one of four different LEGO sensors: touch sensor, light sensor, rotation sensor, and temperature sensor. Sensors are connected to the RCX using the same type of wiring used to connect motors to the RCX output ports.

Each type of sensor has unique requirements for reading and interpreting its values; therefore the RCX must configure each sensor port before it can be used. There are actually two different settings configured: the *sensor type* and the *sensor mode*. The sensor type determines how the RCX interacts with the sensor; for example, the RCX will passively read a touch sensor but must supply power to a light sensor. In general, the sensor type should match the actual type of sensor attached (touch, light, rotation, or temperature).

The sensor mode tells the RCX how to interpret a sensor's values. Some programming languages, such as RCX Code, automatically set the sensor mode based on the sensor type. Other languages, such as NQC, provide the additional flexibility of using any sensor mode with any sensor type (although some combinations are of little practical value).

Every sensor has three separate values associated with it: the *raw value, boolean value,* and *processed value.* The raw value is the actual reading of the sensor's voltage level, converted to a digital number from 0 to 1023 (inclusive). Every 3ms, the RCX reads the raw value for the sensor, then converts it to both a boolean value and a processed value.

Boolean Values

A sensor's boolean value can have one of two values: 0 or 1. Boolean values have their most obvious uses with a touch sensor, but occasionally other sensors can make use of boolean values as well.

The sensor mode includes a special parameter, called the *sensor slope,* which can range from 0 to 31 and determines how the raw value is converted into a boolean value. When the slope is 0, the RCX uses the conversion shown in Table 2-1.

Table 2-1. Boolean Conversion When Slope Equals Zero

CONDITION	RAW VALUE
raw > 562	0
raw < 460	1
460 ≤ raw ≥ 562	unchanged

Note that a high raw vala ue results in a boolean value of 0, while a low raw value is a boolean value of 1.

The cutoff points (460 and 562) represent approximately 45% and 55% of the sensor's maximum value. It is not unusual for the raw values to bounce around by a few points; thus if a single cutoff was used, the boolean value would be susceptible to lots of jitter if the raw value was hovering near the cutoff. This method of reducing the amount of jitter in a boolean signal is called *hysteresis*.

When the slope parameter is nonzero, a different boolean conversion is used. Each time the sensor is read, its raw value is compared to the previous raw value. If the absolute value of this difference is less than the slope parameter, then the boolean value remains unchanged. If this difference exceeds the slope parameter, then the boolean value will be set to indicate whether the raw value increased (boolean value of 0) or decreased (boolean value of 1). Special cases exist at the extremes of the raw value range. This conversion is summarized in Table 2-2.

Table 2-2. Boolean Conversion Using Nonzero Slope

CONDITION	BOOLEAN VALUE
change > slope	0
change < –slope	1
current > (1023–slope)	0
current < slope	1

slope = value of the slope parameter

current = current raw value

change = current value minus previous value

For example, consider the case where the slope is 10, and the initial raw value is 1020. This will result in a boolean value of 0. Let's say the raw value slowly decreases until it is 300. Even though a value of 300 is below the 45% threshold normally used for boolean values, the slope parameter causes the cutoff to be ignored and the boolean value will remain 0. If the raw value suddenly decreases, perhaps to 280 in a single reading, then the boolean value will become 1.

When set properly, the slope parameter can be used to configure a light sensor to ignore moderate variations and detect only abrupt changes. For example, the program in Listing 2-1 configures sensor 2 to be a light sensor in boolean mode with a slope of 10 (more information on sensor types and modes appears later in the chapter). The program plays a high-pitched tone whenever the sensor rapidly goes from dark to light (sensor value equals 1) and a low-pitched tone during a rapid transition from light to dark (sensor value equals 0).

Listing 2-1. NQC Program with a Slope Conversion

```
task main()
{
    SetSensorType (SENSOR_2, SENSOR_TYPE_LIGHT);
    SetSensorMode (SENSOR_2, SENSOR_MODE_BOOL + 10);

    while(true)
    {
        until (SENSOR_2 == 1);
        PlayTone (880, 10);
        until (SENSOR_2 == 0);
        PlayTone (440, 10);
    }
}
```

If you are using NQC and feel like experimenting with the slope parameter, then download this program to the RCX, attach a light sensor to sensor port 2, and run the program. Aim the sensor directly into a bright light, then try blocking and unblocking the light by covering the sensor with your finger. Rapid changes from light to dark (or vice versa) will cause the sensor's boolean value to change and the program will play a tone. Gradual changes such as slowly turning the sensor away from the light will not result in a change to the sensor's boolean value.

Small triangles on the RCX's display (below the sensor ports) indicate when a sensor's boolean value is 1.

Sensor Modes

There are eight different sensor modes, some of which only make sense for certain sensor types. For each mode, a brief description of how it converts raw values into processed values is given in the following sections. The default modes (those automatically selected within RCX Code programs) for each sensor type are also indicated.

Raw Mode

Raw mode is the simplest mode of all. In this mode the processed value of a sensor is always equal to its raw value (an integer between 0 and 1023).

Boolean Mode

When *boolean mode* is selected, the sensor's processed value is set to the boolean value determined by the conversion described previously. For sensors other than the touch sensor, a proper slope parameter is often essential for meaningful boolean values. This is the default mode for a touch sensor.

Edge Count Mode

When *edge count mode* is selected, the RCX counts how many times the boolean value changes value. This count is initially 0 and increments by 1 each time the boolean value changes from 0 to 1 or from 1 to 0. This mode is only useful when the boolean value is meaningful.

Mechanical switches (such as the touch sensor) tend to chatter a bit; that is, they will rapidly turn on and off several times in the process of being pressed or released. The RCX uses a *de-bouncing* process to filter out the chatter (see Figure 2-3). This de-bouncing causes the RCX to ignore edges for 300ms after a transition occurs. This increases the reliability of edge counting for most purposes, but also limits it to detecting edges that are at least 300ms apart.

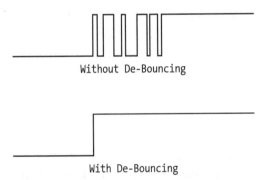

Without De-Bouncing

With De-Bouncing

Figure 2-3.
De-bouncing a sensor

Pulse Count Mode

The *pulse count mode* is similar to the edge count mode except that the counter is only incremented when a boolean value goes from 1 to 0. Like edge counting, the boolean value is de-bounced to eliminate chatter. This mode is ideal for counting the number of times a button is pressed, for example.

Percentage Mode

In *percentage mode*, the raw value is converted into a value between 0 and 100 (higher raw values correspond to a lower percentage value). This is the default mode for a light sensor.

Rotation Mode

Rotation mode uses an algorithm that decodes the special output of the rotation sensor. This mode is the default for the rotation sensor, and it is meaningless when combined with any other sensor type. The resulting value from rotation mode is a cumulative rotation in increments of 22.5 degrees (a value of 16 represents a full revolution).

Celsius and Fahrenheit Modes

Celsius mode uses a special function to convert the raw value into a temperature reading. This function compensates for the specific characteristics of the temperature sensor. *Fahrenheit mode* uses the same function as Celsius mode to convert a raw value into a temperature, but then converts the temperature from Celsius to Fahrenheit.

Internally the RCX multiplies temperature values by 10, so that a value of 22.5 degrees is represented as 225. The LCD, however, will still display the actual temperature (e.g., 22.5). A preference setting in RCX Code development software determines whether Celsius or Fahrenheit mode is used as the default for temperature sensors.

Sensor Types

Sensors provide a mechanism for the RCX to learn about its environment. There are four different types of LEGO sensors, each of which detects a different sort of stimulus. The sensor types, along with short descriptions of how they work, are presented in the following sections.

Touch Sensor

The *touch sensor*, shown in Figure 2-4, is the simplest of the LEGO sensors; it consists of a small pushbutton built into the end of a 2×3 brick. Multiple touch sensors may be connected in parallel—this is when more than one touch sensor is connected to the same input sensor port on the RCX. When used this way, the RCX would be able to detect when any of the sensors were pressed, but would not be able to distinguish which of the sensors was actually pressed. The touch sensor is often used in boolean mode, although edge counting and pulse counting can also be useful.

Figure 2-4.
Touch sensor

Care needs to be taken when attaching a wire to a touch sensor. Only the front four "nubs" have electrical contacts in them. If the wire is over these front contacts, then it can be attached in any direction. However, if the wire connector only overlaps two of the contacts, then it must be in the lengthwise direction as shown in Figure 2-5.

Right　　　　Right　　　　Right　　　　Wrong

Figure 2-5.
Wiring a touch sensor

Light Sensor

The *light sensor*, shown in Figure 2-6, consists of a red light-emitting diode (LED) and a phototransistor that responds to incoming light. It is an active sensor, which means it requires power from the RCX in order to operate properly. The light sensor is typically used in percentage mode, so its values may range from 0 to 100, although values between 40 and 60 are more typical.

Figure 2-6.
Light sensor

A light sensor can be used to measure the amount of light present in a room. For example, if you wanted to build a robot that took some action as soon as a room's lights were turned on, you could add a light sensor to the robot and have it wait until the light sensor's readings were higher than some threshold value. One potential problem is that you need to be careful about the placement of the sensor, since shadows or a small nearby light could fool the light sensor into believing the room is either darker or lighter than it really is.

Another potential problem is that light sensor readings can vary significantly between two different sensors, or even from the same sensor under different conditions. The amount of background light, colors and textures of nearby surfaces, and even the condition of the RCX's batteries can all affect the sensor's reading. Because of this, most programs that use a light sensor will need some adjustment in order to run properly. As the batteries in the RCX get weaker (or old batteries are replaced with new ones), programs that use the light sensor are likely to need further adjustment.

The light sensor responds to light coming from a fairly wide angle. Sometimes it is desirable to limit its detection to light coming from a specific direction. An example would be a robot that wanted to look around and find a bright light. This can be done quite easily by using one or more 1×2 beams to narrow the sensor's field of vision, as shown in Figure 2-7. Black beams work best since they reflect the least amount of light. It is important that the sensor's phototransistor line up with the beam's hole, which is easily accomplished by making the beam and the sensor's bottom flush with one another.

Figure 2-7.
Narrowing the light sensor's field of vision

The previous examples used the light sensor to detect some external light source. Another use for the light sensor is to determine the color of some nearby surface. For example, a robot that sorts bricks by color needs to determine the color of each brick. Dependence on the ambient light in a room can make such a decision very difficult. Fortunately the light sensor contains its own light source (the LED), which allows it to measure reflected light from a nearby surface rather than taking a chance on the room's lighting conditions. For best results, the light sensor should be placed as close as possible to the target surface since this minimizes the influence of external light.

With a proper slope parameter, the boolean-based modes (boolean, pulse count, and edge count) may also be used with a light sensor to detect sudden increases or decreases in light.

Rotation Sensor

The *rotation sensor*, shown in Figure 2-8, is an optional sensor that is not included in the Robotics Invention System. It is an active sensor that only has a meaningful value when used in rotation mode.

Figure 2-8.
Rotation sensor

Unlike the other sensors, which measure things on an absolute scale, the rotation sensor measures relative rotation (its readings are always relative to some base position). By default, the position when the program is started is used as the base position (rotation of 0), but a special command allows you to reset the sensor so that the current position gets used as the base position.

In the base position, the sensor's value is 0. Turning the sensor in one direction will increase the sensor value, while turning it in the other direction will decrease the value. The sensor measures in increments of 22.5 degrees; thus a full revolution in one direction is equivalent to a sensor value of 16.

Gear reduction can be used to increase the accuracy of measurement. In Figure 2-9, a worm gear has been meshed with a 24-tooth gear to provide a 24:1 gear reduction. Placing the angle sensor on the worm gear axle yields $16 \times 24 = 384$ increments per revolution of the 24-tooth gear. The resulting accuracy is better than 1 degree.

Figure 2-9.
Increasing the accuracy of a rotation sensor

Due to technical reasons, the RCX must closely monitor the rotation sensor, otherwise it may miss some rotation and yield incorrect readings. The RCX will reliably measure rotation at speeds up to 1250 revolutions per minute (rpm). This is more than fast enough for the standard LEGO MINDSTORMS motor, which spins at about 350 rpm when unloaded.

Temperature Sensor

The *temperature sensor*, shown in Figure 2-10, is another optional sensor that is not part of the Robotics Invention System. Temperature readings can be made in either Celsius or Fahrenheit degrees. The operational range for the sensor is –20° C to +70° C (–3° F to +157° F). Temperatures outside this range are displayed as 999.9.

Figure 2-10.
Temperature sensor

Due to the slow response of the temperature sensor, it is unsuitable for boolean use with a slope parameter. The temperature sensor also exhibits what is called a *nonlinear* response. What this means is that if you plotted the raw sensor reading versus temperature it would not appear as a straight line. The Celsius and Fahrenheit modes know how to correct for the nonlinearity, but raw and percentage modes do not. As a result, the raw and percentage modes are not very useful with a temperature sensor.

Because the rotation and temperature sensors are not included in the Robotics Invention System, their use is minimized within this book. The rotation sensor is only used once in Chapter 10. The temperature sensor is used for part of Chapter 18. For more information about obtaining these sensors, consult Appendix B.

OTHER CAPABILITIES

The RCX also provides an assortment of other capabilities including sound, timers, variables, and a datalog. A brief description of these additional capabilities follows.

Sound

The RCX contains six built-in sounds that it can play. It can also play individual tones where you specify the frequency and duration of the tone. The RCX allows sounds to be *queued*. This means that a program can request the RCX to play a new sound while a previous sound is still being played. Rather than interrupt the first sound, ignore the second sound, or force the program to wait for the first sound to complete, the RCX will simply add the second sound to the queue of pending sounds. Once the first sound completes, the second sound will begin to play immediately. Of course, the RCX has limited resources, so it cannot queue an unlimited number of sounds—it only provides room to queue eight sounds, in addition to the one currently being played. This means that nine sounds can be requested and played, but if a tenth sound is requested before the first one finishes, the tenth request will be ignored.

When using sounds as a means of debugging a program, it is important to take into account the fact that the sounds are queued. Just because you hear a sound at a certain time doesn't mean the program is currently at the instruction that plays the sound. It is possible that the instruction was executed a little while ago, but because another sound was already playing, the current one was queued and didn't play until much later in the program's execution. Even so, inserting a few sounds into a program is a great way to keep track of when the RCX gets to certain parts of your program.

Keeping Time

The RCX provides a system clock, called the *watch,* which keeps track of the number of minutes since the RCX was turned on. In the default display mode, the LCD shows the current watch time in hours and minutes. Although the watch's current time is available to a running program, most programs require more accurate timing information than can be provided by the watch.

The RCX also provides four *timers,* which measure time in increments of 100ms (^{1}/10th second). The timers are running whenever the RCX is turned on. A program may reset each timer independently at any time. The timers themselves will wrap around to 0 after about 55 minutes.

Variables

The RCX provides 32 storage locations that can be used by a program to store global variables available to all tasks. Each task can have an additional 16 private variables (which are not accessible from other tasks). Each location can store a single 16-bit signed integer (an integer in the range −32,768 to 32,767). The locations are shared across all of the programs and are not reset when changing programs. This makes it possible for one program to store information that will later be used by another program.

   Variables can be assigned nearly any kind of value including constants, timer values, sensor readings, or random numbers. The firmware also provides a set of basic math operations for variables: addition, subtraction, multiplication, division, bitwise AND, bitwise OR, sign, and absolute value.

Datalog

The RCX provides a data logging capability. A program may create a datalog of a fixed size, then add data points to the log. The data points may be sensor readings, variables, timer values, or the system watch. The datalog may then be uploaded to a host computer for analysis or some other function.

   Both the datalog and RCX programs must share the same 6K of user memory (6101 bytes to be exact). Since each data point requires 3 bytes of memory, the largest possible datalog will hold 2033 points. However, a datalog this large would leave no room for any programs.

   The RCX's display includes a datalog indicator, which consists of a circle cut into four quadrants. If no datalog exists, then the indicator remains off. When a datalog is in use, one or more of the quadrants is shown, indicating roughly how much of the datalog is currently filled up. One of the quadrants will be flashing as long as there is still room for additional points. Once the datalog is full, all four quadrants will become solid.

Automatic Power Down

In order to conserve batteries, the RCX will automatically turn itself off after several minutes of inactivity. The amount of time before the RCX turns itself off is called the *power down time* and is initially set to 15 minutes. It is worth noting that the RCX will turn itself off even while a program is running, so in order to run a program unattended for a long time, it is necessary to change the power down time.

The specifics of changing this setting vary depending on the software used to program the RCX. To change this setting from within the RIS software, go to the **Settings** screen, then click on the **Advanced** button. Enter the desired number of minutes for power down time or select "infinity" to disable the automatic power down.

If you are using BricxCC, the power down time can be changed by selecting **Diagnostics** from the **Tools** menu and entering the appropriate time in the dialog box. A time of o minutes indicates that the RCX should never turn itself off.

For MacNQC, select **Miscellaneous Panel** from the **RCX** menu and enter the desired number of minutes in the **Sleep** field. As with BricxCC, a value of o indicates that the RCX should never turn itself off.

CONCLUSION

This chapter discussed the different features of the RCX including tasks, motor outputs, sensors, and timers. The next chapter discusses how to use these features from within NQC. Then, starting with Chapter 5, a series of robots are presented, each demonstrating how these features can be combined to make robots that carry out predefined tasks and respond to their environment.

Chapter 3
Introduction to NQC

This chapter provides an introduction to the NQC programming language. Many of the more commonly used NQC features are presented. For a complete treatment of NQC syntax and commands, refer to the *NQC Programmer's Guide* (downloadable from the NQC web site at http://www.baumfamily.org/nqc).

It is assumed that the reader has already installed NQC (or an NQC-based development environment such as BricxCC) and has already gone through the basic process of creating, compiling, and downloading a program as described in Chapter 1. It also assumes that you are using the 2.0 firmware for the RCX and have enabled the 2.0 features for NQC (by adding -Trcx2 to the command line for NQC or setting the appropriate preference in your development environment).

A SIMPLE PROGRAM

Our first program, shown in Listing 3-1, assumes that there is a motor attached to output A and a touch sensor on input 1. When run, the program will turn on the motor, wait until the touch sensor is pressed, then stop the motor.

Listing 3-1. A Simple NQC Program

```
task main()
{
    SetSensor(SENSOR_1, SENSOR_TOUCH);

    On(OUT_A);
    until(SENSOR_1 == 1);
    Off(OUT_A);
}
```

In general, the amount of white space (spaces, tabs, and carriage returns) doesn't matter in a program, but punctuation is critical. The compiler is also case sensitive, so "On" is not the same as "on."

The first line of the program is a comment. Comments are ignored by the compiler and allow the programmer to provide explanations or annotations to the code itself. There are two types of comments. A single-line comment starts with two forward slashes (//), which cause the compiler to ignore the remainder of the line.

```
// this is a single-line comment

/ NOT a comment - only one slash
/ / NOT a comment - space between the slashes
```

The second type of comment can span multiple lines. It starts with /* and ends with */.

```
/* comment */ no longer a comment

/* this is a multiline comment
    still a comment
    last line */

/* start the comment
    /* <--this is ignored--no nesting
    end the comment --> */
    we are no longer in the comment
*/ <--NOT part of the comment--already ended
```

Which type of comment you use is largely a matter of personal style. I prefer to use the // form most of the time. This allows the use of /* */ to comment out large pieces of code (with their embedded // comments) during testing and debugging.

Programs are built from code blocks (*tasks* and *subroutines*), each of which starts with its type (task or sub), followed by its name and a pair of parentheses (the (and) symbols). The code itself is enclosed in braces (the { and } symbols). The intro_1.nqc program shown earlier contains a single task, named "main," whose structure looks like this:

```
task main()
{
    //...body of the task...
}
```

Every program must contain a task named "main"; this is the task that is activated when the program is run. The other tasks may be named however the programmer desires. Names in NQC must start with a letter or the underscore (_). Remaining characters in the name can be a letter, a numeric digit, or an underscore. For tasks and subroutines, the name must be unique; that is, you cannot use the same name to refer to two different code blocks. NQC also reserves a number of names (called *keywords*) for its own use. A complete list of keywords appears in Appendix D.

A code block (such as a task) contains a list of statements. Each statement is an instruction for the program to do something. Statements must always end with a semicolon (;).

The RCX must be told what sort of sensor is attached to each sensor port. This is done by the SetSensor command, which takes two arguments: the sensor port and the sensor configuration. NQC uses the names SENSOR_1, SENSOR_2, and SENSOR_3 for the RCX's sensor ports. Other names (such as SENSOR_TOUCH) are used to define the different sensor configurations. In this case, sensor 1 is configured for a touch sensor.

```
SetSensor(SENSOR_1, SENSOR_TOUCH);
```

The next statement uses the On command to turn on a motor. NQC uses the names OUT_A, OUT_B, and OUT_C for the RCX's output ports. In this case, output A is turned on.

```
On(OUT_A);
```

Our previous statements were both examples of commands, which always allow execution to continue on to the next statement once their work is complete. Control structures, on the other hand, allow constructs such as loops and conditional tests to be written. Our next statement uses the until control structure, which waits until a condition is true before proceeding. The condition itself must be enclosed in parentheses ((and)). In this case our condition is that the value of sensor 1 (which is the touch sensor) must be equal to 1 (which means it is pressed). When the RCX gets to this statement it will keep checking sensor 1 until the condition is met, and only then will it move on to the next statement.

```
until(SENSOR_1 == 1);
```

Our last statement uses the Off command to turn the motor off.

```
Off(OUT_A);
```

Although our program is very simple, it is built from the same basic elements that all NQC programs are constructed from: tasks, statements, control structures, and conditions. The following sections will explain all of these capabilities in more detail as well as present some of the more advanced features of NQC.

CONTROLLING OUTPUTS

In the previous section we used the On and Off commands to start and stop a motor attached to output A. Since controlling motors (or other output devices such as lights) is one of the primary activities of a program, NQC provides a variety of commands for this.

The commands to control an output's mode are On(*outputs*), Off(*outputs*), and Float(*outputs*). Each of these commands takes a single argument, which must be a set of outputs. NQC uses the names OUT_A, OUT_B, and OUT_C to refer to the three outputs. Multiple outputs may be combined with the + operator, so that a single command can control multiple outputs simultaneously.

```
On(OUT_A + OUT_B);   // turn on outputs A and B
Off(OUT_A);          // turn off A
Float(OUT_B);        // let B "coast"
```

Turning an output on is self-explanatory, but turning an output off is a little more complicated. Take the example of an output that is used to power a motor that in turn propels a vehicle forward. Once the vehicle has started moving it has some momentum. Even if power is no longer applied to the motor, the vehicle may continue to coast for a bit. This is similar to what happens when one is riding a bicycle and stops pedaling. In NQC, this is accomplished by making an output float. It is also possible to control a motor so that it resists any further motion. Returning to the bicycle analogy, this is like applying the brakes. In NQC, this is done by turning an output off.

When an output is on, it can be running in one of two directions: forward or reverse. There are three commands to control direction: Fwd(*outputs*), Rev(*outputs*), and Toggle(*outputs*), each of which takes a set of outputs as an argument. Fwd and Rev set the direction to forward and reverse, respectively. Toggle changes the direction to the opposite of whatever it was previously. Note that these commands can be used even when the output is off (or floating); the direction will then be remembered the next time the motor is turned on.

```
Fwd(OUT_A);  // set A to the forward direction
Rev(OUT_B);  // set B to the reverse direction
Toggle(OUT_A + OUT_B);  // toggle A and B
```

Turning a motor on and setting its direction are so often done together that NQC provides commands combining these actions.

```
OnFwd(OUT_A);  // turn on A in the forward direction
OnRev(OUT_B);  // turn on B in the reverse direction
```

These commands are merely for the programmer's convenience. The preceding two statements are functionally identical to the following sequence of statements:

```
// OnFwd(OUT_A)...
Fwd(OUT_A);
On(OUT_A);

// OnRev(OUT_B)...
Rev(OUT_B);
On(OUT_B);
```

It is also common to turn on a motor for a specified amount of time, then turn it off. The OnFor(*outputs, duration*) command is a convenient way to do this. The duration is specified in hundredths of a second.

```
// turn on OUT_A for 1 second
OnFor(OUT_A, 100);

// same thing, but without using OnFor
On(OUT_A);
Wait(100);
Off(OUT_A);
```

The RCX is also capable of changing the power level of each output. Like direction, the power setting can be set when an output is off and will be remembered for the next time the output is turned on. The command for setting an output's power level is SetPower(*outputs, power*). Outputs are specified just like in all of the other output commands. The power level should be an integer between 0 and 7, where 0 is the lowest power level and 7 is the highest. NQC also defines the names OUT_LOW and OUT_FULL to represent minimal and full power respectively.

```
SetPower(OUT_A + OUT_B, 0);  // set lowest level for A and B
SetPower(OUT_C, 7);  // set highest level for C
SetPower(OUT_C, OUT_FULL);  // set highest level for C
```

When displaying a power level, the RCX adds one to the actual power level; thus the lowest power level is displayed as 1 and the highest as 8.

MISCELLANEOUS COMMANDS

The `Wait(time)` command causes the task to pause for a specified amount of time, which is measured in hundredths of a second.

```
Wait(200);  // pause for 2 seconds
```

The `PlayTone(frequency, duration)` command plays a single tone of specified frequency and duration. Both the frequency and duration must be constants. The duration is measured in hundredths of a second.

```
PlayTone(440, 25);  // play a note for 1/4 second
```

The `PlaySound(number)` command plays one of the RCX's six built-in sounds. The number argument must be a constant between 0 and 5 inclusive. NQC also defines constants representing each of the sound and is shown in Table 3-1.

```
PlaySound(SOUND_CLICK);  // play a sound
```

Table 3-1. Sounds

NAME	NUMBER	TYPE OF SOUND
SOUND_CLICK	0	short click
SOUND_DOUBLE_BEEP	1	two beeps
SOUND_DOWN	2	descending sweep
SOUND_UP	3	ascending sweep
SOUND_LOW_BEEP	4	very low tone
SOUND_FAST_UP	5	fast ascending sweep

The `ClearTimer(number)` command resets a timer's value to 0. The number argument must be a constant between 0 and 3 inclusive, and it specifies which of the four timers to reset. The timers themselves may be read using the `Timer(number)` expression (see the "Expressions" section for more information).

```
ClearTimer(0);  // reset timer 0
```

USING #DEFINE

In our first example we referred to the sensor and motor by the name of the sensor or output port they were attached to (SENSOR_1 and OUT_A). For such a simple program this is fine, but for larger programs it can be a little cumbersome to always remember which sensor and which output to use. Wouldn't it be nice if we could assign our own names to the input and output ports?

NQC provides a preprocessor that allows you to do just that. As its name suggests, the preprocessor works on your program before handing it to the compiler proper. Commands for the preprocessor are called *directives* and always start with a pound sign (#). One of the most powerful directives is #define, which allows you to assign a name to an arbitrary sequence of tokens. Such a definition is called a *macro*. For example, the following line creates a macro called CRANE_ARM that is defined as OUT_A.

```
#define CRANE_ARM  OUT_A
```

Whenever it sees the macro's name, the preprocessor will act as if the definition were used instead. For example, if the program contains

```
On(CRANE_ARM);
```

the preprocessor will act as if the program contained

```
On(OUT_A);
```

Using #define to create more meaningful names for the sensors and outputs makes programs easier to read. It also makes them easier to modify. Let's say you were changing the way your robot was built and, in the process, you moved the crane arm motor from output A to output B. Without a #define, you may have had many references to OUT_A sprinkled throughout your program—all of which would have to be changed to OUT_B. If a #define was used as shown previously, and the rest of the program used CRANE_ARM, rather than referring to OUT_A directly, then the program could be adapted to the new robot simply by changing the macro:

```
#define CRANE_ARM  OUT_B
```

Although the previous example simply defined one name as a synonym for another, macros work just as well if their definition contains several items. For example:

```
#define ALL_MOTORS  OUT_A + OUT_B + OUT_C
On(ALL_MOTORS);  // turn on all motors!
```

Macros can also be defined with a list of arguments. The argument list appears within parentheses, and a comma (,) is used to separate the argument names. For example, the following macro turns one or more outputs on for a specified number of seconds:

```
#define OnForSeconds(outs, secs)  OnFor(outs, (secs)*100)
```

OnForSeconds is a fairly simple macro—all it needs to do is multiply the number of seconds by 100 and then call OnFor.

When defined with an argument list, the macro must be accompanied by the correct number of arguments wherever it is used. This applies even if the #define has an empty argument list.

```
#define OnForSeconds(outs, secs)  OnFor(outs, (secs)*100)

OnForSeconds(OUT_A, 5);  // ok, turn on A for 5 seconds
OnForSeconds;  // ERROR—no argument list!
OnForSeconds(OUT_A);  // ERROR—not enough arguments!

#define OnA()  On(OUT_A)

OnA();  // ok, turn on A
OnA;    // ERROR—no argument list!
```

The definition of OnForSeconds contains parentheses around the use of secs. Without these parentheses the macro could result in some surprising behavior. Consider the following:

```
#define OnForSeconds(outs, secs) OnFor(outs, secs*100)
OnForSeconds(OUT_A, 2+3);
```

At first glance it would appear that output A would be turned on for 5 seconds; however, using a macro results in literal substitution of its arguments into the definition. In this case, OUT_A would be substituted for outs and 2+3 would be substituted for secs, resulting in the following:

```
OnFor(OUT_A, 2+3*100)
```

Because multiplication has higher precedence than addition, the preceding call will turn on the output for 3.02 seconds rather than 5 seconds. Using parentheses within the macro definition avoids this potential problem. An even better solution is to use functions (described later in the chapter) instead of macros whenever possible.

Even so, the macro facilities are so useful that many of the commands and names that NQC provides are actually macros defined internally within the NQC compiler. For example, the until control structure is implemented using the following macro:

```
#define until(cond) while(!(cond))
```

USING SENSORS

The RCX has three sensor ports (labeled 1, 2, and 3), each of which can be connected to a sensor. The RCX has no way of knowing what type of sensor is connected to each sensor port, so an NQC program must contain statements to configure the sensor ports. The primary command for this is SetSensor (*sensor_port, sensor_config*). In NQC, sensor ports are named SENSOR_1, SENSOR_2, and SENSOR_3 (more meaningful names can be assigned using macros as described earlier). The value used for *sensor_config* consists of both sensor type and sensor mode information. NQC predefines the type/mode combinations listed in Table 3-2.

Table 3-2. Sensor Configuration

CONFIGURATION	TYPE	MODE
SENSOR_TOUCH	touch	boolean
SENSOR_LIGHT	light	percentage
SENSOR_ROTATION	rotation	rotation
SENSOR_CELSIUS	temperature	celsius
SENSOR_FAHRENHEIT	temperature	fahrenheit
SENSOR_PULSE	touch	pulse count
SENSOR_EDGE	touch	edge count

For example:

```
// sensor 1 is a touch sensor
SetSensor(SENSOR_1, SENSOR_TOUCH);

// sensor 2 is a light sensor
SetSensor(SENSOR_2, SENSOR_LIGHT);
```

Additional information on the sensor types and modes themselves was presented in Chapter 2.

Several sensor modes (rotation, edge count, and pulse count) measure relative quantities and can be reset using the `ClearSensor(`*sensor_port*`)` command.

```
SetSensor(SENSOR_3, SENSOR_ROTATION);
ClearSensor(SENSOR_3); // reset rotation to 0
```

Unlike the outputs, multiple sensor ports cannot be combined into a single command.

```
SetSensor(SENSOR_1 + SENSOR_2,  IN_TOUCH);  // ERROR!
```

Sensor type and mode may be set individually using the commands `SetSensorType(`*sensor_port, sensor_type*`)` and `SetSensorMode(`*sensor_port, sensor_mode*`)`. The sensor slope (if desired) may be added to the *sensor_mode* parameter.

```
// set up sensor 2 as a boolean light sensor with slope 10
SetSensorType(SENSOR_2, SENSOR_TYPE_LIGHT);
SetSensorMode(SENSOR_2, SENSOR_MODE_BOOLEAN + 10);
```

A sensor is read simply by using its name within an expression. For example, the simple program at the start of this chapter used the following statement to wait for a touch sensor to be pressed:

```
until(SENSOR_1 == 1);
```

Further details on expressions and conditions are given later in the chapter.

USING VARIABLES

Each of the RCX's 10 tasks has its own set of 16 local storage locations. In addition, there are 32 global storage locations (shared across all tasks), for a total of $32 + 16 \times 10 = 192$ storage locations available to a program. NQC uses these locations for a program's variables as well as holding the values of any intermediate calculations needed when evaluating expressions.

The terms *global* and *local* have slightly different meanings when applied to RCX storage locations versus NQC variables. When discussing a storage location, the distinction between global and local locations is simply that global locations may be shared across multiple tasks, while local locations are private to each task. When discussing NQC variables, the meanings are somewhat different. Variables that are declared outside of a task, function, or subroutine are global variables, which means that they can be accessed from anywhere in the program. Variables declared within a task, function, or subroutine are local variables and can only be accessed with the block that declares them. In both cases the variable must be declared prior to its first use. A variable declaration is the keyword int, followed by a comma-separated list of variable names, and terminated by a semicolon (;). Optionally, a variable may be assigned an initial value in the declaration. The program in Listing 3-2 shows how global and local variables may be declared and where they can be accessed.

Listing 3-2. Global and Local Variables

```
int g=1; // g is a global variable, initialized to 1

task main()
{
    int x; // x is a local variable
    while(true)
    {
        int y; // y is another local variable
        // x, y, and g can all be accessed here
    }
    // x and g can be accessed here, y cannot
}

task foo()
{
    // only g can be accessed here
}
```

When NQC compiles a program it must map each variable to a specific storage location. In general, global variables must be mapped to global locations, but local variables can use either global or local locations. It is important to note that NQC still enforces the restrictions for access to local variables even when they are mapped to global locations. In the previous example, task foo would not be able to use variables x and y even if they were placed in global locations.

To maximize the number of variables you can use in a program, it is a good idea to use local variables instead of global ones whenever possible. This gives the NQC compiler the freedom to put the variables in either global or local storage. It can thus try to find the best arrangement of variables.

In some cases, such as within complicated expressions or conditions, NQC must allocate one or more temporary variables for its own use. In general, NQC tries to reuse these temporary variables as much as possible and place them in local locations, but they still deplete the total number of locations available for your own variables. If NQC is unable to assign storage for all of the variables, it will report an error.

Variables may be assigned a value using an assignment statement.

```
int bar;
bar = 7;   // set the value of bar to 7
```

There are also several variants of the assignment operator that allow a variable to be operated on arithmetically.

```
bar += 7;  // add 7 to bar
bar -= 3;  // subtract 3 from bar
bar *= 5;  // multiply bar by 5
bar /= 2;  // divide bar by 2
```

Although the preceding examples used constant integers on the right-hand side of the assignment, any legal expression may be used (see the following section).

EXPRESSIONS

The simplest expression is an integer constant. Constants are interpreted as decimal values unless they are preceded by 0x, in which case they are interpreted as hexadecimal values.

```
bar = 10;    // set the value of bar to 10
bar = 0xa;   // also set the value of bar to 10
```

Variable names and sensor port names are also legal expressions, and they refer to the value of the variable or sensor. Additionally, the expression Random(x) uses the RCX's random number generator to pick a number between 0 and x (inclusive).

```
bar = baz;       // assign the value of baz to bar
bar = SENSOR_1;  // assign the value of sensor 1 to bar
bar = Random(4); // assign a number between 0 and 4 to bar
```

Two other expressions provide access to the RCX's timers and message capability:

```
bar = Timer(0);  // assign value of timer 0 to bar
bar = Message(); // read the last received IR message
```

Expressions may be combined using several different arithmetic operations:

```
bar = 1 + Random(4);  // random between 1 and 5
bar = SENSOR_1 - 7;   // sensor 1 minus 7
bar = SENSOR_1 * 4;   // sensor 1 times 4
bar = SENSOR_1 / 3;   // sensor 1 divided by 3
bar = 100 % 7;        // 100 modulo 7
bar = baz & 0x7;      // bitwise AND
bar = baz | 0x4;      // bitwise OR
```

There are also three unary operators:

```
bar = - baz;     // negation
bar = abs(baz);  // absolute value
bar = sign(baz); // sign (-1, 0 or +1)
```

Several operators require constants for one or both of their arguments. The shift operators can have a variable (or other expression) as the left argument, but require a constant for the right-hand side. The exclusive OR and one's complement operators can only operate on constant values. It is an error to use a nonconstant expression such as a variable or input sensor in a case where a constant value is required.

```
bar = x << 2;    // left shift x by 2 bits
bar = x >> 1;    // right shift x by 1 bit
bar = 5 ^ 4;     // bitwise exclusive OR
bar = ~0x80;     // one's complement (bitwise negation)
```

Two special operators, ++ and --, provide the ability to increment and decrement a variable. Since they implicitly modify their operand, they can only be used on variables. In addition, the operators may be applied as prefix or postfix operations, meaning they can take effect before or after the value of the variable is used.

```
baz = 1;
bar = baz++; // postfix: bar=1, baz=2
bar = ++baz; // prefix: bar=3, baz=3
baz--;       // baz=2
bar = 123++; // ERROR--123 cannot be incremented!
```

The precedence and associativity of all of the operators follow that of C, and this is summarized in Appendix D. Parentheses may be used to change the order of computation.

```
bar = 2 + 3 * 4;   // bar = 14
bar = (2 + 3) * 4; // bar = 20
```

CONDITIONS

Our sample program needed to wait until the touch sensor was pressed. This was done with the until statement, which waits until a specified condition becomes true.

```
until(SENSOR_1 == 1);
```

Most conditions involve comparing one expression with another; in the preceding example the value of sensor 1 was compared to the constant 1. There are six different relational operators that can be used in a condition: ==, !=, <, >, <=, and >=. An example of each of these, along with a description of the condition to be met, is shown here:

```
until(SENSOR_1 == 1);  // sensor 1 equal to 1
until(SENSOR_1 != 1);  // sensor 1 not equal to 1
until(SENSOR_1 < 10);  // sensor 1 less than 10
until(SENSOR_1 > 20);  // sensor 1 greater than 20
until(SENSOR_1 <= 15); // sensor 1 less or equal to 15
until(SENSOR_1 >= 25); // sensor 1 greater or equal to 25
```

Of course, the expressions in a condition aren't limited to sensors and constants.

```
until(SENSOR_1 > bar); // use the value of bar
until(Timer(0) < 100); // wait for timer
```

Technically, conditions and expressions are the same thing. Any expression can be used as the condition: if the expression evaluates to a value of zero, then the condition is considered to be false, if it evaluates to a nonzero value, then the condition is true. Conversely, the relational operators (e.g., ==) can be used in any expression. They will evaluate to some nonzero value if the relationship is true, and zero if the relationship is not true.

Conditions may be combined using && (logical AND) or || (logical OR). Note that these operators are different from the bitwise AND and bitwise OR operators for expressions (& and |). Bitwise operators act on the individual bits in a variable and are not suitable for use in combining conditions.

```
// wait until SENSOR_1 between 10 and 20
until( SENSOR_1 > 10 && SENSOR_1  <  20);
// wait until either SENSOR_1 or SENSOR_2 equals 1
until (SENSOR_1 == 1 || SENSOR_2 == 1);
```

Conditions may also be negated with the ! (logical negation) operator. This operator has a higher precedence than && and ||, but parentheses may be used to change the grouping.

```
until (! SENSOR_1 == 1);   // wait until sensor 1 does NOT equal 1
// wait until neither SENSOR_1 or SENSOR_2 are equal to 1
until (! (SENSOR_1 == 1 || SENSOR_2 == 1));
```

Finally, there are two constant conditions: true and false.

```
until(false);  // wait forever
until(true);   // no wait at all...always true
```

CONTROL STRUCTURES

Control structures can be used to make decisions or create conditional and unconditional loops. Most control structures make use of a condition, which must always be enclosed in a set of parentheses. The `if` statement allows a statement to be executed if a condition is true.

```
// turn off output A if sensor 1 equals 1
if (SENSOR_1 == 1)
    Off(OUT_A);
```

The indenting makes the statement easier to read but has no effect on its execution. Only the statement immediately following the condition is considered part of the `if` structure. If multiple statements need to be executed conditionally, they should be grouped together using braces (the { and } symbols). This concept of grouping multiple statements together with braces that are to be treated as a single statement applies to all of the control structures.

```
// not quite right...
if (SENSOR_1 == 1)
    Off(OUT_A); // this is executed conditionally
    On(OUT_B);  // this is executed unconditionally

// better--both Off() and On() are conditional
if (SENSOR_1 == 1)
{
    Off(OUT_A);
    On(OUT_B);
}
```

An `if` condition may also have an `else` clause, which is executed if the condition is false.

```
if (SENSOR_1 == 1)
    On(OUT_A);  // executed if SENSOR_1 equals 1
else
    On(OUT_B);  // executed if SENSOR_1 does not equal 1
```

The while statement causes a statement (or statements) to be repeatedly executed so long as the condition is true. If the condition is initially false, then the body of the while statement will not be executed at all.

```
// keep reversing output A as long as sensor 1 equals 1
while(SENSOR_1 == 1)
    Toggle(OUT_A);
```

The do while statement is the same as the while statement, with the exception that the condition is checked after the body instead of before. As a result, the body will always be executed at least once.

```
do
{
    Toggle(OUT_A);
} while(SENSOR_1 == 1);
```

The repeat statement executes a statement a specified number of times. Unlike the previous control structures, it relies on a numerical expression rather than a condition. The expression is evaluated a single time, and the result of that expression is used to determine the number of repetitions.

```
// repeat 10 times...
repeat(10)
{
    Toggle(OUT_A);
}
```

The for statement is a souped-up version of a while loop. It consists of three clauses, separated by semicolons, and then the body: for(*initial*; *test*; *iterate*) *body*. The *initial* clause is a statement that is executed one time, *test* is an expression that determines if the body of the loop should be executed (just like in a while statement), and *iterate* is a statement that is executed after the body each time through the loop. In essence, the for loop is just shorthand for writing

```
initial
while(test)
{
    body
    iterate
}
```

When programming in C, the `for` loop is often used to iterate a loop a predetermined number of times:

```
int i;
for(i=0; i<5; ++i)
{
    // code in here will get executed 5 times
}
```

USING TASKS

The `main` task must always exist—it is the task that is started when a program is run. An NQC program may contain up to nine additional tasks, which are defined by the same syntax as the `main` task, but have unique names.

```
task main()
{
    // this is the main task
}

task foo()
{
    // this is another task
}
```

When a program is run, only the main task is active. The other tasks may be started or stopped using the `start` and `stop` statements. The example in Listing 3-3 starts two tasks, then stops one of them 10 seconds later.

Listing 3-3. Using Multiple Tasks

```
// intro_2.nqc - using multiple tasks
task main()
{
    start fast_beep;
    start slow_beep;
    Wait(1000);
    stop slow_beep;
}

task fast_beep()
{
    while(true)
    {
```

```
        PlayTone(440, 10);
        Wait(50);
    }
}

task slow_beep()
{
    while(true)
    {
        PlayTone(880, 10);
        Wait(100);
    }
}
```

Even though the main task ends (after stopping the slow_beep task), the program continues to run. This is because the fast_beep task is still active. In order to stop a program completely, all tasks must be stopped. This can be done with the StopAllTasks command.

```
StopAllTasks();
```

FUNCTIONS

So far, all of the example code has been very simple, and the statements for a task have appeared directly within the task's body. When writing larger programs, however, it is often desirable to break up a program into several smaller pieces. These pieces are called *functions* and make programs easier to read, maintain, and reuse. A function's definition looks similar to that of a task, but it uses the keyword void rather than task.

```
void onUntilPressed()
{
    On(OUT_A);
    until(SENSOR_1 == 1);
    Off(OUT_A);
}
```

The function can then be invoked from within a task (or another function).

```
task main()
{
    SetSensor(SENSOR_1, SENSOR_TOUCH);
    onUntilPressed();
}
```

This example does the same thing as the intro_1.nqc example at the start of the chapter; specifically it turns on motor A until a touch sensor attached to input 1 is pressed. Functions really start to pay off when a piece of code needs to be executed more than once. For example, let's say we want to run motor A until the touch sensor is pressed, then we want to run motor B for one second, then resume A until the touch sensor is pressed again. We can use the previous onUntilPressed function and simply call it twice from the main task.

```
task main()
{
    SetSensor(SENSOR_1,  SENSOR_TOUCH);
    onUntilPressed();
    OnFor(OUT_B,  100);
    onUntilPressed();
}
```

Functions can also have one or more arguments, which are declared after the function name. Each argument is specified as a type followed by a name, and multiple arguments are separated by commas. For example, consider the following function, which turns output A on and off a specified number of times and for a specified duration:

```
void pulse(int count, int duration)
{
    repeat(count)
    {
        OnFor(OUT_A, duration);
        Wait(duration);
    }
}
```

The arguments are named count and duration and are both of type int. When calling a function, the appropriate number of arguments must be supplied. Using the preceding function, a program could send 5 pulses of 1 second each by making the following call:

```
pulse(5, 100);
```

Although all numbers within the RCX are the same data type (signed 16-bit integers), argument types are still required in order to determine how an argument is passed from the code calling the function (the caller) to the function itself (the callee).

The first type, int, is perhaps the most basic and was used in the preceding definition of pulse. It represents a temporary variable that gets used within the function. Argument passing is done by copying the value of the actual argument into this temporary variable. The function then can use this temporary variable however it wants. This is known as *pass by value.* There are two important features of passing by value: the actual argument cannot be altered by the function (it can only alter the temporary variable), and the value of the actual argument is latched into the temporary variable when the function is called. This second feature is of particular importance in NQC since arguments are often dynamic sources such as sensor values (e.g., SENSOR_1). The downside to passing by value is that it typically requires using up one of the RCX's storage locations to hold the temporary variable and can be less efficient than using one of the other types.

The second type, const int, carries with it the restriction that only constant expressions (numbers or arithmetic operations on constant expressions) may be used as actual arguments. There is no corresponding notion in C—this is purely an NQC invention due to some limitations in the RCX firmware. This argument type is especially useful when the argument needs to be used in a place where only constant values are allowed. For example, outputs are always identified by constant expressions, so a const int argument could be used to pass an output name to a function.

```
void pulse2(const int out, int count, int duration)
{
    repeat(count)
    {
        OnFor(out, duration);
        Wait(duration);
    }
}
```

This function could then be called like this:

```
pulse2(OUT_A, 5, 100);
```

If the out argument were of type int rather than const int, the function would not compile. This is because the OnFor command requires its first argument to be a constant expression, and if out were of type int the compiler would not be able to ensure that it is always constant. Many of the standard NQC functions for controlling the RCX (e.g., On, Off, Fwd) make extensive use of const int arguments.

The third type, int &, represents *pass by reference*. In this case, instead of allocating a temporary variable and copying the actual argument into it, the argument itself is used within the body of the function. This allows a function to modify the argument so that the caller will see the modified value. For example:

```
void swap1(int x, int y)
{
    int temp;
    temp = x;
    x = y;
    y = temp;
}

void swap2(int &x, int &y)
{
    int temp;
    temp = x;
    x = y;
    y = temp;
}
```

The definitions of swap1 and swap2 are identical, except for the types of the arguments. The intent behind both functions is to swap the values of the two arguments. The problem with swap1 is that it uses call by value, so when called like this:

```
swap1(a, b);
```

the values of a and b will be copied into temporary variables. The contents of these temporary variables will then get swapped, but a and b will remain unchanged. By using pass by reference, swap2 avoids this problem. No temporary variables are created, and the function operates on its arguments directly. Note that it is illegal to use anything other than a variable as an actual argument for type int &.

```
swap2(a, 123); // ERROR, 123 is not a variable!
```

The fourth type, const int &, is a strange beast. It is passed by reference, but with the restriction that the item being passed will not be directly modified by the function. This means that the argument may not be used as the target of assignment or as the operand of an increment or decrement operation. In effect, this is a promise from the function to its caller that the value will not be changed. The most significant benefits to this are that any expression may be passed this way (not just variables), and it is often more efficient than an ordinary int argument. For example, the following function is like the original definition of pulse, with the exception that it uses const int & arguments.

```
void pulse3(const int &count, const int &duration)
{
    repeat(count)
    {
        OnFor(OUT_A, duration);
        Wait(duration);
    }
}
```

It can be called just like its predecessor, but unlike the original version, no temporary variables are used to hold copies of the arguments.

```
pulse3(5, 100);
```

What argument type should be used? There are no hard and fast rules, but a couple of guidelines will suffice most of the time. If a constant expression is required (perhaps because the argument will in turn be used in a command like On), then the argument type must be const int. If the argument is to be modified by the function (and the modified value returned to the caller), then int & is required. In most other cases const int & is probably the right choice. The only reason to fall back on int is if a copy of the actual argument is desired.

The four different argument types are summarized in Table 3-3.

Table 3-3. Argument Types

TYPE	SEMANTICS	COMMENTS
int	by value	uses up a variable, actual argument is not altered
int &	by reference	efficient, actual argument must be a variable
const int	n/a	efficient, actual argument must be a constant
const int &	by reference	efficient, argument cannot be modified

DISPLAYING VALUES

The RCX's LCD display can operate in several different modes. The default mode is for it to display the value of the RCX's watch (its internal clock). Other modes—all selectable by using the **View** button—allow it to show the current value of a sensor or the status of an output. Programs have access to an additional mode, called *user display*, which can be used to monitor just about any kind of value in the RCX. The most obvious use for this mode is to display constant numbers. However, it can also be used to display the contents of dynamic sources, such as variables or timers. The NQC function SetUserDisplay(*source, decimal_point*) tells the RCX to display the value of *source*. The second argument specifies where the decimal point (if any) should be drawn.

```
SetUserDisplay(123, 0);  // display "123"
SetUserDisplay(123, 2);  // display "1.23"
SetUserDisplay(Timer(0), 0); // display the value of timer 0
```

The behavior of displaying a timer may surprise you. At first glance, it looks like Timer(0) will be evaluated, and its current value will then be passed to SetUserDisplay(), presumably to be written to the LCD. The RCX operates a little differently—the function tells it to display timer 0, so it will keep displaying it, and as the timer's value changes (it keeps ticking 10 times a second), the display will be updated with the latest value. Run the program shown in Listing 3-4 to see this effect in action.

Listing 3-4. Viewing a Timer

```
task main()
{
    ClearTimer(0);
    SetUserDisplay(Timer(0), 0);
    until(false); // keep the program running
}
```

If you get errors when trying to compile the program in Listing 3-4, then it is likely that you have not told the NQC compiler that you want it to enable the RCX 2.0 functions (by default it assumes you are generating code for the original RCX 1.0 firmware, which did not support user display mode). If you are using a command line version of NQC, then add -Trcx2 at the start of the command. If you are using an IDE, such as BricxCC or MacNQC, then make sure you have selected RCX2 as the "target" for the programs you are writing.

If the program compiles, but does not run as expected, then it is possible you are still using RCX 1.0 firmware. In order to use some of the new features, such as user display mode and events, you will need to download the RCX 2.0 firmware to your RCX.

The RCX normally returns to the default display mode (the watch) whenever a program ends. In the preceding program, the until statement prevents the program from finishing, thus allowing the display to stay in user mode. Note that the RCX will only reset the display mode when a program ends normally— interrupting the program by pressing the **Run** button will leave the display mode unchanged. Thus the value of Timer(0) in this case would continue to be displayed even after the program was stopped.

The fact that the RCX will continuously update the display in user mode has some interesting consequences. First, it must be possible for the RCX to read the value to be displayed. Because the LCD does not belong to any specific task, local storage locations (which are only valid within their own task) cannot be used. If you want to display the value of a variable, you generally need to make the variable global (by declaring it outside a task, function, or subroutine).

Another consequence of displaying a variable is that you may occasionally see its value partway through a calculation because it is continuously being updated on the LCD. For example, the program in Listing 3-5 gives the impression that it will always be showing the value of 1 plus timer 0. However, if you run the program you will notice that although the timer continues to count upwards, every once in a while the value 1 is shown on the LCD. This is because sometimes the LCD grabs the value of x in the middle of the calculation x = 1 + Timer(0).

Listing 3-5. Viewing a Calculation

```
int x = 0;

task main()
{
    ClearTimer(0);
    SetUserDisplay(x, 0);
    while(true)
    {
        x = 1 + Timer(0);
    }
}
```

This program can be fixed by latching the calculated value into a separate global variable that actually gets displayed, as shown in Listing 3-6. Even though the value of x moves around during the calculation of x = 1 + Timer(0), the LCD will always show the correct value since the update to displayValue happens in a single operation. Since x is no longer displayed directly, it can be moved to a local variable.

Listing 3-6. Viewing the Results of a Calculation

```
int displayValue = 0;

task main()
{
    int x;

    ClearTimer(0);
    SetUserDisplay(displayValue, 0);
    while(true)
    {
        x = 1 + Timer(0);
        displayValue = x;
    }
}
```

One of the best uses of the display is to assist in debugging a program. In cases where you want to inspect a variable's value, just insert the appropriate call to SetUserDisplay in a program. Another useful technique is to display constant values at various points in the program. Then by observing the value on the LCD you can tell what part of the program was last executed.

EVENTS

Nearly every program needs to detect changes in a robot's sensors and respond accordingly. One way to do this is to use control structures, such as `if` and `while`, to check a sensor's current value, and then execute certain statements if a condition is true. This technique is relatively straightforward to use, but it also has a few limitations. Consider a `while` loop like this:

```
while(SENSOR_1 == 1)
{
    // do something
}
```

The sensor is checked at the top of the loop, and if it is not equal to 1 then the body of the loop ("do something") is executed. If the body takes a long time to execute, the sensor may not be checked for quite a while. If the sensor's value changes rapidly (perhaps by a quick press of a touch sensor), it is possible for the loop to completely miss the change. Furthermore, there is no way for a sensor to interrupt the body of the loop—it must complete all of its work before the sensor can be checked again.

NQC provides another mechanism, called *event monitoring,* which solves both of these problems. The tradeoff is that event monitoring is a little more complicated to use, and in some cases having a sensor change interrupt a sequence of statements actually causes more problems than it solves. The tradeoffs between using conditions and events are explored more in Chapter 7. For now, we will just concentrate on how to use events in NQC.

There are three steps to using events: *configuring* the event, *monitoring* the event, and *handling* the event when it occurs. The RCX has 16 events, numbered 0 to 15, each of which can be configured to detect a different condition. Events are configured using the function `SetEvent(number, source, type)`, where *number* specifies which event you are configuring, *source* is the thing that the event should read (a sensor for example), and *type* is the kind of condition that will trigger the event. For example, to configure event 0 to be triggered when a touch sensor attached to sensor port 1 is pressed, you could use the following statement:

```
SetSensor(0, SENSOR_1, EVENT_TYPE_PRESSED);
```

Sensors are the most common sources for events, but timers and communication messages can also be used. There are 11 different types of events, which are listed in Table 3-4.

Table 3-4. Event Types

EVENT TYPE	CONDITION	EVENT SOURCE
EVENT_TYPE_PRESSED	value changes to *on*	sensors only
EVENT_TYPE_RELEASED	value changes to *off*	sensors only
EVENT_TYPE_PULSE	value changes from *off* to *on* to *off*	sensors only
EVENT_TYPE_EDGE	value changes from *off* to *on* or vice versa	sensors only
EVENT_TYPE_FASTCHANGE	value changes rapidly	sensors only
EVENT_TYPE_LOW	value changes to *low*	any
EVENT_TYPE_NORMAL	value changes to *normal*	any
EVENT_TYPE_HIGH	value changes to *high*	any
EVENT_TYPE_CLICK	value from *low* to *high* and back to *low*	any
EVENT_TYPE_DOUBLECLICK	two clicks within a certain time	any
EVENT_TYPE_MESSAGE	new message received	Message() only

The first four event types (pressed, released, pulse, and edge) are most useful with touch sensors because those sensors have obvious *on* and *off* conditions. However, these event types can be used with other sensors provided that their boolean conversion (described in Chapter 2) is acceptable. Most of the remaining event types (low, normal, high, click, and doubleclick) use several parameters to determine what constitutes a low or high value. The functions SetUpperLimit(), SetLowerLimit(), and optionally SetHysteresis() should be used to set these parameters when those event types are being used. An additional parameter, set with SetClickTime(), is used to specify how fast a click must be for the click and doubleclick event types. For now, we will just be using a touch sensor, so no parameters need to be set.

The second step in using events is to *monitor* them during portions of your program. You do this by using the monitor statement, which looks a little bit like a while loop. Instead of a condition, the argument to a monitor statement determines which events are going to be monitored inside the body of the statement. Events are specified using *masks* instead of the event number. The macro EVENT_MASK converts an event number into a mask, and multiple event masks can be combined by adding them together. For example, the following code monitors events 1 and 2:

```
monitor(EVENT_MASK(1) + EVENT_MASK(2))
{
    // the body of the monitor statement
}
```

It is critical to place the monitor statement around the entire region of your program that you want to detect events within. If an event is triggered when your program is not monitoring it, then the event is ignored. However, when a monitored event is triggered, the code within the monitor statement will be interrupted immediately. Sometimes that is a sufficient response to the event, but in other cases a program will need to do something more in response to the event. This can be accomplished by adding a catch phrase at the end of the monitor statement. An example of a program that uses events is shown in Listing 3-7. The program expects a touch sensor to be attached to sensor port 1, and a motor to be attached to output A. The program begins by setting up the sensor, configuring an event to trigger whenever the sensor is pressed, and turning on the motor.

Listing 3-7. Using Events

```
#define MY_EVENT 1

task main()
{
    SetSensor(SENSOR_1, SENSOR_TOUCH);
    SetEvent(MY_EVENT, SENSOR_1, EVENT_TYPE_PRESSED);

    On(OUT_A);

    while(true)
    {
        monitor(EVENT_MASK(MY_EVENT))
        {
            while(true)
            {
                PlayTone(440, 50);
                Wait(50);
                PlayTone(880, 50);
                Wait(50);
            }
        }
        catch
        {
            ClearSound();
            Toggle(OUT_A);
        }
    }
}
```

The program then enters a `while` loop that will repeat forever. Within this loop, the program plays alternating low and high notes while monitoring the event. When the event is triggered, the program will interrupt what it is doing to run the `catch` clause, which calls `ClearSound()` to turn off whatever sound is currently playing and then reverses the direction of the motor.

CONCLUSION

Although far from a complete reference on NQC, the material presented in this chapter serves well as an introduction to the commonly used NQC features. The robots in this book, starting with Chapter 5, provide a more hands-on approach to learning NQC. While working with those sample programs, it may be helpful to refer back to this chapter or the summary provided in Appendix D.

These first few chapters have concentrated on the electrical and programming aspects of robots. Mechanical aspects are equally important, which is why Chapter 4 introduces various techniques and principles used in actually building robots.

Chapter 4
Construction

This chapter describes the various mechanical principles and techniques used in constructing LEGO robots. A number of structures will be introduced, followed by examples of using special pieces such as gears, pulleys, and the differential. Builders who have spent years constructing LEGO Technic models will find many of the procedures to be second nature already. However, those unfamiliar with these special pieces will find many helpful hints in the following material.

STRUCTURES

When building a robot it is tempting to think only of the motors, sensors, and gears that will make the robot come alive. The use of motors, however, subjects these creations to unusual forces, and without a solidly constructed body a robot may fall apart at the most inopportune moment. The following pages present several structures that can be used to make more robust robots.

Frames

When constructing a rectangular structure, it is often desirable to make it sturdy while still using a minimal number of pieces. Our first attempt, shown in Figure 4-1, is about as simple as it gets. The frame itself is made up of 1×12 and 1×4 beams. To hold the beams together, 1×6 plates are used both above and below the 1×4 beams.

Figure 4-1.
Simple frame

 When discussing LEGO, it is convenient to use LEGO units, rather than actual measurements in inches or centimeters. After all, which is more descriptive: a 2×4 brick or a $^{10}/_{16}$"×1$^1/_4$" brick? A LEGO unit is equal to the distance between adjacent "studs" on an ordinary brick, which happens to be $^5/_{16}$".

This structure stays together well enough, but it has a little too much wiggle to be of much practical use. The problem is that the 1×6 plates do not lock the corners at right angles. This can be remedied by using wider plates. In fact, a single 2×6 plate makes the entire structure much more rigid, as shown in Figure 4-2.

Figure 4-2.
Improved frame

Long Beams

It is often necessary to build structures that are longer than the largest beam. The simplest way is to join one beam to another using plates (or bricks) above and below the seam, as shown in Figure 4-3. This arrangement is relatively compact and quick to build; however, it is not strong enough to support a large weight. Thus it would not be good for something like the arm of a crane.

Figure 4-3.
Simple long beam

A more robust way to join two beam lengths is to use *friction pegs* to attach a third beam that overlaps the seam. The overlapped beam must be at least a 1×6 (in order to have room for all four friction pegs), and longer beams will result in a stronger structure. The placement of the friction pegs is important—they should be at the very ends of the beams in order to maximize stability, as shown in Figure 4-4.

Figure 4-4.
Better long beam

This arrangement is capable of supporting a significant weight, but it flexes slightly from side to side. If this is a concern, the structure can be reinforced by top and/or bottom plates as shown in Figure 4-5.

Figure 4-5.
Best long beam

Vertical Beams

So far, we have only used beams in a horizontal orientation. What if we need to attach them vertically? The friction pegs will allow us to connect beams at any angle, but when we try to put a second peg in the vertical beam, we find that the holes don't quite line up, as shown in Figure 4-6.

Figure 4-6.
Vertical miss

This is because of the unfortunate fact that a 1×1 brick is a little taller than it is wide. In fact, a brick is 1.2 LEGO units tall. Since three plates stack up to make a brick, a plate is 0.4 LEGO units tall. It just so happens that a stack of one brick and two plates is exactly 2 LEGO units tall (1.2 + 2 × 0.4 = 2.0). Taking this into account, we can build the structure in Figure 4-7.

Figure 4-7.
Vertical beam

The vertical beam arrangement is quite sturdy. In extreme cases, a third beam can be used to reinforce it further as shown in Figure 4-8. The key is to form a right triangle with integral lengths for all three sides. The most common dimensions for such triangles are 3–4–5 and 5–12–13 (or multiples thereof).

Figure 4-8.
Triangular structure

Bracing

Vertical beams can also be used to provide bracing for a structure. The resulting arrangement, shown in Figure 4-9, is extremely strong. This can be used quite effectively on larger robots—vertical bracing from the top to the bottom of a robot ensures the integrity of everything in between because the brace will prevent any individual horizontal pieces from pulling apart.

Figure 4-9.
Vertical bracing

Wide Beams

Let's say you need a small platform at the end of a long beam. In Figure 4-10, a small platform is created by using two 1×4 beams alongside the main 1×12 beam, and two plates hold everything together.

Figure 4-10.
Simple platform

An alternative, shown in Figure 4-11, is to eliminate the plates and use double-pegs to hold the beams together. (The name "double-peg" is actually somewhat of a misnomer since it is only 1.5 times as long as a normal peg.)

Figure 4-11.
Wide-beam platform

This technique of attaching beams together with pegs often comes in handy when building motors into structures that are just a little too wide, as demonstrated in Figure 4-12. Beams provide much better structural support than plates, so the motor is less likely to pop off your model if it starts or stops suddenly.

Figure 4-12.
Using wide beams to mount a motor

BASIC GEARS

Motors supply the mechanical power to bring a robot alive, but in many cases the motor itself may be in the wrong position, turning at the wrong speed, or providing the wrong amount of torque. The following pages discuss how gears can be used to transfer mechanical power and to convert speed into torque.

Gear Reduction

Consider what happens as the pulley with the handle is turned clockwise in the model shown in Figure 4-13. The pulley is on the same axle as a small gear, which then meshes with a larger gear, which in turn is attached to a second pulley. The numbers in the illustration indicate the length of the axle.

Figure 4-13.
Gear reduction (3:1)

You may have noticed that the second pulley rotates differently than the first one. First of all, it is spinning in the opposite direction. This is one of the basic properties of the way gears mesh with one another—the direction of rotation is reversed.

The second observation is that the second pulley turns much more slowly than the first one. If you count, you'll find that the first pulley must make three complete revolutions for the second pulley to turn once. This difference in speed occurs because the two gears have different numbers of teeth. If you feel like counting, you'll find that the small gear has 8 teeth and the larger one has 24. Thus, in order for the larger gear to make one complete revolution, all 24 teeth must move past the point where the gears mesh. Since the small gear only moves 8 teeth past this point per revolution, it must turn three times (24 divided by 8) for each revolution of the larger gear. Since the number of teeth on a gear determines how it meshes with other gears, it is worth remembering that the four standard LEGO gears, shown in Figure 4-14, have 8, 16, 24, and 40 teeth, respectively.

8   16   24   40

Figure 4-14.
Standard gears

Reducing the number of revolutions is called *gear reduction,* or *gearing down.* The exact amount of gearing down can be written as the ratio that specifies how many turns of the first gear equal a certain number of turns of the second gear. In the preceding example, the gear ratio is 3:1.

Speed and Torque

In the previous example we used gears to reduce the speed of rotation. We can also arrange things so that we increase speed. This is called *gearing up,* and it can be accomplished by having a large gear turn a smaller one. The example in Figure 4-15 uses a 40-tooth gear to turn an 8-tooth gear; it thus has a gear ratio of 8:40 = 1:5 (you can reduce gear ratios just like you reduce fractions).

Figure 4-15.
Gearing up (1:5)

If you start turning the pulley with the handle, you'll find that the second pulley spins much faster (five times as fast to be exact). All of this extra speed seems like we're getting something for nothing. Unfortunately, physics gets in the way and prevents us from having a free lunch.

A rotating axle has both speed and torque. Speed represents how fast the axle is spinning, and it is typically measured in units such as revolutions per minute (rpm). Roughly speaking, torque represents how much force the rotating axle is capable of supplying. Higher torque means that the axle will be able to propel a heavier vehicle or lift a heavier weight.

 Technically, torque is a product of force and distance. If an axle has torque of 1 foot-pound (ft lb), it means that if a wheel of a radius of 1 foot were attached to the axle, there would be 1 pound of force at the edge of the wheel. For a given force, the amount of torque increases as the radius of the rotating object increases. That's why screwdrivers with fat handles are better at loosening tight screws.

When gears are used to change the speed of an axle (gearing up or down), they also affect the torque in the opposite manner. For example, if you gear down using a 2:1 ratio, the speed will be cut in half, but the torque will be doubled. Conversely, when you increase speed, you reduce torque. In the 1:5 example earlier, the torque was reduced by a factor of 5. The total amount of work that can be done (speed times torque) remains unaffected by gear ratios (aside from the small amount of energy that is wasted due to friction whenever two gears mesh).

Compound Gear Trains

Our previous examples used only two gears. It is also possible to combine multiple stages of gears to form a compound gear train. When compounded, the ratios of the individual stages are multiplied together to determine the overall gear ratio. This allows the creation of gear ratios far larger (or smaller) than those available from a single pair of gears.

The example in Figure 4-16 is a three-stage gear reduction, with each stage consisting of an 8-tooth and a 24-tooth gear. Note how the end of one stage (24-tooth gear) is attached to the start of the next stage (8-tooth gear). Each stage has a ratio of 3:1. The ratio of the compound arrangement is 3:1 × 3:1 × 3:1 = 27:1 (ratios multiply just like fractions).

Figure 4-16.
Compound gear reduction

We can use the RCX to power the motor. First you'll need to download the START program from Chapter 1 to the RCX. Attach the motor to RCX output A and run the program. The motor should start spinning quite fast (as you can see by the left pulley), while the right pulley at the end of the gears moves very slowly. By grasping the left pulley you should be able to prevent the motor from turning. Now try stopping the motor by grasping the right pulley. In the first case it was fairly easy to overcome the motor's torque. In the second, we have to deal with 27 times more torque.

Distances Between Gears

Some combinations of gears, such as a 24-tooth and an 8-tooth, line up perfectly along a beam. For other combinations, such as a 16-tooth and a 24-tooth gear, the spacing of holes in a beam just won't work.

So far we have been describing gears by the number of teeth they have. Gears also have another important measurement: their radius. When you are meshing two gears, the distance between their axles should be equal to the sum of their radii. The radii (in LEGO units) for the four standard gears are shown in Table 4-1.

Table 4-1. Gear Sizes

TEETH	RADIUS
8	0.5
16	1.0
24	1.5
40	2.5

Now it should become clear why the 16/24 combination doesn't work—we need a spacing of 2.5 units, and the holes in a beam have whole-number spacing (no pun intended). Note that the 8-, 24-, and 40-tooth gears can mesh with each other along a beam, and the 16-tooth gear can mesh with itself. It is only when combining the 16-tooth with one of the others that we have difficulty.

With a little cleverness, however, we can get the gears to mesh. The example in Figure 4-17 shows how to use two *crossblocks* separated by a *half bushing* to achieve the proper spacing for an 8-tooth gear and a 16-tooth gear.

Figure 4-17.
Nonstandard spacing

A more flexible solution is to use vertical and horizontal distance to create a diagonal spacing that works. To compute the diagonal distance, you use the Pythagorean theorem. There is a slight complication in that a brick is actually 1.2 units tall (see the "Structures" section earlier in this chapter for more discussion of this).

$$distance = \sqrt{width^2 + (1.2 \times height)^2}$$

In Figure 4-18, the gears are separated horizontally by 2 units, and vertically by one brick and one plate. The resulting distance is just a touch over 2.5 units, but it is still close enough to mesh 16- and 24-tooth gears together.

Figure 4-18.
Diagonal spacing

$$distance = \sqrt{width^2 + (1.2 \times height)^2} = \sqrt{2^2 + (1.2 \times (1 + \tfrac{1}{3}))^2} \approx 2.56$$

SPECIALIZED GEARS

Besides the "vanilla" gears discussed in the previous sections, specialized gears such as the crown gear, the bevel gear, the worm gear, the rack, and the differential are also available. The following pages describe the uses for each of these special gears.

Crown and Bevel Gears

The *crown gear* is the same size as a standard 24-tooth gear, but its teeth are curved to allow it to mesh with a gear at right angles to it, as shown in Figure 4-19. The meshing involves a lot of friction, so this is not a good arrangement for something where speed or power is at a premium. However, for auxiliary functions the crown gear can be quite useful. It is also important that the crown gear have ample support directly behind the meshing point; otherwise it will tend to slip.

Figure 4-19.
Using a crown gear

The *bevel gear,* used in Figure 4-20, is a more compact alternative to the crown gear. Its 12 teeth can only mesh with other bevel gears, but when used properly it can transfer power a bit more efficiently than the crown gear. It is critical that the bevel gear be backed up against something solid, preferably a beam, although bushings can be used to fill empty space.

Figure 4-20.
Using bevel gears

Worm Gear

The *worm gear* is unique. Each full rotation of the worm gear results in the movement of one tooth of the gear it is meshed with. In Figure 4-21, it is meshed with a 24-tooth gear, and the resulting gear ratio is thus 24:1. Needless to say, the worm gear provides an extremely compact mechanism for gear reduction.

Figure 4-21.
Using the worm gear

The worm gear also provides a one-way mechanism. Try turning the left pulley shown in Figure 4-21. There will be some wiggle (due to the fact that the worm gear is just a little shorter than 2 units), but no amount of force will cause the worm gear itself to rotate. This means that the worm gear can transfer power from its axle to a gear meshed with it but will not allow power to be transferred in the reverse direction.

This feature can be exploited when building something like a crane, where a motor is used to lift some heavy weight and the weight must remain lifted even after the motor is turned off.

The wiggle I mentioned is actually one of the more troublesome aspects of using the worm gear. In some cases, a little wiggle is acceptable, but in other cases it needs to be eliminated. One option is the vertical arrangement shown in Figure 4-22. If such an arrangement is used, then suitable vertical bracing must be used; otherwise the vertical forces on the worm gear tend to pop the structure apart.

Figure 4-22.
Using the worm gear vertically

Multiple worm gears may be placed end to end to create a longer worm gear. Care must be taken, however, to align the gears. If they are twisted with respect to one another, then the meshing will be uneven at the seam between the two worm gears, as shown in Figure 4-23.

Right   **Wrong**

Figure 4-23.
Multiple worm gears

The Rack

A *rack* can be used to convert the rotation of a gear into linear movement. It is common to use an 8-tooth gear in combination with a rack. Larger gears will still mesh properly, but in most applications the finer control afforded by the smaller gear makes it the best choice.

The rack needs to be able to slide freely back and forth; hence it must rest on a smooth surface. Specifically, you don't want it sitting on top of a normal brick or plate. LEGO makes some smooth-topped pieces (called *tiles*) that work well for this; however, the MINDSTORMS Robotics Invention System doesn't include any tiles. A little creativity will solve the problem, though. In Figure 4-24, we use two *half-beams* to create a smooth surface for the rack. Turning the crank will cause the rack to move back and forth.

Figure 4-24.
Using a rack

The rack itself is only 4 units long, so it doesn't take much turning for it to be pushed completely out of the mechanism. A longer rack can be built by placing multiple racks end to end.

The Differential

The *differential* is the most complicated gear assembly, but it is also one of the most useful. Internally, it uses three bevel gears to connect the two independent axles with the shell of the differential. The axles may rotate at different speeds, but their average speed must equal the rotation of the differential shell. Assembling the differential can be a bit tricky. The "middle" bevel gear (the one not attached to an axle) must be placed inside the differential shell first. Then each axle may be inserted through the differential to its own bevel gear. The completed assembly is shown in Figure 4-25.

Figure 4-25.
The differential

The best way to understand the differential's operation is to play a little; start by building the model shown in Figure 4-26.

Figure 4-26.
Differential example

Pulley A turns the shell of the differential; pulleys B and C are connected to the differential's independent axles. Turning pulley A one full rotation causes the differential to also make one full rotation. This results in pulleys B and C also making one full rotation (assuming neither one has too much friction). This is the simplest case: everything turning at the same speed.

If you turn pulleys B and C at the same speed but in opposite directions, the differential (and pulley A) will remain motionless. In this case, the average speed of the independent axles is zero, so the differential remains still.

Play with other combinations until you feel you are comfortable with how the differential works. What happens if you turn the differential but keep one of the other axles frozen in place?

The Clutch Gear

The *clutch gear* is a white gear that is the same overall size as an ordinary 24-tooth gear (RIS 1.0 does not include a clutch gear, it was added for RIS 1.5 and 2.0). What makes this gear unique is that an axle connects to the gear by sliding through a gray sleeve in the center of the gear. Friction between the sleeve and the rest of the gear is what makes the gear turn. This combines some of the advantages of pulleys (described in the next section) with the compactness of an ordinary gear. In practice, however, I find that the gear "slips" too easily for most of the things I design, so I tend not to use the clutch gear.

PULLEYS AND BELTS

Like gears, *pulleys* can be used to convert between speed and power, but the similarity ends there. Whereas gears reverse direction when they mesh, pulleys turn in the same direction. And, unlike gears, which have teeth to be counted, the ratio between pulleys is determined strictly by their size. While you should never rely on pulleys for exact ratios (due to slippage), their relative sizes are shown in Figure 4-27 and Table 4-2.

small   **friction**   **medium**   **large**

Figure 4-27.
Pulleys

Table 4-2. Pulley Sizes

PULLEY	RELATIVE SIZE
small	2
friction	3
medium	7
large	11

Pulleys do not mesh with each other directly; power is transferred from one pulley to another via a rubber *belt*. This means that the distance between pulleys is a little more flexible than the distance between gears. In some cases this allows pulleys to be used in places where a combination of gears wouldn't fit. In the model shown in Figure 4-28, it takes roughly $3^1/2$ turns of the crank for the larger pulley to complete one revolution.

Figure 4-28.
Pulley example

Now try holding the second axle (the one with the larger pulley) still while turning the crank. The belt will start to slip. The tightness of the belt determines how much power can be transferred before the belt starts to slip. At first thought, such slipping may seem to be a limitation, but it is actually a very important feature of pulleys that can be exploited in designs. It can provide a sort of safety valve in systems where a motor is powering something with limited range of motion.

For example, let's try to motorize the rack mechanism from the previous section. Instead of a crank, we use a 24-tooth gear, as shown in Figure 4-29. We also build "stoppers" to prevent the rack from moving too far. Finally, we add a motor that drives the track in a 3:1 ratio. Use the RCX program from Chapter 1 to power the motor and test the motorized rack. When I tried it, my model broke apart; the force of the motor was too much for the stoppers to handle.

We could reinforce the stoppers, but then something else would probably break. The forces from the motor will just find the weakest link and break it. Perhaps the beams will separate, or the motor itself will pop off. Reinforcing every single weak point in a large and complex model can be quite an undertaking.

Pulleys and belts provide us with a simpler solution. We can replace the 24-tooth gear with a medium pulley and replace the 8-tooth gear on the motor with a small pulley. A blue belt completes our model, shown in Figure 4-30.

Figure 4-29.
Motorized rack

Figure 4-30.
Motorized rack with pulleys

Not only is the pulley-and-belt solution simpler than reinforcing the entire model, it is also a better solution. If you reinforce a model to the point where the forces from the motor will not be able to break it, then the motor will be prevented from turning once the rack hits a stopper. This is known as *stalling* the motor, and it tends to put more strain on the motor than normal operation. Ironically, a motor also consumes more energy when it is stalled than when it is running. This means that a stalled motor will also drain your batteries faster.

RATCHETS

A *ratchet* is a mechanism that freely allows rotation in one direction but prevents rotation in the opposite direction. There aren't any special LEGO ratchet pieces, but we can fashion our own ratchets using the pieces at hand.

A Simple Ratchet

Our first example, shown in Figure 4-31, is a simple ratchet mechanism built from a gear and a beam. As the pulley is turned clockwise, the teeth on the gear hit the arm in such a way that it is briefly lifted out of the way. As the arm repeatedly lifts and falls into place, you can hear the characteristic clicking sound of a ratchet mechanism. Now try turning the pulley counterclockwise. Instead of lifting the arm out of the way, the gear's teeth actually push it more firmly into place, thus preventing movement.

Figure 4-31.
A simple ratchet

Finally, try giving the pulley a very quick clockwise spin. If you spin it fast enough, it will kick the arm hard enough that it swings completely behind the gear, rendering the ratchet ineffective. For this reason, it is sometimes desirable to build some sort of stop to prevent the arm from swinging too far out of position.

Our simple ratchet relies on gravity to hold the arm in place. Sometimes the ratchet may not be able to count on gravity (perhaps it needs to operate upside down). In these cases, another mechanism, such as a rubber band, must be provided to keep the arm in place. However, a strong rubber band will require the gear to supply more force when lifting the arm out of the way, thus sapping some of the power that is presumably destined for some other function. Like many other techniques, building a good ratchet is a balancing act between efficiency and robustness.

The Ratchet Splitter

Sometimes a robot needs to do more than three things. Since the RCX has only three outputs, it is necessary to find a way for multiple functions to share the same motor (and hence the same RCX output). The *ratchet splitter* provides a way for a single motor to control two separate functions. The catch is that each function can only operate in a single direction, and only one function may operate at a time. The design is relatively simple, relying on a differential and two ratchets. Assembly of the mechanism is shown in Figure 4-32.

Figure 4-32.
The ratchet splitter

As discussed before, a ratchet allows rotation in one direction but prevents the reverse motion. The two ratchets in this model are set up so that one axle may rotate only clockwise, while the other may rotate only counterclockwise. Power is then applied to the shell of the differential. Consider what happens when the motor turns the differential in the forward direction: the "normal" operation would be for both axles to rotate forward at the same speed as the differential, but one axle is prevented from going in this direction (by the ratchet); therefore the other axle must spin twice as fast (so the average axle speed equals that of the differential shell). If the motor is reversed, the previously spinning axle is held in place by its ratchet while the other axle is free to rotate (again at twice the speed).

Levers

The *lever* is one of the most basic machines. With it, a small force can be used to lift a large weight. Consider the example in Figure 4-33. Placing one brick on each side will result in the long beam being balanced.

Figure 4-33.
A balanced lever

Placing the bricks closer together, as in Figure 4-34, still leaves the beam balanced.

Figure 4-34.
Another balanced lever

Now if we place two bricks on the left side while leaving only one brick on the right, the beam no longer balances—it tips completely to the left, as shown in Figure 4-35. This should come as no surprise because two bricks obviously weigh more than a single brick.

Figure 4-35.
Two bricks are heavier than one.

In Figure 4-36, however, things have changed. There are still two bricks on the left and a single brick on the right, but somehow the right side is "heavier" than the left.

Figure 4-36.
Making one brick "heavier" than two

In our example, the beam is actually a lever. The point at which the axle goes through the beam is called the *fulcrum* of the lever. When a force is applied to a lever, both the magnitude of the force and the distance between the force and the fulcrum must be taken into account. The product of the force and distance is called the *moment*. In our example, the beam will tip to the side with the greater moment, or balance if the moments are equal. In the first three cases, the distances for the left and right bricks were equal, so only the number of bricks (and hence the weight on the beam) mattered. In the preceding example, the distances are not equal. In this case, the left side has two bricks that are 2 units away from the fulcrum, which equals a moment of 4. The right side has only one brick, but it is 7 units away, for a moment of 7. Since 7 is greater than 4, the beam tips to the right. If we put the right-hand brick 4 units away from the fulcrum, then its moment will be the same as that of the left-hand side, and the beam will once again balance, as shown in Figure 4-37.

Figure 4-37.
Balancing bricks

All of our examples have shown the fulcrum in the middle, with the forces applied on either side, but this does not have to be the case. The fulcrum can be at one end, and the forces can both be applied to the same side. Bottle openers, the claw end of a hammer, and crowbars are all examples of using a lever so that a modest force at one end can create a much larger force nearer to the fulcrum.

CONCLUSION

This chapter has presented a lot of different topics: frames, gears, pulleys, levers, differentials, vertical bracing, levers, and ratchets. Don't worry if it seems like a lot to remember; practice makes perfect, and the remaining chapters of the book will provide plenty of practice. This concludes Part One of the book, and we are now ready to start building some robots.

Part Two
Robots

Chapter 5
Tankbot

Tankbot is a rather simple robot; in fact calling it a robot may be a bit of a stretch. Tankbot has no sensors, so it cannot respond to the environment. All it can do is follow a preprogrammed set of directions (e.g., drive straight for 2 seconds, turn right, etc.). However, Tankbot itself will become the base for some more complicated robots presented in later chapters.

Like a tank, Tankbot uses caterpillar treads instead of wheels to propel itself (this is also known as a tracked vehicle). Caterpillar treads, hereafter referred to simply as treads, are often a good choice for general-purpose robotic vehicles. They are easy to construct and program and have the ability to rotate a vehicle in place.

CONSTRUCTION

Construction of Tankbot begins with a frame to support the RCX and motors. In Figure 5-1, beams are prepared with a number of friction pegs. These pegs will be used to join other beams together in later steps.

Figure 5-1.
Tankbot step 1

In Figure 5-2, the frame is completed with an additional set of beams and a pair of 2×8 Technic plates. The reason for doubling up the beams is that the RCX is 8 units wide, but because of its tapered design, it needs to be supported somewhere other than its edges. The doubled-up beams provide a frame that is as wide as the RCX while still providing interior support. 2×8 plates were chosen instead of 1×8 plates in order to make the frame more rigid. Two axles, which will eventually connect to one tread, are also put in place. A similar pair of axles for the other tread are added in Figure 5-3. Note that the axles are 12 units apart—this is the ideal spacing for the treads that are to be used on Tankbot.

Figure 5-2.
Tankbot step 2

Figure 5-3.
Tankbot step 3

The rear axles have 24-tooth gears, which will later mesh with gears on the motors. On all four axles, bushings are used inside to lock the axles in place and to provide adequate spacing for the tread hubs (to be added later).

In Figures 5-4 and 5-5, a platform to support the motors is constructed. The motors do not have a flat bottom, so sometimes rather unusual constructions must be used to support them. In this case, the recessed center area provides space for the rounded bottom of the motors.

Figure 5-4.
Tankbot step 4

Figure 5-5.
Tankbot step 5

The motors themselves are added in Figures 5-6 and 5-7, and the RCX is added in Figure 5-8. It is important to connect the wires exactly as shown. This will ensure that when the RCX activates an output in the forward direction, the motors will spin in the proper direction to propel Tankbot forward. For consistency with some of the later examples, we will consider the motors to be at the back of Tankbot and the IR window of the RCX to be at the front.

Figure 5-6.
Tankbot step 6

Figure 5-7.
Tankbot step 7

Figure 5-8.
Tankbot step 8

Figure 5-9 is the final step for Tankbot. Four 1×6 beams are used to secure the RCX to the frame. This is actually quite important since it is tempting to pick up Tankbot by grasping the RCX itself. Without the 1×6 beams, the top of the RCX could then separate from the bottom—often dumping the batteries on the ground.

The easiest way to attach a tread is to wrap the tread around the hubs, then slide the tread and both hubs onto the axles. This is far easier than attempting to stretch the tread around hubs that are already in place. The hubs themselves slide and spin freely on axles, which makes it necessary to secure them in place. In the case of the rear treads, 16-tooth gears must be used. This ensures that the hub will turn whenever the axle turns. For the front hubs, it is not necessary to lock them to the axle; simple bushings are sufficient to hold them in place (in fact, using gears on the front axles would lead to increased friction and actually degrade overall performance).

Figure 5-9.
Tankbot step 9

DRIVING STRAIGHT

Our first program is very simple—all it does is turn on both motors so that
Tankbot travels in a forward direction. Versions of this program in both RCX Code
(Figure 5-10) and NQC (Listing 5-1) are shown.

Figure 5-10.
Tankbot program 1 in RCX Code

Listing 5-1. Tankbot Program 1 in NQC

```
// tankbot1.nqc - drive straight ahead

#define LEFT OUT_A
#define RIGHT OUT_C

task main()
{
    On(LEFT+RIGHT);
    until(false);
}
```

Download the program to the RCX and try running it. Does Tankbot start driving straight ahead? If Tankbot moves backward, or spins with one tread moving forward and one tread backward, then you need to change the wiring so that the RCX's notion of "forward" matches reality.

In some cases Tankbot will curve slightly to one side or the other as it is driving. This is quite normal and is a consequence of the slight differences between the individual motors, treads, and axles. These slight variations can cause one side to encounter a little more friction than the other, and thus turn at a slightly slower speed. In later chapters, we will discuss other drive mechanisms that avoid this problem, but for now we'll just have to live with it.

If you are new to using NQC, then a few comments about the code are probably in order. First of all, note how the first two lines define the symbols LEFT and RIGHT to be OUT_A and OUT_C, respectively. This isn't strictly necessary, since without those definitions, we could just use

```
On(OUT_A + OUT_C);
```

However, it is a good programming practice to assign names to each output and sensor near the top of the program. Within the body of the program, they can be referred to by function (e.g., LEFT) rather than having to remember which output or sensor was being used. This makes the program more readable and allows it to be adapted easily if you change how the motors or sensors are connected later on.

The second detail about the code is the last statement:

```
until(false);
```

Without this statement, the program would finish running right after turning on the motors. The motors would then be left running, and the only way to stop them would be by turning the RCX off. The RCX does allow you to stop a running program by pressing the **Run** button, and this also has the side effect of turning off all of the motors. However, since the program would already be finished, pressing **Run** couldn't stop it—instead it would start running the program a second time! Using the until statement causes the program to enter an infinite loop (waiting for something that will never be true), thus the program runs forever. This allows us to use the **Run** key to stop the program and the motors.

TURNING

Most of the wheeled vehicles we encounter in real life, such as bicycles and automobiles, can be steered by changing the direction that some of the wheels face, thereby directing the entire vehicle to start curving left or right. Tankbot, however, has no means of changing the angle of its treads. How can we steer it?

The answer comes from geometry. Consider a car driving in a circle. If we were to look at the tracks left by the car's wheels, we would see that they form two concentric circles; the outer wheels traveling in a circle that is slightly larger than the inner wheels (see Figure 5-11). Since both sets of wheels take the same amount of time to complete the circle, the outer wheels must cover more ground per second. Assuming that the wheels are all the same size, this means the outer wheels are turning slightly faster than the inner wheels.

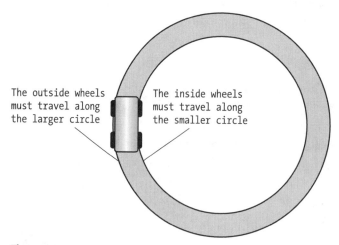

The outside wheels must travel along the larger circle

The inside wheels must travel along the smaller circle

Figure 5-11.
Turning

We can apply this fact in reverse to steer Tankbot. We simply run one side's tread faster than the other side and Tankbot will start turning.

We'll start with a program that causes Tankbot to weave back and forth. We can do this by repeating the following steps:

■ Turn right.

■ Drive straight.

■ Turn left.

■ Drive straight.

Turning is accomplished by running one motor at half the power while the other one is at full power. The RCX Code version of this program is shown in Figure 5-12, and the NQC program is in Listing 5-2.

Listing 5-2. Tankbot Program 2 in NQC

```
// tankbot2.nqc - drive and turn

// motors
#define LEFT OUT_A
#define RIGHT OUT_C

// how much time to spend turning or moving forward
#define TURN_TIME        200
#define STRAIGHT_TIME    100

// speed to run a turned motor
#define TURN_POWER    3

task main()
{
    // start with both motors on
    On(LEFT+RIGHT);

    // repeat the following steps forever
    while(true)
    {
        // turn right by slowing down the right tread
        SetPower(RIGHT, TURN_POWER);
        Wait(TURN_TIME);
```

Figure 5-12.
Tankbot program 2 in RCX Code

```
        // resume going straight
        SetPower(RIGHT, OUT_FULL);
        Wait(STRAIGHT_TIME);

        // turn left
        SetPower(LEFT, TURN_POWER);
        Wait(TURN_TIME);

        // resume going straight
        SetPower(LEFT, OUT_FULL);
        Wait(STRAIGHT_TIME);
    }
}
```

As usual, we define anything that we may want to change later (such as the output ports, the time spent turning, and the speed to use for turns) as constants near the top of the NQC program.

The results were probably less than spectacular. The amount of turning may have been barely noticeable, and the sharpness of the right turns was probably different from that of the left turns. Why didn't this work?

The RCX cannot directly control the speed of a motor. Instead, it varies the amount of power supplied to the motor. The LEGO motors were designed to be very power efficient, and they have an internal flywheel, which acts as a sort of energy storage tank. The flywheel is most effective when the motor has very little physical resistance (called *load*). Starting the motor consumes a lot of energy since the flywheel must also be spun up to speed. Once running, however, a lightly loaded motor (perhaps a motor that is turning a gear that isn't connected to anything else) can maintain its speed with very little external power. In this case, it doesn't matter if the RCX is sending lots of power or just a little bit to the motor, it will turn at the same speed regardless. Under a heavy load (propelling a vehicle across a carpeted surface), the flywheel is less effective, and changing power levels will have a more noticeable effect on speed.

With Tankbot, we could try adjusting the power level used for turns (by setting TURN_POWER), or even turn a motor completely off. However, one of the unique features of a tread-based design is that it is quite good at turning in place by reversing one tread while leaving the other running. In fact, it is so good that we can reduce the amount of time spent turning from 2 seconds to $1/2$ second and thereby increase the time spent driving forward. The resulting RCX Code program is shown in Figure 5-13, and an NQC version appears in Listing 5-3.

Listing 5-3. Tankbot Program 3 in NQC

```
// tankbot3.nqc - improved turning

// motors
#define LEFT OUT_A
#define RIGHT OUT_C

// how much time to spend turning or moving forward
#define TURN_TIME        50
#define STRAIGHT_TIME    200

task main()
{
    // start with both motors on
    On(LEFT+RIGHT);

    // repeat the following steps forever
    while(true)
    {
        // turn right by reversing the right tread
        Rev(RIGHT);
        Wait(TURN_TIME);

        // resume going straight
        Fwd(RIGHT);
        Wait(STRAIGHT_TIME);

        // turn left by reversing the left tread
        Rev(LEFT);
        Wait(TURN_TIME);

        // resume going straight
        Fwd(LEFT);
        Wait(STRAIGHT_TIME);
    }
}
```

Figure 5-13.
Tankbot program 3
in RCX Code

CONCLUSION

Congratulations, you have completed the first robot in this book. Although relatively simple, the construction and programming techniques used in Tankbot serve as a foundation for many of the other robots in this book.

Tankbot itself can be adapted for a variety of tasks. In the next few chapters, a variety of sensors will be added to Tankbot. Bumpbot and Bugbot use touch sensors to navigate around obstacles. Linebot uses a light sensor to follow a line drawn on the floor. Scanbot uses a light sensor (and an extra motor) to look around and seek out bright lights.

Chapter 6
Bumpbot

The goal of Bumpbot is to drive around randomly without getting stuck against a wall or in a corner. To accomplish this, Bumpbot needs some way of detecting a collision with an obstacle. This can be achieved by adding a "bumper" to the basic Tankbot chassis. This chapter presents two different versions of Bumpbot, each with its own bumper design.

A SIMPLE APPROACH

A simple bumper can be constructed from a touch sensor as shown in Figures 6-1 and 6-2. A #12 axle is used as the bumper itself, which is attached to a #6 axle that presses against a touch sensor. We mount this sensor on the front of our previous robot (Tankbot), and presto—Bumpbot is born.

Figure 6-1.
A simple bumper

Figure 6-2.
A simple Bumpbot

All that remains is a little programming. Let's start by programming Bumpbot to drive forward until it hits something, then back up a little, spin around a bit, and resume going forward. A suitable program in RCX Code is shown in Figure 6-3.

A similar program can also be created in NQC, as shown in Listing 6-1.

Listing 6-1. Simple Bumpbot Program in NQC

```
// bumpbot1.nqc - a simple bumper

// sensors
#define BUMP SENSOR_1

// motors
#define LEFT OUT_A
#define RIGHT OUT_C

// constants
#define REV_TIME     50
#define SPIN_TIME    70

task main()
{
    // configure the sensor
    SetSensor(BUMP, SENSOR_TOUCH);

    // start going forward
    On(LEFT+RIGHT);

    // do this forever
    while(true)
    {
        // wait for bumper to hit something
        until(BUMP==1);

        // back up
        Rev(LEFT+RIGHT);
        Wait(REV_TIME);

        // spin around
        Fwd(LEFT);
        Wait(SPIN_TIME);

        // resume
        Fwd(RIGHT);
    }
}
```

Figure 6-3.
Simple Bumpbot program
in RCX Code

Because Bumpbot uses a sensor, there are a few new elements to our NQC program. The first thing we must do whenever sensors are being used is to tell the RCX what type of sensor is connected to the sensor port. This is done with the SetSensor command, which takes two arguments: a sensor port and a sensor type. In the preceding example, BUMP was simply defined as another name for SENSOR_1—just like we've been defining LEFT and RIGHT to be names for OUT_A and OUT_C.

We've used the until statement before, but this time the sensor is used as part of the condition. A task will stay in the until statement until its condition becomes true. In this case, we are waiting for BUMP == 1. BUMP is just another name for the touch sensor, meaning that we are waiting for the touch sensor's value to be equal to 1.

NQC inherits much of its syntax—both good and bad—from the C language. In C, = and == mean very different things. Specifically, = is used to assign a value to a variable, whereas == is used to test equality (compare two values). This is often confusing to those new to the language. There's good reason for such a distinction in C, but less so in NQC. Nevertheless, NQC sticks with the C syntax.

A BETTER BUMPER

Our first bumper is very simple to build, but it does have a problem in that anytime it hits something, the force of impact is transmitted directly to the touch sensor, and hence to the rest of the model. In addition, the RCX cannot respond instantaneously, so for a short time the motors keep running, resulting in even more pressure being applied to the bumper and sensor. The most noticeable effect of this is that after enough collisions, the bumper will just fall off.

Although we could mount the bumper more securely (perhaps using some vertical bracing), this still wouldn't eliminate the stress to the touch sensor. Such repeated impact is something to be avoided, so what we really need is a bumper that will give way during impact and allow more time for the RCX to respond.

We begin constructing the improved Bumpbot by removing the treads and front 1×6 beams from Tankbot as shown in Figure 6-4.

Figure 6-4.
Bumpbot step 1

Supports for the bumper assembly are then constructed in Figures 6-5 and 6-6. The bumper itself is going to be a pivoting structure held in the "forward" position by a rubber band. The gray peg at the front of the 1×16 beam serves as the pivot point, while the black peg serves as an anchor point for the rubber band. Although these pegs look alike (except for color), they have slight differences, which alter how they are used. The gray peg is slightly smaller than the holes in the beams (and other parts), and as a result parts joined with this peg can pivot freely. In contrast, the black peg is slightly larger and holds parts together more firmly. For that reason, the black peg is often called a *friction peg,* and it should be used whenever pivoting is not required.

Figure 6-5.
Bumpbot step 2

Figure 6-6.
Bumpbot step 3

Figure 6-7 shows the construction of one half of the bumper. The black *angle beam,* along with an axle, makes for a nice bumper, and the yellow *double-angle beam* provides a convenient way to extend the bumper in front of the RCX. Both of these parts are often good choices when designing bumpers. The black angle beam is attached to the axle using a special piece called a *catch* (see Figure 6-9 later for a better view of this).

Figure 6-7.
Bumpbot step 4

One end of the double-angle beam has a bushing and #2 axle attached to it. These parts serve a dual purpose: they provide the other anchor point for the small black rubber band, and they also provide the means for the bumper to activate the touch sensor, which is added in Figure 6-8. The sensor should be connected to port 1 on the RCX. The extra 1×2 plates on top of the touch sensor have an important function, which will become clear a little later.

The other half of the bumper is completed in Figure 6-9. This half is almost identical to the first half, with the exception that it does not need the #2 axle and bushing.

Figure 6-8.
Bumpbot step 5

Figure 6-9.
Bumpbot step 6

Figure 6-10 shows the finished robot. Tankbot used four 1×6 beams to secure the RCX to the bottom frame. In Bumpbot, a pair of 1×6 beams is still used to secure the back of the RCX, while the front is braced using 1×10 beams that go from the bottom frame all the way up to the 1×16 beams supporting the bumper itself. This vertical bracing keeps the bumper intact even after multiple collisions. As a final detail, the treads and hubs must be attached and locked into place (once again with bushings on the front and 16-tooth gears in back).

Figure 6-10.
Bumpbot step 7

This new bumper design has a larger range of motion than the simple bumper presented at the start of the chapter. The bumper is normally held forward by the tension of the rubber band. In this position, the touch sensor is pressed by the small arm at the end of the double-angle beam. During a collision, the front of the bumper gets pushed in, leading to a rotation of the double-angle beam and lifting the arm away from the touch sensor. After the touch sensor is released, the bumper can continue to be pushed in a little further without any serious impact to Bumpbot itself. This gives the RCX extra time to react to the sensor. Even in the worst case, any impact would be felt by the structure of the bumper and not by the touch sensor itself.

Remember those extra plates on top of the touch sensor? The double-angle beams used for the bumper tend to wiggle a bit. Without those plates it would be possible for the bumper to get stuck on top of the touch sensor. The additional plates ensure that the double-angle beam remains "in its place" as it pivots.

A BETTER PROGRAM

We'll need to change the program slightly since the touch sensor is now pressed during normal operation and then released when the bumper hits something. This can be accommodated simply by changing the until statement:

```
until(BUMP==0);
```

Bumpbot is also a bit too predictable; it would be a little more interesting if it spun around a different amount each time it ran into something. The RCX has the ability to generate a random number between 0 and a number of our choosing. We can then use this number as the amount of time to spin. Unfortunately, that tends to result in Bumpbot's frequently spinning just a very small amount extra, and Bumpbot may take many tries to turn away from a wall. What we really want is for Bumpbot to always turn some minimum amount, but also to turn some additional random amount. We can do this in NQC simply by adding a constant value to the random value:

```
Wait(SPIN_MINIMUM + Random(SPIN_RANDOM));
```

Incorporating both of these changes, the new Bumpbot code looks like Listing 6-2.

Listing 6-2. Improved Bumpbot Program in NQC

```
// bumpbot2.nqc - improved sensor design

// sensors
#define BUMP SENSOR_1

// motors
#define LEFT OUT_A
#define RIGHT OUT_C

// constants
#define REV_TIME   50
#define SPIN_MIN   70
#define SPIN_RANDOM 50

task main()
{
    // configure the sensor
    SetSensor(BUMP, SENSOR_TOUCH);

    // start going forward
    On(LEFT+RIGHT);

    // do this forever
    while(true)
    {
        // wait for bumper to hit something
        until(BUMP==0);

        // back up
        Rev(LEFT+RIGHT);
        Wait(REV_TIME);

        // spin around
        Fwd(LEFT);
        Wait(SPIN_MIN + Random(SPIN_RANDOM));

        // resume
        Fwd(RIGHT);
    }
}
```

Similar changes can also be made to the RCX Code program as shown in Figure 6-11.

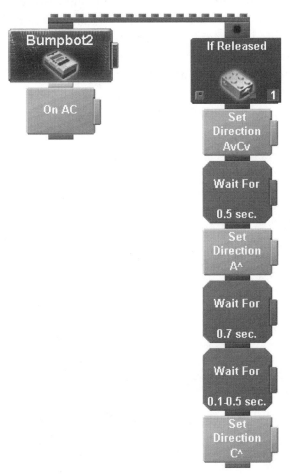

Figure 6-11.
Improved Bumpbot in RCX Code

CONCLUSION

With the ability to respond to its environment, Bumpbot is a bit more interesting than Tankbot. More sophisticated versions could be built with both front and rear bumpers, or perhaps a more complicated bumper that could discern between obstacles on the left or right side and respond accordingly. In any case, the basic ability to drive around while avoiding obstacles can be used as a stepping stone for more complicated vehicles.

Chapter 7
Bugbot

Bugbot once again extends the chassis introduced with Tankbot, this time by adding two antennalike feelers that give Bugbot its distinctive appearance. With its more sophisticated sensors and programming, Bugbot is much better at navigating around obstacles than the previous Bumpbots. The RCX's timer and counter capabilities are also utilized, and the concepts of *concurrent* and *synchronous* behavior are introduced.

CONSTRUCTION

In order to create Bugbot, you will first need to build Tankbot as shown in Chapter 5. If you have just completed Bumpbot, you will need to undo those changes and restore Tankbot to its original form.

In the previous robots, motors and sensors were put in place, then wires were attached between the motors or sensors and the RCX itself. With Bugbot, however, the feeler assembly is built above the RCX input ports; therefore it is necessary to attach two wires (short ones will do) to inputs 1 and 3 ahead of time. Figure 7-1 shows the addition of these wires and four *cross beams* to the original Tankbot. Cross beams are similar to regular beams, except the hole is shaped like a cross instead of a circle. Because of this design, cross beams can be used to prevent an axle from rotating. They also hold an axle in place more firmly than regular beams do.

Figure 7-1.
Bugbot step 1

Figures 7-2 and 7-3 build up the structure that will support the feelers. The pieces at the ends of the axle are called *1×3 crossblocks*. These pieces (and their shorter cousins) are quite versatile: one end has a cross hole (which prevents rotation), and the other end has a circular hole (allowing rotation). Bushings are used as spacers between the crossblocks and the cross beams. Without the spacers, it would be difficult to place both crossblocks the exact same distance from the cross beams, thus the feelers would not be symmetrical. A pair of touch sensors are also added; these will be activated by the feelers as Bugbot approaches an obstacle.

Figure 7-2.
Bugbot step 2

Figure 7-3.
Bugbot step 3

A #6 axle is passed through both touch sensors and secured in place by two bushings in Figure 7-4. These bushings are used later to hold two rubber belts in place. The feelers are built around #6 axles in Figure 7-5. Crossblocks are used to connect the axle to the peg that serves as a pivot point, and bushings are once again used as spacers. Rubber belts are used to hold each feeler against its corresponding touch sensor. The blue belts are a little too loose, but if they are wrapped a second time around the rear bushing, the tension is just right.

Figure 7-4.
Bugbot step 4

Figure 7-5.
Bugbot step 5

Only a few final touches are needed. The touch sensors must be attached to the RCX using the wires from step 1, and a piece with the unlikely name of *catch cross* is added to each of the feeler axles. This piece serves two purposes: it prevents the rubber belt from slipping off the feeler, and it provides better contact with the touch sensor than the axle alone. Flexible-ribbed tubing is added to extend the feelers (the longer magenta tubing works best). This tubing forms a sort of lever. The rubber belt is pulling on one side of the pivot, and an obstacle will push the feeler the other way. The distance from the pivot to the end of the tubing is much greater than the distance between the pivot and the rubber belt. Therefore, even a very small force applied to the tubing will counteract the rubber belt and cause the touch sensor to be released. The flexibility of the tubing, combined with the pivot design itself, gives the RCX plenty of time to react to obstacles before any serious impact is felt by Bugbot. The completed robot is shown in Figure 7-6.

Figure 7-6.
Bugbot step 6

RCX CODE BLOCKS

Before digging into the details of writing a program for Bugbot, a little discussion about RCX Code is in order. An RCX Code program is built up from individual *code blocks*. These blocks are grouped together into stacks.

The RCX Code concept of stack should not be confused with the more traditional concept of a stack in computer science. In RCX Code, a stack is just a group of individual code blocks.

All programs start with a *program block* that contains the name of the program. The stack appearing under the program block will be executed whenever the program is run. The remaining code blocks are divided into the following categories: *small blocks*, *wait blocks*, *repeat blocks*, *yes or no*, *sensor watchers*, *my blocks*, and *big blocks*.

Small blocks are colored green and represent a single action such as turning on a motor or playing a sound. In a way, small blocks do all of the real work of a program, and the other types of blocks just serve to organize and coordinate the small blocks.

Wait blocks are colored red and instruct the RCX to wait for either a certain amount of time (**Wait For**) or until a certain event occurs (**Wait Until**).

Repeat blocks are colored orange and can be used to construct *loops* (a sequence of instructions that gets executed over and over again). Blocks inserted between the top and bottom half of the repeat block are called the *body* of the loop. There are four different flavors of repeat blocks: **Repeat For** repeats the body a specified number of times, **Repeat Forever** repeats the body an infinite number of times, **Repeat While** and **Repeat Until** repeat the body until a certain condition is met (the difference between **Repeat While** and **Repeat Until** is discussed later).

Yes or no blocks (also called **If** blocks) are colored purple and instruct the RCX to make a decision based on some condition. Blocks placed under the left side will be executed if the condition is true, while those on the right side will be executed if the condition is not true.

Sensor watchers are colored blue and are used to monitor a sensor (or other condition such as the timer or counter). The RCX continuously checks each sensor watcher, and if the appropriate condition is met, the stack below the watcher will be executed. Unlike other blocks, sensor watchers always appear at the top of stacks; they cannot be placed underneath another block.

My blocks are colored yellow and allow you to group an entire stack of blocks under a single name. This can help organize a large program by breaking a large stack into smaller chunks. It can also help if certain sequences of blocks need to be used more than once in a program since once a *my* block is defined it can be used multiple times in a program. When you create a new *my* block it will be added to both your program and the My Blocks bin. You can add more copies of the *my* block into your program by selecting it from this bin and clicking somewhere in your program. Each copy of the *my* block in the program will contain the exact same blocks—if you add a new block to one copy, all of the others will also receive that new block. Furthermore, any *my* blocks in the bin can be added to other programs as well.

Big blocks are colored dark green and provide some predefined sequences of blocks that can be used in constructing your programs. Think of them as partially assembled pieces that you can use so that you don't have to build every program from scratch.

You may have noticed that there are a lot of different blocks that can be used to respond to stimuli (sensors, time, incoming messages from another RCX, etc.). All of these blocks fall into one of two categories: *condition based* or *event based*.

Condition-based blocks test for the specified condition at one instant in time, then make their decision based on the outcome of that test. The **If** and **Repeat While** blocks are condition based. In the case of the **If** block, it will test the condition a single time, then choose which stack to execute based on that test. The **Repeat While** block will test the condition, and if true will execute its body, then go back to the top and test the condition another time. It continues to do this until one of the tests fails.

Event-based blocks are a little different. They respond to changes in the stimuli rather than tests at specific times. For example, with a touch sensor, pressing it will cause an event to be triggered, but holding it in will not trigger any additional events. In order for a new event to be triggered, the touch sensor would have to be released first. Sensor watchers, **Wait Until**, and **Repeat Until** are event based.

Both mechanisms have their uses. If you were programming an electronic rooster, then you would probably use an event-based block (i.e., make lots of noise when it first becomes bright outside). If the rooster used a condition-based block, then it would continue making noise all day until the sun finally set. On the other hand, a take-out-the-garbage robot might not work very well if it was solely based on event-based blocks. What if it couldn't completely empty out all of the trash cans in its first trip? No new events would be triggered, but there would still be trash to take out. Ideally it would continue its work until all of the garbage was gone—a good indicator that some portion of the robot's programming would use condition-based blocks.

An Event-Based Experiment

The differences between event-based and condition-based blocks are sometimes quite subtle. With Bugbot, both of its touch sensors are normally pressed. When one of the feelers comes in contact with an obstacle, its corresponding touch sensor becomes released. Download the program shown in Figure 7-7 to the RCX and experiment with it a little. Note that the complete settings of a **Wait Until** block do not show up on screen. Specifically, you cannot tell if it is waiting for the sensor to be pressed or released. Whenever a block's screen shot is ambiguous, annotations are used in the illustration to show the block's full settings.

Touch 3
Release

Figure 7-7.
Event experiment program

Pull the left feeler back so that the touch sensor becomes released. The RCX should emit a high-pitched note. At this point the program has responded to the sensor watcher and is in the **Wait Until** block. Let go of the feeler and then pull it again. The RCX should emit another high-pitched tone. Even though the program is in the block waiting for sensor 3, it still responds to the new event that occurs for sensor 1. This is one of the special abilities of event-based blocks—they can interrupt whatever else is happening in order to respond to an event.

If you pull back the right feeler, you should hear a low-pitched tone. Pulling the right feeler back a second time will not emit a second tone. Once the **Wait Until** block has been satisfied (and the tone has been played), the stack of blocks has finished its work and only the sensor watcher will be active.

If you pull back the feeler and let it snap back quickly, you may hear several tones emitted in a row. This is because the feeler bounces a little as it comes in contact with the touch sensor. Sometimes it bounces enough to make the RCX think that the sensor was pressed and released several times in a row, and each press causes a sound to be emitted. Note that since the RCX queues any sounds that it needs to play, the program can continue onto the next blocks before the sound has finished playing. In the case of the bouncing touch sensor, the sensor watcher gets activated several times very quickly (while the first sound is still being played). These queued up sounds continue to play even after the touch sensor is firmly pressed.

Sensor watchers look for events all of the time. However, other event-based blocks need to become active before they can catch events, and as a result it is possible to miss events if they occur earlier than expected. As a demonstration, run the program and pull back the right feeler first, then while still holding it away from the touch sensor, pull the left feeler back as well. You should hear the high-pitched tone indicating that the RCX is responding to the touch sensor 1 being released. Touch sensor 3 was also released, but since this happened before the **Wait Until** block was activated, the RCX is still waiting for the release to happen.

A Condition-Based Experiment

The previous program waited until touch sensor 3 was released by using the aptly named **Wait Until** block, which is event based. There is no condition-based counterpart to **Wait Until**; however, the **Repeat While** block can be used instead. The trick is to make the condition of the **Repeat While** block the opposite of the thing you are waiting for, and then leave the body of the **Repeat While** block empty. Sometimes it helps if you think of the repeat blocks as meaning "do." In this case, instead of "waiting until sensor 3 is released," we will "do nothing while sensor 3 is pressed." The resulting program is shown in Figure 7-8.

Figure 7-8.
Condition experiment program

Run this program and observe how it responds to the feeler being activated. In most cases, it behaves identically to the previous event-based program. One important exception is when the right feeler is activated first, held so that the touch sensor remains released, then the left feeler is activated. The program will play the high-pitched tone, immediately followed by the low-pitched tone. Where the event-based program was still waiting for sensor 3 to change from pressed to released, this program checks the sensor, sees that it is currently released, and moves on.

As mentioned earlier, both event-based and condition-based blocks have their uses. Sometimes, the operation of the program will strongly dictate which kind of block needs to be used, but often it comes down to a matter of personal style. The programs in this book generally use sensor watchers to invoke some action, then use condition-based blocks during the action.

MULTIPLE WATCHERS

The idea behind Bugbot's programming is to have Bugbot drive forward until it hits something. If the obstacle is sensed by the right-hand feeler, then Bugbot should turn to the left while backing away slightly. If the obstacle is on the left, the Bugbot should back and turn to the right. The most obvious way to do this in RCX Code is to use a sensor watcher for each feeler as shown in Figure 7-9. As you can see, backing and turning is accomplished by reversing one motor while stopping the other. We only back and turn until the feeler clears the obstacle.

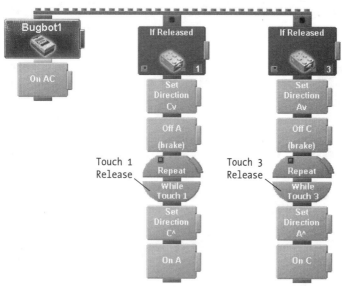

Figure 7-9.
Multiple watchers in RCX Code

In order to completely understand the operation of the preceding program, it is important to remember that the RCX supports multitasking. A program may define multiple tasks, and any number of them may be active at a given time. When only a single task is active, its instructions are executed one after another. However, when multiple tasks are active, the RCX rotates through each of the active tasks, executing a single instruction from each task, then proceeding to the next one. Conceptually, this is similar to playing a board game with several people. Each person gets a turn and makes one move, then control passes to the next player. After everyone has had a turn, the first player gets to move again. The RCX adds the additional twist that tasks may become active or inactive as a program executes. Returning to our board game analogy, this is the equivalent of players leaving the game (tasks becoming inactive) or new players entering the game (tasks becoming active).

In RCX Code, the main program stack (the blocks underneath the program's name) executes in one task, while the stacks beneath any sensor watchers are executed in their own separate tasks (one task per stack). Thus, in the previous example, the RCX could be executing the stack below the first sensor watcher while at the same time checking to see if the second sensor watcher has been triggered.

An NQC version of this program appears in Listing 7-1. Note how each watcher is its own task (within a while loop) and uses a monitor statement to respond to events. The main task starts the watcher tasks after performing initialization (configuring the sensors and events, and starting the motors). This is certainly more cumbersome than using if statements (as was done with Bumpbot), but it is a more accurate representation of the RCX Code program, and using separate tasks is relevant to our discussion.

Listing 7-1. Bugbot NQC Program Using Multiple Tasks

```
// bugbot1.nqc - using multiple tasks

// sensors
#define LBUMP SENSOR_1
#define RBUMP SENSOR_3

// motors
#define LEFT OUT_A
#define RIGHT OUT_C

// events
#define LEFT_EVENT 1
#define RIGHT_EVENT 2
```

```
task main()
{
    // configure the sensor
    SetSensor(LBUMP, SENSOR_TOUCH);
    SetSensor(RBUMP, SENSOR_TOUCH);

    // configure the events
    SetEvent(LEFT_EVENT, LBUMP, EVENT_TYPE_RELEASED);
    SetEvent(RIGHT_EVENT, RBUMP, EVENT_TYPE_RELEASED);

    // start going forward
    On(LEFT+RIGHT);

    start watch_left;
    start watch_right;
}


task watch_left()
{
    while(true)
    {
        monitor(EVENT_MASK(LEFT_EVENT))
        {
            while(true);
        }
        catch
        {
            Off(LEFT);
            Rev(RIGHT);

            until(LBUMP==1);
            On(LEFT);
            Fwd(RIGHT);
        }
    }
}


task watch_right()
{
    while(true)
    {
        monitor(EVENT_MASK(RIGHT_EVENT))
        {
            while(true);
        }
```

```
        catch
        {
            Off(RIGHT);
            Rev(LEFT);

            until(RBUMP==1);
            On(RIGHT);
            Fwd(LEFT);
        }
    }
}
```

Try running either of these programs on Bugbot and see how well it can maneuver. Overall, it does pretty well when it hits an obstacle with one feeler or the other, such as when approaching a wall at an angle. However, if both feelers hit an obstacle at about the same time, Bugbot has a tendency to stop dead in its tracks. Occasionally it will even stop when only one feeler has hit an obstacle. Why does this happen? Nowhere in the program have we instructed Bugbot to turn off both of its motors.

 *If the RCX Code program causes Bugbot to sometimes stop when only one feeler is touching an obstacle, then check to make sure **Smart Tasking** in the **Settings** menu is unchecked (see the sidebar "Smart Tasking" later in this chapter for more information).*

The problem arises from the fact that the actions associated with the right and left sensors may run concurrently (at the same time). In the NQC program, the watch_left and watch_right tasks are both active. In the RCX Code program, the two sensor watchers are active at the same time. Now consider what happens if the two feelers come into contact with an obstacle at about the same time. Let's say the left feeler is detected first. The watch_left task (or the watcher on sensor 1 in RCX Code) will stop the left motor, reverse the direction of the right motor, and wait for the feeler to return to normal. Now what happens if the right feeler suddenly is noticed (because the watch_right task or second sensor watcher decided to check)? The right motor will be stopped, and the left motor will be reversed. Of course, the left motor is already stopped, so reversing it has no effect. The net result is that both motors are stopped and both watchers are waiting for sensors to be pressed, which, of course, won't happen since Bugbot isn't moving away from the obstacle. This is an example of the type of subtle problems that make it difficult to program and debug concurrent systems.

Perhaps you think the problem can be fixed by making the tasks (or watchers) turn the motor on in addition to reversing its direction before waiting for the sensor. In NQC, the fix for the watch_left task might look something like the code shown in Listing 7-2 (accompanied by a similar fix for the watch_right task).

Listing 7-2. Trying to Fix the Problem

```
task watch_left()
{
    while(true)
    {
        monitor(EVENT_MASK(LEFT_EVENT))
        {
            while(true);
        }
        catch
        {
            Off(LEFT);
            On(RIGHT);
            Rev(RIGHT);

            until(LBUMP==1);
            On(LEFT);
            Fwd(RIGHT);
        }
    }
}
```

Although this will prevent Bugbot from stopping completely, we will still have a potential problem when both feelers hit an obstacle. Basically, the watchers are fighting against one another. Each one is trying to correct its own situation but is making the other one's situation worse. In many cases, the watchers will fight back and forth, causing Bugbot to bounce back and forth until one of the watchers eventually "wins" and Bugbot returns to normal. In some situations this may be completely acceptable, but sometimes more dependable behavior is needed.

SMART TASKING

RCX Code has a special feature, called Smart Tasking, that can sometimes be used to solve the problem of two portions of a program fighting against one another. RCX Code programs are always split into multiple tasks. If the **Show Smart Tasking** item in the **Settings** menu is checked, light blue dashed lines will show you how your program has been divided.

The RCX has several resources: the speaker (for making sounds) and the three motors. When Smart Tasking is enabled (by checking the **Smart Tasking** item in the **Settings** menu), the computer will examine each task and look to see which (if any) resources get used. It then inserts special invisible instructions in your program that try to ensure that only a single task uses each resource at any given time.

SYNCHRONOUS BEHAVIOR

An alternative to the multiple watcher problem is to ensure that only one feeler is being reacted to at a time and that we clear the condition on that feeler before checking the other one. This is called synchronous behavior. The idea is to have our program consist of a loop (sometimes called the *main loop*) that checks for the sensors being released, then responds to these events by executing the appropriate code.

If the program were created as a single RCX Code stack, it would get to be quite long—a bit too long to work with comfortably. Instead, the program will be broken into three parts: the main loop, checking the left feeler, and checking the right feeler. As shown in Figure 7-10, the main loop consists of a **Repeat Forever** block that then calls both the left and right check blocks (which are **My Blocks**). Checking is completely condition based since both the **If** and **Repeat While** blocks use conditions rather than events.

Figure 7-10.
Synchronous behavior in RCX Code

A similar program written in NQC appears in Listing 7-3. Note that the check_left and check_right functions in the NQC program correspond to the **BUG_LEFT** and **BUG_RIGHT** blocks in the RCX Code program.

Listing 7-3. NQC Program for Synchronous Behavior

```
// bugbot2.nqc - syncrhonous behavior

// sensors
#define LBUMP SENSOR_1
#define RBUMP SENSOR_3

// motors
#define LEFT OUT_A
#define RIGHT OUT_C


void check_left()
{
    if (LBUMP == 0)
    {
        Off(LEFT);
        Rev(RIGHT);
```

```
            until(LBUMP==1);
            On(LEFT);
            Fwd(RIGHT);
        }
}

void check_right()
{
    if (RBUMP == 0)
    {
        Off(RIGHT);
        Rev(LEFT);
        until(RBUMP==1);
        On(RIGHT);
        Fwd(LEFT);
    }
}


task main()
{
    // configure the sensor
    SetSensor(LBUMP, SENSOR_TOUCH);
    SetSensor(RBUMP, SENSOR_TOUCH);

    On(LEFT+RIGHT);

    while(true)
    {
        check_left();
        check_right();
    }
}
```

How does Bugbot work with the new program? When one feeler touches an obstacle, it should behave the same as it did with the original program. When both feelers hit an obstacle, however, Bugbot will no longer stop. Instead, it will pay attention to either the right or left feeler (depending on exactly where in the program it was when the feelers were touched), and only after that condition is cleared will it check the other feeler.

STUCK IN A CORNER

Bugbot has a tendency to get trapped in a corner. The reason for this is that the right feeler will hit, Bugbot will turn left, then the left feeler will hit, Bugbot will turn right, and so on. Taking care of the corner problem requires two things: detecting that Bugbot is in a corner, and then taking corrective action. The corrective action is relatively easy: backing up and spinning around a bit should get Bugbot headed away from the corner.

Detecting the corner, however, is a bit more troublesome. The feelers don't know the difference between a corner and any other obstacle. All they know is if the obstacle is on the right, or the left, or possibly both. Corners can seem like any of these. Clearly we need some other way of deciding that we're in a corner.

When Bugbot encounters an obstacle, it usually can deal with it. There will be a little course correction to the right or left—sometimes even a few such corrections are needed—but eventually Bugbot heads away from the obstacle. A corner, however, causes Bugbot to thrash about: turning right, then left, then right again, never making much progress. Perhaps that is how we can tell if Bugbot is in a corner—we just need to determine when Bugbot is thrashing about. Instead of trying to detect the cause (being in a corner), we will attempt to detect the symptom (thrashing back and forth).

One way to do this is to keep track of how often Bugbot hits something. If we ever see a large number of hits within a fixed time period, then we'll assume that Bugbot is stuck and that is it time to panic. To make this determination, we need to introduce two new programming features: *variables* and *timers*.

The RCX contains 32 global variables, which are a kind of memory. Each variable can hold a single number. The RCX also has functions that operate on the variables. For example, you can set a variable to a specific value, add a number to a variable, or check to see if a variable's value is equal to some other value.

When using RCX Code, you create a new variable by selecting **Add a Variable** from the **Edit** menu. You will then be prompted to enter the variable's name. Variables can hold a value in the range –3,276.8 to +3,276.7 and have a resolution of 0.1. That means you could store the value 3.1 in a variable, but not 3.14.

When a program is run, it automatically sets all of the variables to 0; after that it is up to your program to set and check any variables. An entire group of small blocks are available to set variables and perform calculations. All of the control blocks (sensor watchers, repeat loops, etc.) can also be configured to use a variable instead of a sensor for its event or condition.

We can use a variable to keep track of how many times Bugbot has hit an obstacle simply by incrementing the variable each time the right or left feeler is triggered. However, for our corner detection to work we also need a way to reset the variable to 0 every so often. This is where timers come in.

The RCX contains four timers that, like variables, are memory locations that hold a value which can be examined and checked. Unlike variables, timers change their value automatically; every tenth of a second each timer is incremented by 1. A program may reset a timer back to 0 at any time. After doing this, the timer will simply continue counting up from 0. This allows us to perform periodic tasks: if we need to do something every 3 seconds, then we create a task that waits for a timer's value to hit 30, reset the timer, perform the desired action, and go back to waiting for the timer.

Using variables and timers, our new program for Bugbot is shown in Figure 7-11. The program plays a short tone every time the timer task is triggered. This has no real function other than to let the user know that the timer task has been triggered. Sometimes adding a few tones or beeps within a program can be very helpful while trying to debug it. In this case, the tone gives an indication of how often the counter is being reset. A series of descending tones (**Beep 3**) tells us when Bugbot thinks it is in a corner and is about to take corrective action.

Figure 7-11.
Corner detection in RCX Code

NQC also provides access to variables, although in a slightly different way. A program has access to the RCX's 32 global variables as well as an extra 16 variables per task that are local to that particular task. The nice part is that the programmer rarely has to worry about what kind of memory the variable is coming from. The NQC compiler will assign a particular variable name to a specific location based on where it was declared in your program and how it is used. Variables that are declared outside of a task or function are always placed in global memory and all tasks can use them. Variables declared inside a task or function can sometimes take advantage of local memory—preserving those precious 32 global memory locations for other uses. In general, you should try to make your variable declaration as local as possible to the statements that use it. If you only use a variable within a while loop, then place the declaration at the start of the while loop rather than at the top of the task or function. This gives the compiler the greatest flexibility in assigning (and possibly reusing) storage for your variables, thus allowing you to use more than 32 total variables.

Unlike RCX Code (which measures things in tenths), variables in NQC always hold integer values in the range −32,787 to 32,767. Another important difference is that unless you explicitly initialize a value (by assigning it a value in its declaration), NQC will not clear a variable automatically when a program starts. Forgetting to initialize a variable is a very common bug, and can sometimes be difficult to track down since the behavior might differ from one run to the next (whatever was left in the memory location last time will still be there when the program starts again).

Using timers and variables, the NQC version of a corner detecting Bugbot program is shown in Listing 7-4.

Listing 7-4. Corner Detection in NQC

```
// bugbot3.nqc - now with corner detection

// sensors
#define LBUMP SENSOR_1
#define RBUMP SENSOR_3

// motors
#define LEFT OUT_A
#define RIGHT OUT_C

#define TIMER_LIMIT 50
#define BUMPS_LIMIT 10

int bumps;
```

```
void check_left()
{
    if (LBUMP == 0)
    {
        Off(LEFT);
        Rev(RIGHT);
        until(LBUMP==1);
        On(LEFT);
        Fwd(RIGHT);
        bumps += 1;
    }
}


void check_right()
{
    if (RBUMP == 0)
    {
        Off(RIGHT);
        Rev(LEFT);
        until(RBUMP==1);
        On(RIGHT);
        Fwd(LEFT);
        bumps += 1;
    }
}


void check_bumps()
{
    if (bumps > BUMPS_LIMIT)
    {
        // we're in a corner...
        PlaySound(SOUND_DOWN);
        bumps = 0;

        // back up, spin around, and continue
        Rev(RIGHT+LEFT);
        Wait(100);
        Fwd(RIGHT);
        Wait(300 + Random(300));
        Fwd(LEFT);
    }
}
```

```
task main()
{
    bumps = 0;

    // configure the sensor
    SetSensor(LBUMP, SENSOR_TOUCH);
    SetSensor(RBUMP, SENSOR_TOUCH);

    On(LEFT+RIGHT);
    start watch_timer;

    while(true)
    {
        check_left();
        check_right();
        check_bumps();
    }
}


task watch_timer()
{
    while(true)
    {
        until(Timer(0) > TIMER_LIMIT);
        PlayTone(440, 10);
        ClearTimer(0);
        bumps = 0;
    }
}
```

The check_left and check_right functions both contain the following statement:

```
bumps += 1;.
```

This statement uses the += operator, which can take a while to get used to. When we use a normal assignment, such as $x = y + 4$, the meaning is fairly intuitive: take the value of y, add 4 to it, and stick the result into x. In order to increment bumps, we could have written:

```
bumps = bumps + 1;.
```

NQC (like C and Java) provides special assignment operators that perform calculation and assignment together. For example, x += y adds x and y together and sticks the result back into x. There are similar assignment operators for most calculations (-=, *=, etc.).

Many programmers (myself included) prefer using the special operators such as += because they are more compact and easier to maintain (if you want to change the variable being modified, you only need to change it in one place, instead of on both the right and left sides of a normal assignment).

Note how the bumps variable is checked within the main loop, but the timer is watched in its own task. This is because after the bumps check, the program may need to control the motors. If this check were done in its own task, we would encounter problems similar to the very first Bugbot program. For example, consider what would happen when Bugbot was stuck in a corner. The main loop would be checking the right and left feelers, and it would be responding by turning Bugbot appropriately and incrementing bumps. At some point, bumps would exceed the limit set for corner detection. The code responsible for checking bumps would want to make Bugbot back away from the corner. However, if this code were in its own task, the main loop would continue to check the feelers while this was happening. Depending on the circumstances, one of the feelers may have hit an obstacle before the bumps checking task had reversed the motors. In this case, the feeler checking code would be fighting against the bumps checking code. The results of two tasks fighting for control, as shown in our first Bugbot example, are unreliable at best.

The timer, however, does not directly interact with the motors, so there are no adverse side effects to letting it remain in its own task. In fact, keeping it a separate task actually makes for a cleaner program.

TUNING THE CORNER DETECTOR

Our corner detection algorithm relies on two parameters: how many obstacle hits constitute a "corner" and how often this counter should be reset. The program shown in Listing 7-4 uses a limit of 10 hits within a 5-second period. Depending upon the type of obstacles Bugbot must negotiate, some trial and error may be required to determine the right values. The remaining paragraphs will refer to these values by their NQC names: BUMPS_LIMIT and TIMER_LIMIT. If you are using RCX Code, then BUMPS_LIMIT is the value used in the **If** block at the top of **BUG_CHECK**, and TIMER_LIMIT is the value used in the sensor watcher for the timer. Keep in mind that times in NQC are measured in tenths of a second, so a value of 50 means 5 seconds, while in RCX Code 5 seconds is specified as "5.0".

To find a set of values, first pick an amount of time that you are willing to let Bugbot thrash about in a corner before panicking and use that to set TIMER_LIMIT (actually Bugbot may thrash in the corner for twice that much time in the worst case). Now set BUMPS_LIMIT to something large (99 is a nice number) and send Bugbot running into a corner. Listen for the tones that indicate the timer triggering and count the number of collisions that occur between those tones. For best results you should repeat this several times, then set BUMPS_LIMIT to one less than the smallest count you made.

Now try running Bugbot around the room and see how it behaves. Try sending it into a corner and listen for the panic sound. If you don't hear the panic sound, then BUMPS_LIMIT is too high; try using a slightly smaller value. In the other extreme, if Bugbot panics even when negotiating normal obstacles such as a wall, then TIMER_LIMIT needs to be increased and a new value for BUMPS_LIMIT should be found.

If Bugbot is still panicking too frequently, a small delay can be inserted into the turning code so that Bugbot turns a little more after each collision, and presumably will negotiate obstacles with fewer collisions. For example, the check_left function for the NQC program could be modified as follows (with a similar modification to check_right):

```
#define TURN_DELAY 10

void check_left()
{
    if (LBUMP == 0)
    {
        Off(LEFT);
        Rev(RIGHT);
        until(LBUMP==1);
        Wait(TURN_DELAY); // turn a little extra
        On(LEFT);
        Fwd(RIGHT);
        bumps += 1;
    }
}
```

CONCLUSION

The mechanical design of Bugbot was simple enough, but it led us to some rather complicated programming issues. Specifically, using a concurrent behavior led to some subtle problems that could be avoided with a synchronous behavior. In addition, the timer and variable facilities of the RCX were introduced to solve the problem of getting stuck in a corner.

Chapter 8
Linebot

Linebot is a robot that follows a path drawn on the floor. This simple behavior can be used as a building block in more complex robots. Linebot introduces the light sensor and also explains the concept of *feedback*, and how it can be used in programming robots.

CONSTRUCTION

Following a line requires more precise movement than our previous robots, so the Tankbot chassis will need some minor modification. Instead of driving the treads using a 1:1 gear ratio, Linebot will use a 3:2 ratio, which results in a slightly slower speed. The only other modification is the mounting of a light sensor at the front of Linebot.

Construction starts with Tankbot stripped down to its bottom frame (Tankbot step 3 minus the 2×8 plate) as shown in Figure 8-1.

Figure 8-1.
Linebot step 1

Tankbot used 24-tooth gears on the rear axles and the motors (1:1 gear ratio). For Linebot, we want to add some gear reduction, so 16-tooth gears will be used on the motors while 24-tooth gears remain on the axles (3:2 gear reduction). Because the 16-tooth gear has a smaller radius than the 24-tooth gear, the motors must be placed slightly lower than before in order for the gears to mesh properly. The space between the frame and the motors is now only one plate height instead of two. Figures 8-2 and 8-3 illustrate this revised motor arrangement. Note that since the motors are one plate lower than before, an extra 1×4 plate (for a total of two) must be added on top of the motors to make them flush with the RCX.

Figure 8-2.
Linebot step 2

Figure 8-3.
Linebot step 3

The light sensor itself is positioned just barely above the floor. The light sensor responds to *ambient light* (the overall light in the room) as well as to *reflected light* from its own LED. By placing the light sensor close to the floor, the amount of ambient light is minimized, thus increasing the overall reliability of measuring reflected light. When attempting to detect reflected light, it is a good design practice to get the sensor as close as possible to the object to be seen. Figures 8-4 and 8-5 show the light sensor being added to Linebot.

Figure 8-4.
Linebot step 4

Figure 8-5.
Linebot step 5

In contrast to some of the previous designs (such as Bumpbot), Linebot is somewhat fragile (especially the mounting of the light sensor). Even the slightest impact will snap off the light sensor. A more robust mounting, perhaps utilizing cross beams and some vertical bracing, could be designed, but since we don't expect Linebot to bump into things during normal operation, we'll stick with this simple (yet fragile) design. A note of caution: don't try to use Linebot on a carpeted floor. The rough surface of the carpet will typically knock the light sensor off of Linebot.

SEEING THE LINE

The goal of Linebot's program is to allow it to follow the path of a black line drawn on a white surface. The test mat included with the Robotics Invention System can be used, or you can create your own test course. The line should be a solid dark color and at least $1/2$" wide. Although such a course can be drawn with markers, I prefer to use colored flexible tape since it creates a line of uniform color and width with crisp edges. Another option is to cut out strips of construction paper and tape or glue them into place on a poster board.

It is tempting to have the robot follow a line by attempting to keep the light sensor centered directly over the line. Since the light sensor can easily differentiate between black and white, the robot will be able to tell whether it is still following the line or has wandered astray. Unfortunately, just knowing that it has gone astray is not enough. The robot must also know whether to correct by turning to the right or to the left. Since both sides of the line look the same (white), what can the RCX do?

The answer has to do with the way that the light sensor sees things. The sensor measures the total amount of light falling on it. In the case of Linebot, most of this light is light from the built-in LED that is reflected back up from the surface. White paper reflects much of the light, while black absorbs most of it. But the sensor sees more than just a single point directly below it; light bouncing back anywhere in a small region will cause the sensor to respond. When this entire field of vision is over the white paper, the sensor reads a very high value. When the entire field is over the black line, a very low value is read. When the field is only partly over the line, however, an intermediate value is read.

Knowing this, we can change our strategy slightly. Instead of trying to keep the sensor centered over the line, we will try to keep it centered on the edge between the blank surface and the line. When correctly centered, we should read an intermediate value. We will detect a high value if the robot wanders too far to the left and a low value if it wanders too far to the right. Our program can then correct the situation by turning a little to the right or left to remedy the situation.

This is an example of a *feedback system,* and it is an important enough concept to warrant some extra discussion.

FEEDBACK

Consider a household thermostat that has a single temperature setting. Let's say the thermostat is set for 70 degrees and it is winter time, so a furnace is being used to heat the house. When the temperature falls below 70 degrees, the thermostat starts the furnace, which slowly begins to heat the house. The furnace remains on until the temperature rises above 70 degrees, at which point the thermostat turns it off. The condition used to control the furnace (temperature) is the same thing that is actually affected by the furnace. This is called *feedback*, and it is a very powerful technique for programming robots. The operation of this thermostat is illustrated in Figure 8-6.

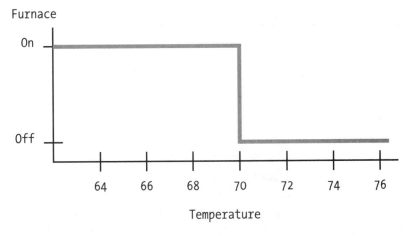

Figure 8-6.
Operation of thermostat

When using feedback, it is often important to keep the system from reacting too quickly. Returning to our thermostat example, consider what would happen if the thermostat turned on the furnace as soon as the temperature was 69.9999 degrees, then turned it off the moment it hit 70.0000. The furnace would be perpetually turning on and off rapidly, with the slightest air current causing it to change state.

To make matters worse, the temperature of the house would still oscillate a few degrees above or below 70 degrees. This is because houses rarely heat in a uniform manner, and a good deal of air circulation is usually necessary to average out the air temperature. In addition, it takes a certain amount of time for the effects of the furnace to be detected by the thermostat.

A better solution is to make the threshold for turning on the furnace a few degrees cooler than the threshold for turning it off. For example, we could turn on the furnace when it is 68 degrees, and turn it off when it is 72 degrees. For any value in between (e.g., 70 degrees), the furnace would remain in its current state. This technique is known as *hysteresis* and is illustrated in Figure 8-7.

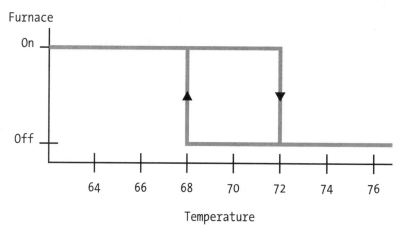

Figure 8-7.
Adding hysteresis to a thermostat

This graph is a bit unusual in that there are two possible states for the furnace (on and off) when the temperature is between 68 and 72 degrees. This is because the decision for turning the furnace on or off depends both on the current temperature and whether or not the furnace is already on. Consider what happens when the temperature is 64 degrees. The furnace will be running and will begin to heat up the house. Even when the temperature is 70 degrees the furnace will remain on. Only when the temperature rises above 72 degrees will the furnace turn off. Presumably the house will then slowly begin to cool, but rather than turning on the furnace right away, the thermostat waits until the temperature drops to 68 degrees.

Most thermostats use some form of hysteresis, although it usually isn't as extreme as in our example.

FOLLOWING THE LINE

As discussed previously, when the light sensor is completely over the black surface, it will read a low value. When the light source is over the white surface, it will register a significantly higher value. While it is over the edge between black and white, it will register a value somewhere in the middle. Since we are going to be using a feedback algorithm with hysteresis, we will need two threshold values: one for turning left, the other for turning right.

As long as the sensor reads between these two thresholds, the robot can continue moving straight ahead. If the sensor reads too low, then the robot is too far to the right and needs to turn left. This can be accomplished simply by turning off the left motor. The case where the sensor reads too high is similar, but the right motor is turned off instead.

Specific threshold values can be determined by using the view function of the RCX to monitor the light sensor's value while manually positioning it over the white surface or the black line. To view the sensor's value, the RCX must first be told that sensor 2 is a light sensor. One way to do this is to download and run a program that uses sensor 2 as a light sensor—any of the programs in this chapter will work fine. The program doesn't have to run for very long; just starting it will configure the RCX properly. Pressing the **View** button twice will then switch the RCX from the default display mode to viewing sensor 2.

The threshold for turning left should be a little larger than the reading over the black line. The threshold for turning right should be a little smaller than the reading over the white surface. For example, if the sensor reads a value of 50 over the white surface and 42 over the black line, then thresholds of 48 and 44 could be tried. When thresholds are close together, Linebot is pickier about what it considers "over the line," and this can result in a lot of adjustments as it attempts to follow the line. On the other hand, thresholds that are too far apart run the risk of letting Linebot wander too far astray. The light sensor readings are susceptible to many factors including the ambient lighting in the room, the condition of the RCX's batteries, and the exact colors and surfaces used. Because of this, proper calibration of the thresholds will often require a bit of trial and error. If you observe that Linebot is constantly adjusting back and forth, even over a straight line, then the thresholds are probably too close together. If Linebot tends to wander completely off the line (perhaps even spinning in circles), the thresholds are probably too far apart.

An RCX Code program that uses this simple line following strategy is shown in Figure 8-8. Three sensor watchers are used to respond to "too dark," "too bright," and "just right." The numbers used in the sensor watchers are the thresholds discussed previously.

Figure 8-8.
Simple line following program in RCX Code

A similar program written in NQC is presented in Listing 8-1. Since the thresholds might need to be adjusted a bit, they are set using #define near the top of the file. The RCX Code program was event based and this one is condition based, but in this case there is little difference between the two approaches.

Listing 8-1. Simple Line Following Program in NQC

```
// linebot1.nqc
//     turn by stopping one tread

// sensor and motors
#define EYE     SENSOR_2
#define LEFT    OUT_A
#define RIGHT   OUT_C

// thresholds
#define TOO_DARK    44
#define TOO_BRIGHT  48

task main()
{
    SetSensor(EYE, SENSOR_LIGHT);
    On(LEFT+RIGHT);

    while(true)
    {
        if (EYE <= TOO_DARK)
        {
            Off(LEFT);
            On(RIGHT);
        }
        else if (EYE >= TOO_BRIGHT)
```

```
    {
        Off(RIGHT);
        On(LEFT);
    }
    else
    {
        On(LEFT+RIGHT);
    }
  }
}
```

DYNAMIC THRESHOLDS

The process of continually adjusting thresholds to accommodate changes in the batteries or ambient lighting can become quite tedious after a little while. It would be much nicer if the program could run reliably without any manual adjustments.

For following the edge of the line, the thresholds were set a little lower than the reading over the line and a little higher than the reading over the background. We can instruct Linebot to do this measurement and calculation itself. Figure 8-9 shows two **My Blocks** that can be used to accomplish this. This first block, **LB2_SETUP**, assumes that Linebot starts out over the white background, and reads in a preliminary value for the value **tooBright**. It then plays a sound and waits 3 seconds for you to reposition the robot directly over the center of the line. It will then read in a preliminary value for **tooDark**.

Figure 8-9.
Threshold calculation in RCX Code

Measurement of the bright and dark values is only the first step—Linebot then needs to calculate the actual thresholds. Consider the range of values between the dark center of the line and the bright background. We will divide the range roughly into thirds, with the middle third representing when Linebot is over the edge of the line. The **LB2_CALC** block first calculates one third of the range between dark and light and stores the result in a variable named **delta**.

RCX Code doesn't allow us to write equations, so we have to break the calculation into tiny steps. Each step can either copy a value into a variable, or perform some operation on a variable (adding, subtracting, etc.). The value we wish to compute is (**tooBright** – **tooDark**) / 3, and we do this in three steps:

1. Set **delta** to **tooBright**.
2. Subtract **tooDark** from **delta**.
3. Divide **delta** by 3.

Once we know how big one third of the range is, we can adjust **tooDark** and **tooBright** inwards by **delta**.

Now that we have calculated the thresholds, we can use our line following algorithm from before. The only problem is that we can't use sensor watchers. Since sensor watchers are always active, they would be trying to do their work even during the initial calibration of **tooBright** and **tooDark**. We don't want anything to happen until we have finished calculating the thresholds, so we need to make sure the line following code is underneath the main program stack. Figure 8-10 shows the line following algorithm implemented in its own block called **LB2_FOLLOW**. The main program stack simply calls **LB2_SETUP**, **LB2_CALC**, and **LB2_FOLLOW** in sequence.

To try out the program, place Linebot away from the line and press the **Run** button. It will play a sound almost immediately, which is your signal to move it so that the light sensor is positioned over the center of the line. In a few seconds it will then start following the line. Because the thresholds are recomputed each time the program is run, it will work in almost any environment. The only potential problem is if there isn't enough contrast between your line and the background.

Listing 8-2 shows a similar program written in NQC. The main task is nearly identical to the previous version, except that the thresholds have been changed from constants to variables, and the new `setup` function is called. The `setup` function performs both the measurement and calculation of thresholds. Unlike RCX Code, NQC allows the use of simple equations (such as `(tooBright - tooDark) / 3`). This tends to make a program a little easier to read, and is one reason that NQC is often preferred for programs that do a lot of calculations.

Figure 8-10.
Line following with dynamic thresholds in RCX Code

Listing 8-2. Dynamic Thresholds in NQC

```
// linebot2.nqc
//      automatic thresholds

// sensor and motors
#define EYE       SENSOR_2
#define LEFT      OUT_A
#define RIGHT     OUT_C

// use variables for thresholds
int tooDark;
int tooBright;


void setup()
{
    // remember bright value
    tooBright = EYE;
    PlaySound(SOUND_UP);

    // wait 3 seconds
    Wait(300);
```

```
        // get dark value
        tooDark = EYE;

        // move values in
        int delta = (tooBright - tooDark) / 3;
        tooDark += delta;
        tooBright -= delta;
    }


    task main()
    {
        SetSensor(EYE, SENSOR_LIGHT);

        setup();

        On(LEFT+RIGHT);

        while(true)
        {
            if (EYE <= tooDark)
            {
                Off(LEFT);
                On(RIGHT);
            }
            else if (EYE >= tooBright)
            {
                Off(RIGHT);
                On(LEFT);
            }
            else
            {
                On(LEFT+RIGHT);
            }
        }
    }
```

IMPROVED LINE FOLLOWING

Our previous tracking algorithm tried to keep the robot positioned over the edge between a white surface and a black line. It is also possible to design an algorithm to follow the line itself. The algorithm is somewhat more complicated—using multiple variables, several loops, and a timer. This added complexity, however, is not without its rewards. If we make the line itself gray rather than black, and design an algorithm to follow the gray line, then we can also place black *stoppers* along the line and instruct Linebot to take some action whenever it encounters one of these stoppers.

The theory behind this algorithm is to drive forward until the light sensor exceeds some threshold indicating that the robot has wandered off the line. The robot will then start searching alternately right and left looking for the line. Once it finds the line, it will continue moving forward. This first threshold represents the brightest value that could still be consider "on the line," and will be represented by the variable **lineValue**. Another variable, named **stopValue**, will represent the threshold between the color of the line and the color of the stopper (which must be darker than the line).

Searching back and forth is an easy thing to describe in English, but a bit harder to explain to the RCX. We want it to start turning a little to the left, then a little to the right, then a little more to the left, etc. But how much should we turn each time? Let's say we spend 1 unit of time turning to the left for the first scan. For the second scan we need to turn to the right for at least for 1 unit of time just to get back to center. Ideally, we'd continue to turn even further and explore a little of the area to the right of the RCX. A simple strategy is to start with a small amount of time for the first scan, and then double it for each successive scan afterwards. So we start with 1 unit to the left, then 2 to the right, 4 to the left, etc.

In RCX Code, the heart of the algorithm is a pair of **My Blocks** named **LB3_FIND** and **LB3_SCAN**, which are shown in Figure 8-11. When **LB3_SCAN** starts, it assumes that the motors have already been set to spin Linebot in one direction or another (it doesn't care which). The **Repeat Until** loop will continue until it is interrupted by the light sensor reading a value darker than **lineValue** (a threshold that will be calculated beforehand). Note that **Repeat Until** is event driven, so execution of the loop stops as soon as the light sensor meets the specified condition. This allows the loop to stop as soon as the light sensor moves over the line. If a **Repeat While** loop were used instead, then it would only stop if the light sensor read a dark value at the end of sweep.

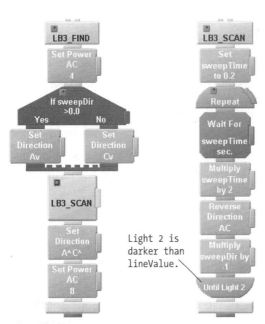

Figure 8-11.
Finding the line in RCX Code

Each iteration of the loop waits for **sweepTime** seconds. If the line hasn't been found yet, then it will prepare for the next sweep by doubling **sweepTime**, reversing the direction of both motors (thus reversing the direction of the spin), and also multiplying the variable **sweepDir** by –1.

The **sweepDir** variable is used to keep track of which direction Linebot was spinning the last time a scan was successful. It will be initialized to the value 1 early in the program, then change polarity (to –1, then back to +1) after each change of direction. Why is this important? Whenever Linebot loses the line, it must guess whether it needs to spin right or left to correct its heading. Guessing correctly means that Linebot will probably find the line faster. It turns out that in most cases, the direction it should use is the same one it used last time. This is because a single curve might take several adjustments as Linebot moves along it.

The **LB3_FIND** block does all of the preparation and cleanup for **LB3_SCAN**. The preparation reduces the power to the motors (so the spin will be a little slower), and picks an initial direction to spin based on **sweepDir**. The cleanup consists of restoring full power and setting both motors to the forward direction.

Pulling **LB3_SCAN** into its own **My Block** was a decision completely based on personal style. I could have just as easily written **LB3_FIND** as a single stack of blocks without any nested **My Blocks**. However, I prefer to work with chunks of code that can completely fit on the screen. Scrolling up and down can be a bit tedious, and it is easy to miss details when zoomed out. By breaking **LB3_FIND** up into two stacks, I could place them side by side and see the entire thing on screen at once.

Now that the RCX knows how to find the line, the rest of the program, shown in Figure 8-12, is relatively simple. The **LB3_FOLLOW** block turns on the motors, then uses a loop to follow the line until it sees the stopper, at which point it finishes its work by turning off the motors. Following the line involves a single check—if the light sensor reads too bright a value, then Linebot must have wandered off the line and **LB3_FIND** is used to correct the situation. Otherwise, Linebot must be doing okay, so nothing needs to be done, and Linebot will continue moving straight ahead.

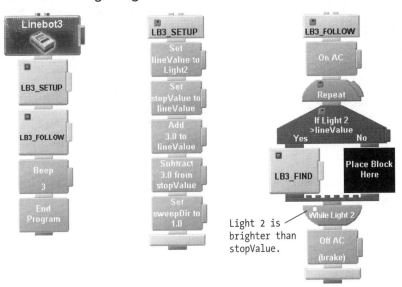

Figure 8-12.
Improved line following program in RCX Code

The **LB3_SETUP** block takes care of the initial preparation and calibration. Unlike the previous program, which required two measurements to determine the thresholds, this program only takes a single measurement—the sensor reading of being directly over the line. It then sets **lineValue** to a number a little brighter than the line, and **stopValue** to a number slightly lower. The program currently adjusts each number by 3, but feel free to experiment with other values. A larger adjustment will make Linebot a bit sloppier (but perhaps faster), while a smaller adjustment will keep Linebot following the line closer. **LB3_SETUP** also initializes **sweepDir** to 1.0 (so that it can be used for the left/right decision later on).

To run the program, start Linebot in a position such that the light sensor is directly over the center of the line. It should then follow the line until it sees the dark sensor, at which point it will play some sounds and the program will end.

As with the previous Linebot programs, creating a suitable test course may require some experimentation. The test course should be designed to have excellent contrast between the blank surface, the line to be followed, and the stoppers. It is also important to make the turns gradual and smooth. An extremely sharp turn may cause Linebot to lose track of the line. I constructed my test course on white poster board and used 3/4" gray tape for the line with a 6" radius for the sharpest turns. Black tape, also 3/4" wide, was used for the stoppers. Each stopper was about 1" long. If you place the stoppers on or near a curve, then they may need to be a little wider and/or longer.

An NQC version of the same program appears in Listing 8-3. As usual, we start with the definitions of constants and variables for the program. The setup function has to do a little more work than its RCX Code counterpart. Specifically, it has to configure the sensor and set the event parameters. One thing setup does not need to do is initialize sweepDir. Recall that in NQC, variables are not automatically initialized to 0 when the program runs. Instead, you must explicitly set them. One way is to assign a value to the variable near the start of the program (or at least somewhere before you use the variable). Another option is to specify an initial value right in the variable's declaration, as done for sweepDir in this program.

Listing 8-3. Improved Line Following Program in NQC

```
// linebot3.nqc
//      improved line following

// sensor and motors
#define EYE      SENSOR_2
#define LEFT     OUT_A
#define RIGHT    OUT_C

#define LINE_EVENT 1

// global variables
int lineValue;
int stopValue;
int sweepDir = 1;


void setup()
{
    SetSensor(EYE, SENSOR_LIGHT);

    lineValue = EYE;
    stopValue = lineValue - 3;
    lineValue += 3;
```

```
        SetEvent(LINE_EVENT, EYE, EVENT_TYPE_LOW);
        LowerLimit(LINE_EVENT) = lineValue;
}


void find()
{
    SetPower(LEFT+RIGHT, 3);
    if (sweepDir > 0)
    {
        Rev(LEFT);
    }
    else
    {
        Rev(RIGHT);
    }

    int sweepTime = 20;

    monitor(EVENT_MASK(LINE_EVENT))
    {
        while(true)
        {
            Wait(sweepTime);

            sweepTime *= 2;
            sweepDir *= -1;
            Toggle(LEFT+RIGHT);
        }
    }

    Fwd(LEFT+RIGHT);
    SetPower(LEFT+RIGHT, OUT_FULL);
}


void follow()
{
    On(LEFT+RIGHT);

    while(EYE > stopValue)
    {
        if (EYE > lineValue)
        {
            find();
        }
    }
```

```
        Off(LEFT+RIGHT);
}


task main()
{
    setup();

    follow();
    PlaySound(SOUND_DOWN);
}
```

The find function combines the functionality of **LB3_FIND** and **LB3_SCAN** from the RCX Code program. NQC tends to be a lot more compact, at least in terms of screen space, than RCX Code, so there was no need to split up find—the entire algorithm easily fits on screen.

There is one other difference between the NQC and RCX Code programs that is worth mentioning. The RCX Code program explicitly used an **End Program** block after it followed the line and played the sound. The NQC program has no such block. That is a fundamental difference between RCX Code and NQC. By default, an RCX Code program runs forever, while an NQC program will automatically stop once all of its tasks have reached their end.

CONCLUSION

Several different algorithms for following a line were presented, and the concepts of feedback and hysteresis were introduced. The behavior of following a line is a good building block for more complicated robots. Consider a robotic garbage truck that follows a path on the floor, emptying any garbage cans that it encounters along the way. Another variation would be a robotic mailman that follows its route, dropping off mail at each stop. In the next chapter, a robotic dump truck, Dumpbot, will be built using Linebot as a starting point.

Chapter 9
Dumpbot

Dumpbot is a robotic dump truck based on Linebot. Like its predecessor, it can follow a line to drive from place to place. In addition, it has a motorized bin that can be used to transport cargo and dump it out when desired.

CONSTRUCTION

Because Dumpbot is based on Linebot, the first stage of construction, shown in Figures 9-1 and 9-2, is to add the appropriate support and connecting wire to Linebot so that the cargo bin may be attached later on.

Figure 9-1.
Dumpbot step 1

Figure 9-2.
Dumpbot step 2

Steps 3 and 4, shown in Figures 9-3 and 9-4, illustrate the construction of the dumping mechanism. The 1×4 beams will later be attached to the cargo bin itself, and the #10 axle will be powered by a motor (after suitable gear reduction). The oval-shaped pieces added in step 4 are called 1×3 *liftarms*, and they are remarkably versatile. In this case they are being used just as their name implies: as an arm for lifting something. In later chapters, liftarms will be employed for bracing and other structural purposes as well.

Figure 9-3.
Dumpbot step 3

Figure 9-4.
Dumpbot step 4

The frame for the dumping mechanism is constructed in Figures 9-5 through 9-8. The two 1×2 plates near the back of the frame will serve as a stopper to limit the cargo bin's movement later on.

Figure 9-5.
Dumpbot step 5

Figure 9-6.
Dumpbot step 6

Figure 9-7.
Dumpbot step 7

Figure 9-8.
Dumpbot step 8

The 1×4 plates added in Figure 9-9 are used to support the motor. As usual, we need to accommodate the unusual shape of the motor's bottom by providing support along only the edges of the motor.

Figure 9-9.
Dumpbot step 9

The cargo bin itself is built in Figures 9-10 through 9-12. The friction peg shown in step 10 will hit the 1×2 stopper plates added back in step 6. A 1×4 plate serves as a lip for the cargo bin so that cargo won't roll out until the bin is tipped. Depending on the exact cargo, a larger lip could be built (perhaps using two 1×4 plates, or even a beam).

Figure 9-10.
Dumpbot step 10

Figure 9-11.
Dumpbot step 11

Figure 9-12.
Dumpbot step 12

In Figure 9-13, the cargo bin is attached to the 1×4 beams of the dumping mechanism. The motor is also added, with a blue belt to connect the pulleys. The pulleys provide approximately a 7:2 reduction, which, when combined with the 3:1 gear reduction, yields a total reduction of 21:2. This is suitable to lift and dump a modest amount of cargo quickly. The belt drive also allows the motor to slip when the cargo bin's motion is limited by the stopper.

Figure 9-13.
Dumpbot step 13

The dumping mechanism is attached to the back of Linebot in Figure 9-14. Some minor adjustment of the tread motor wires (outputs A and C) may be required in order to get the dumping mechanism firmly in place. The dumping motor is connected to output B. The best route for this wire is to run it straight backward (over the top of the 1×8 beam), then wrap it up and around to the motor.

Figure 9-14.
Dumpbot step 14

DELIVERING CARGO

Since Dumpbot's construction is based on Linebot, it makes sense that its program is also based on those from Linebot. The program will follow a gray line until the end is reached (indicated by a black stopper). It will then dump its cargo bin, turn around, and follow the line back to the beginning (also marked with a black stopper).

We will use the improved line following algorithm from the end of Chapter 8. That just leaves two actions to program: dumping the cargo bin and turning around.

To dump the cargo bin, the motor is run forward for 0.7 second to tilt the bin, then backward for 1.0 second to restore the bin to a horizontal position. The reason that the motor is run longer in reverse than forward is that there is always some variability in how fast the bin tips. If the forward and reverse times were exactly equal, there would always be the chance that the bin wouldn't get fully restored to a horizontal position. The stopper (the friction peg that hits the 1×2 plates) will prevent the bin from moving too far, and the rubber belt will allow slippage once this happens.

Turning around is accomplished by reversing one of the treads so that Dumpbot spins in place. Since it presumably starts with the light sensor over the line, we first wait for a value brighter than the line, then a value dark enough to be the line. An RCX Code program that pulls all of this together is shown in Figure 9-15. Note that **LB3_SETUP, LB3_FOLLOW, LB3_FIND,** and **LB3_SCAN** are used by the program even though they are not shown in the illustration.

An NQC program for Dumpbot can be created making a few changes to the linebot3.nqc program. First, the new functions for dumping the cargo bin and turning, shown in Listing 9-1, need to be added to Linebot's program.

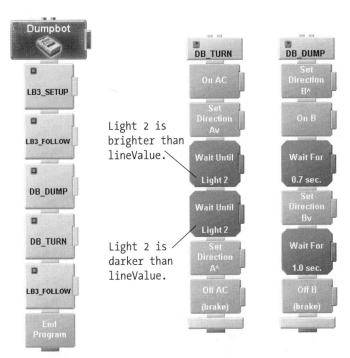

Figure 9-15.
Dumpbot program in RCX Code

Listing 9-1. Dumping Cargo and Turning Around in NQC

```
#define DUMPER OUT_B
#define DUMP_TIME 70
#define UNDUMP_TIME 100

void dump()
{
    // dump the cargo bin
    OnFwd(DUMPER);
    Wait(DUMP_TIME);
    Rev(DUMPER);
    Wait(UNDUMP_TIME);
    Off(DUMPER);
}
```

```
void turn_around()
{
    // start turning
    OnRev(LEFT);
    OnFwd(RIGHT);

    // wait until not over the line
    until(EYE > lineValue);

    // wait until over the line again
    until(EYE < lineValue);
    Off(LEFT+RIGHT);

}
```

The turn_around function is another case where we used event-based blocks in RCX Code, but condition-based statements in NQC. In this particular case there wasn't a significant advantage to either approach, so the choice came down to what was most convenient in each language. Since the RCX Code **Wait Until** block is a bit more intuitive than using a **Repeat While** with the opposite condition, the event-based block was used. In NQC, configuring events is more work than a simple while or until statement, so the condition-based approach was taken. All that remains is to rewrite the main task to call these new functions, as shown in Listing 9-2.

Listing 9-2. Main Task for Dumpbot in NQC

```
task main()
{
    setup();

    follow();
    dump();
    turn_around();
    follow();
}
```

The test surface for Dumpbot should meet the same criteria as for Linebot: specifically, a gray or green line that is $3/4$" thick on a white surface, curves that have a 6" or larger radius, and stoppers that are at least $3/4$" long. Create the path of your choice (I used a large "U" shape) with a stopper at each end. Position Dumpbot near one end with the light sensor directly over the line (but not over the stopper), place some suitable cargo in the cargo bin, then run the program. If all goes well, Dumpbot should follow the line to the other end, dump the cargo, turn around, and return to you.

CONCLUSION

Dumpbot shows how line following can be used as a building block for more sophisticated robots. Dumpbot and its line following program will appear again in Chapter 17 as an example of how two robots can communicate with one another. In the meantime, we will turn to a different sort of navigation in the next chapter with Scanbot.

Chapter 10
Scanbot

$\int$ canbot is a robot that seeks out bright lights. For example, if you stand across
the room and point a flashlight at Scanbot, it will head toward you. If you move
about the room, it will continue to home in on your location. Scanbot even has a
head that turns from side to side as it looks for bright lights, allowing it to proceed
on its current course while simultaneously looking for a better alternative.

CONSTRUCTION

Once again, we use the Tankbot chassis (with the original 1:1 gearing). Figure 10-1 shows Tankbot with the addition of a wire on motor port B.

Figure 10-1.
Scanbot step 1

Scanbot will be using a light sensor as part of a head that can look back and forth searching for light. The head itself is powered by a motor, and the position of the head is determined by a rotation sensor. A frame to support this motor and rotation sensor is built in Figures 10-2 and 10-3 using the "wide beam" construction technique. A #6 axle, which will serve as the neck for Scanbot, is also shown. Don't worry, it won't be floating in space for very long.

Figure 10-2.
Scanbot step 2

Figure 10-3.
Scanbot step 3

The neck is secured in Figures 10-4 and 10-5. There should now be two half bushings on the axle, one above the plate and one below. Make sure that these bushings are pushed close enough to the plate to keep the axle from wobbling, but not so close that it cannot spin freely.

Figure 10-4.
Scanbot step 4

Figure 10-5.
Scanbot step 5

Rather than directly gearing the motor to the neck, a belt-and-pulley combination will be used to transfer power. The pulley used here is called a *friction pulley* because of the small rubber ring inside of it. For our purposes we are ignoring its friction capability and using it simply because it is the correct size.

Figures 10-6 and 10-7 show the assembly of the driveshaft using a #8 axle, which passes through the rotation sensor. Two half bushings are used as spacers between the rotation sensor and the worm gear.

Figure 10-6.
Scanbot step 6

Figure 10-7.
Scanbot step 7

In Figure 10-8, the driveshaft is placed on the frame. A white rubber belt should be used to connect the two pulleys (on the motor and on the drive shaft). The worm gear is a little smaller than 2 LEGO units, so it may wiggle back and forth a little. To correct this, slide the worm gear all the way forward against the 1×6 beam, then push the half bushings up tight against the worm gear. The result of this will be a slight space between the bushings and the rotation sensor. As usual, make things tight enough to prevent wiggle, but loose enough so that everything can turn easily. This problem with the worm gear is the reason that two half bushings were used rather than a single regular bushing. Although the total amount of space occupied is the same in both cases, a pair of half bushings has more friction than a regular bushing and will do a better job of holding the worm gear in place.

Figure 10-8.
Scanbot step 8

This drive mechanism accomplishes two very important things: it reduces the rotation speed of the neck (8:1 gear reduction using the worm gear), and it allows slippage if the neck gets stuck. The position of the rotation sensor is critical. The rotation sensor itself has a resolution of 16 ticks per revolution. For Scanbot, we would like more accurate rotation readings, so the sensor is placed before the gear reduction. As a result, the sensor has an effective resolution of 128 ticks per revolution of the neck (16 ticks per revolution times an 8:1 gear reduction). Furthermore, since the intention is for the sensor to give an accurate reading of the neck position, it is important that any slippage occur between the motor and the rotation sensor, rather than between the rotation sensor and the neck (upon which the light sensor is mounted).

The rotation sensor measures relative rotation rather than absolute rotation. When the program is started, whatever position the sensor is in will be read as the value 0. Rotation in one direction will increment this value, while rotation in the other direction will decrement it. For Scanbot to function, we need to be able to determine if the head is pointing left, right, or straight ahead. This requires knowing an absolute rotation rather than a relative one. You can accomplish this by turning the head to a known position, then resetting the rotation sensor (which sets the value to 0). In Figure 10-9, a small arm is added to the neck, and a $3/4$ peg is used as a stopper. We can then turn the neck to a known position simply by running the motor for a few seconds. No matter where the neck originally was, it will eventually bump up against the stopper and remain there. The consequence of this is that we will sometimes be running the motor while the neck is prevented from turning; hence the use of the belt drive to allow slippage.

Figure 10-9.
Scanbot step 9

Another subtle detail, also shown in Figure 10-9, is the orientation of the bushing at the top of the neck. The two faces of a bushing are not identical—one is circular, and the other is notched. The notched face fits just perfectly between four "studs" on top of a LEGO piece. We will be taking advantage of this feature later on, so it is important that the notched side of the bushing face upward, as shown in the figure.

A bushing also appears at the end of the drive shaft (the #8 axle with the worm gear on it). This bushing provides a convenient way to manually adjust the neck if necessary. Because the worm gear is a kind of "one-way" mechanism, the neck itself cannot be turned. Instead the worm gear must be turned, which in turn will rotate the neck.

Scanbot's head is shown in Figure 10-10. It is built around a light sensor, with a 1×2 beam in front to narrow its field of vision (thus increasing its selectivity).

Figure 10-10.
Scanbot step 10

The head is mounted (upside down) on the neck in Figure 10-11. It is important to have the correct orientation of the head with respect to the small arm on the neck. When the arm is pointed directly away from the stopper peg, the head should point forward. The sensor wires from the rotation and light sensors should be attached to RCX ports 1 and 3, respectively. The sensor frame then sits on top of the wire connectors from the sensors and motors.

Figure 10-11.
Scanbot step 11

LOOKING AND STEERING

The basic operation of Scanbot is as follows: drive forward while looking back and forth until a bright light is spotted, then turn a little bit in the direction of the light, and resume looking back and forth.

The rotation sensor can be used to determine the current angle of the head, but since the rotation sensor measures relative rotation, we must first rotate to a known position and reset the sensor. I call this *aligning* the head. A simple way to do this is to turn the head for a fixed amount of time, then stop and reset the sensor. So long as the fixed amount of time is sufficient to move the head from one extreme to another, this will result in alignment of the head; 3 seconds should be adequate.

In order to look back and forth, we need to reverse the motor whenever the head has rotated to its rightmost or leftmost rotation. It turns out that the "center" position for the head results in a reading of 53 on the rotation sensor (after the head has been aligned). I chose to have the head sweep an area of 270 degrees (135 degrees both right and left). Since the rotation sensor counts 16 steps per rotation, and the head is geared down by 8:1, a full rotation (360 degrees) would be 128 steps. Thus the leftmost rotation is 48 less than the center position (53 − 48 = 5), and the rightmost rotation is 48 more than the center (53 + 48 = 101). Whenever the rotation sensor reads less than 5, the head has turned too far to the left, and the motor should be set to the forward direction. Whenever the sensor reads greater than 101, the head is too far to the right, and the motor should be run backward.

While the head is looking back and forth, the light sensor needs to be monitored. Whenever a bright light is detected, the head is stopped, which results in "freezing" the value of the rotation sensor. This value can then be checked to see if it is to the right or to the left of center. In order to prevent unnecessary zigzagging, a little slop is built into the checks. Any value within 3 of center is considered good enough not to require a turn. The turning itself is quite simple—one tread is reversed for half a second. A complete implementation of this in NQC is shown in Listing 10-1.

Listing 10-1. Simple Scanbot Program in NQC

```
// scanbot1.nqc
//   a simple tracking program for Scanbot

// sensors
#define EYE    SENSOR_3
#define ANGLE SENSOR_1

// motors
#define LEFT  OUT_A
#define HEAD  OUT_B
#define RIGHT OUT_C

// other constants
#define SLOP 3

#define CENTER 53
#define SWEEP  48      // 135 degrees

#define ALIGN_TIME     300     // 3 seconds
#define TURN_TIME      50      // 1/2 second
```

```
#define THRESHOLD    50

void align()
{
    Rev(HEAD);      // begin turning left
    OnFor(HEAD, ALIGN_TIME);
    Off(HEAD);         // stop turning
    Fwd(HEAD);          // prepare for later activation
    ClearSensor(ANGLE);    // make this position "0"
}


void steer()
{
    while(true)
    {
        if (EYE >= THRESHOLD)
        {
            Off(HEAD);     // stop looking
            PlaySound(SOUND_CLICK);

            if (ANGLE < CENTER-SLOP)
            {
                // turn left
                Rev(LEFT);
                Wait(TURN_TIME);
                Fwd(LEFT);
            }
            else if (ANGLE > CENTER+SLOP)
            {
                // turn right
                Rev(RIGHT);
                Wait(TURN_TIME);
                Fwd(RIGHT);
            }

            On(HEAD);      // resume looking
        }
    }
}


task look()
{
    // keep looking back and forth
    while(true)
    {
```

```
        if (ANGLE < CENTER-SWEEP)
        {
            Fwd(HEAD);
        }
        else if (ANGLE > CENTER+SWEEP)
        {
            Rev(HEAD);
        }
    }
}


task main()
{
    // configure sensors
    SetSensor(EYE, SENSOR_LIGHT);
    SetSensor(ANGLE, SENSOR_ROTATION);

    align();

    // look and steer...
    On(LEFT+RIGHT+HEAD);

    // now we can start the looking task
    start look;

    // steer the robot
    steer();
}
```

The same behavior can be implemented in RCX Code. By default, the Robotics Invention System software doesn't show the sensor watchers and stack controllers for optional sensors (such as the rotation sensor). To enable these blocks, you must change one of the preferences. From the main menu screen, select **Settings,** then **Advanced** to get to the Advanced Settings screen. The settings towards the bottom of the screen can be used to enable the rotation and temperature sensors. Click on the option for the rotation sensor if it is not already checked. Now you can return to the main menu and build a program that uses the rotation sensor.

We'll start by programming the head to align itself, as shown in Figure 10-12. The first block in this stack—**Reset Rotation 1**—may seem out of place, but its purpose will be explained later.

Figure 10-12.
Head alignment in RCX Code

The code to steer the robot needs to respond to a light sensor. An initial choice for this might be to use a sensor watcher at the top of the program. The problem is that the sensor watcher will be active even while the head is being aligned. In this case, there's a chance that a bright light will be detected and that the sensor watcher will then stop the head while it attempts to turn. If you get really unlucky, the sensor watcher may even trigger more than once as the head is being aligned. This may prevent the head from rotating all the way to the left, thus preventing true alignment.

Instead of using a sensor watcher, we will create a **My Block** with an infinite loop inside it that waits for the light sensor to be triggered, then performs the necessary actions. As usual, the long sequence of commands for steering has been split into two stacks to make it more manageable. The resulting **My Blocks** are shown in Figure 10-13.

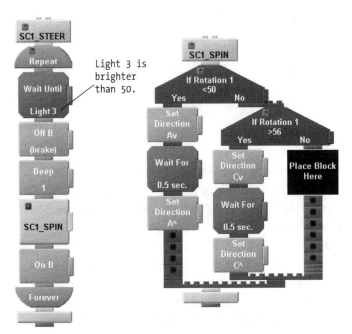

Light 3 is brighter than 50.

Figure 10-13.
Steering in RCX Code

The only thing left to do is make the head sweep back and forth, then pull it all together in a program as shown in Figure 10-14. Sensor watchers are used to control the head. When it moves too far to the left, one sensor watcher will trigger and switch the motor to the forward direction. When the head travels too far to the right, the other sensor watcher sets the motor in reverse. Remember that initial **Reset Rotation 1** block in the **SC1_ALIGN** stack? Its job is to prevent the sensor watchers from interfering with the alignment process. Without that initial block, the sensor value could be anything, and one of the sensor watchers could get triggered as the head is being aligned, which could set the motor to the wrong direction. By resetting the rotation sensor immediately in **SC1_ALIGN**, its value will start at 0 and then decrease during alignment, which will not trigger either sensor watcher.

Figure 10-14.
Program and sensor watchers for simple Scanbot program

Now you are ready to test Scanbot out. One way is to place a bright light near the floor somewhere in a room, and let Scanbot try to find it. Another option is to aim a flashlight at Scanbot and move around the room (always pointing the flashlight at the robot) while Scanbot tries to catch you.

If the head gets stuck to one side, then it is possible that the wire for motor B is not connected properly. If this happens, then running the motor forward (or backward) will not have the expected effect on the rotation sensor, and Scanbot will become confused. One solution would be to switch the motor directions within the program, but a simpler solution is to ensure that the motor is wired correctly. While the RCX is turned off, manually center the head by turning the bushing at the front end of the driveshaft (the axle that holds the worm gear). Once the head is centered, turn on the RCX and run the Scanbot program. The first thing the program does is attempt to align the head by running the motor backward. This should result in a counterclockwise rotation of the head. If the head turns the other way, then the motor's wiring needs to be reversed. Use a different orientation for the wire as it attaches to either the RCX or the motor itself.

Assuming that the wiring is correct, you are ready to let Scanbot run a little. Scanbot will emit a short beep whenever it has detected a bright light. If this beep is going off too often, then you need to increase the threshold for the light sensor (THRESHOLD in the NQC program, and the value in the **Wait Until** block in **SC1_STEER** for the RCX Code program). If Scanbot never detects your light, then the threshold needs to be reduced.

You can also adjust the amount of time that Scanbot turns each time a light is spotted. Smaller values will result in slower, more gradual tracking. Larger values will have a tendency to make Scanbot zigzag as it approaches a light.

IMPROVING THE SCANBOT PROGRAM

Scanbot's program is still rather limited. First of all, the head always takes 3 seconds to align, even if it is already in the leftmost rotation. Second, a light threshold must be explicitly set. It would be much nicer if Scanbot followed the brightest object, not just any object brighter than a certain threshold. The third problem is that Scanbot turns the same amount whether the light is a little or a lot off center. Programming Scanbot to make slight turns and sharp turns would result in much better tracking.

Solving the alignment problem is easy. We can use the rotation sensor to determine when the head is no longer moving, and at that point we'll consider the head to be aligned. A revised version of the align function is shown in Listing 10-2.

Listing 10-2. Improved Alignment in NQC

```
void align()
{
    int previous;

    OnRev(HEAD); // begin turning left

    do
    {
        previous = ANGLE; // save current position
        Wait(10);
    } while(ANGLE != previous); // if position changed, keep going


    Off(HEAD);
    ClearSensor(ANGLE); // make this position "0"
}
```

The improved align function introduces a variable called previous to hold a sensor reading, which is later compared to a more recent reading. This is called *latching* the value. Note that a small delay is necessary between latching the variable and checking it against a second reading. Without the delay, the RCX would take the two sensor readings so close together that the sensor might not change in value even if the head were moving. Now that the head is aligned, we can consider how to use it to scan for a light source.

A simple way would be to start with the head at the leftmost position, then sweep to the right and keep track of the position in which the brightest light was found, as shown in Listing 10-3.

Listing 10-3. Looking Left to Right in NQC

```
int max, level, target;

void scan()
{
    // turn head left
    OnRev(HEAD);
    until(ANGLE <= CENTER-SWEEP);

    // look right
    max = 0;
    Fwd(HEAD);
    while(ANGLE < CENTER+SWEEP)
    {
        level = EYE;
        if (level > max)
        {
            target = ANGLE;
            max = level;
        }
    }
    Off(HEAD);
}
```

There are a couple of subtleties worth pointing out. The reading from the light sensor is latched in the variable level before being compared with, and possibly assigned to, max. The reason for this is that the actual reading of the light sensor may change in the short time between executing the statements that follow. It is important that max get set to the exact same value as was used in the test, otherwise the maximum brightness could be missed.

The second detail is that the rotation sensor is not latched. Since the head is moving, it sounds like a good idea to latch the angle as well. However, even with latching, the value would still be sampled slightly later than the light sensor, and the extra statement would slow down the loop (increasing the chance of missing a small, bright light). As a compromise, the angle is not latched, but it is recorded before max is updated, minimizing the amount of time between sampling the light sensor and the rotation sensor. Overall, this slight inaccuracy in reading the angle will have little effect.

The code is still not ideal, since each time it is called it may spend up to half its time "rewinding" the head to its leftmost position. What we really want is to be able to call scan when the head is at either the leftmost or rightmost position, and then it will perform its scan either left to right or right to left. Since the code to update the maximum light level (and the angle at which it was found) is the same in both cases, it is put into its own inline function as shown in Listing 10-4.

Listing 10-4. Looking in Both Directions in NQC

```
int target, max;

void check()
{
    int level = EYE;
    if (level > max)
    {
        target = ANGLE;
        max = level;
    }
}


void scan()
{
    max = 0;

    if (ANGLE > CENTER)
    {
        // look left
        OnRev(HEAD);
        while(ANGLE > CENTER-SWEEP)
            check();
    }
    else
    {
        // look right
        OnFwd(HEAD);
        while(ANGLE < CENTER+SWEEP)
            check();
    }

    Off(HEAD);
}
```

Now we are ready to address the problem with steering. Instead of a constant amount of turn time, it will be proportional to how far away from center the bright light is, as shown in Listing 10-5.

Listing 10-5. Proportional Steering in NQC

```
#define TURN 2

void steer()
{
    int spinTime;

    target -= CENTER;

    if (target > SLOP)
    {
        Rev(RIGHT);
        spinTime = TURN * target;
    }
    else if (target < -SLOP)
    {
        Rev(LEFT);
        spinTime = -TURN * target;
    }
    else
        return; // no need to steer, just return now

    // turn for a little while, then go forward again
    Wait(spinTime);
    Fwd(LEFT+RIGHT);
}
```

As in the first Scanbot program, the SLOP value allows Scanbot to continue straight ahead if the target is close to center. The amount of proportional turning can be controlled by the constant TURN. The code in Listing 10-5 uses a value of 2 for TURN, but you may have to adjust this slightly in your own designs. Smaller values will cause the Scanbot to curve more gently toward the target, whereas larger values can cause Scanbot to overshoot during its turns and oscillate back and forth.

Only a few details, such as initialization and a main loop, remain. The complete program is shown in Listing 10-6.

Listing 10-6. Improved Scanbot Program in NQC

```
// scanbot2.nqc
//    A better Scanbot program

// sensors
#define EYE      SENSOR_3
#define ANGLE   SENSOR_1

// motors
#define LEFT   OUT_A
#define HEAD   OUT_B
#define RIGHT  OUT_C

// other constants
#define SLOP 3
#define TURN 2

#define CENTER 53
#define SWEEP   48      // 135 degrees


// variables
int target, max;


void align()
{
    int previous;

    OnRev(HEAD); // begin turning left

    do
    {
        previous = ANGLE; // save current position
        Wait(10);
    } while(ANGLE != previous); // if position changed, keep going


    Off(HEAD);
    ClearSensor(ANGLE); // make this position "0"
}


void check()
{
```

```
        int level = EYE;
        if (level > max)
        {
            target = ANGLE;
            max = level;
        }
    }


void scan()
{
    max = 0;

    if (ANGLE > CENTER)
    {
        // look left
        OnRev(HEAD);
        while(ANGLE > CENTER-SWEEP)
            check();
    }
    else
    {
        // look right
        OnFwd(HEAD);
        while(ANGLE < CENTER+SWEEP)
            check();
    }

    Off(HEAD);
}


void steer()
{
    int spinTime;

    target -= CENTER;

    if (target > SLOP)
    {
        Rev(RIGHT);
        spinTime = TURN * target;
    }
    else if (target < -SLOP)
    {
        Rev(LEFT);
        spinTime = -TURN * target;
```

```
    }
    else
        return; // no need to steer, just return now

    // turn for a little while, then go forward again
    Wait(spinTime);
    Fwd(LEFT+RIGHT);
}


task main()
{
    // configure sensors
    SetSensor(EYE, SENSOR_LIGHT);
    SetSensor(ANGLE, SENSOR_ROTATION);

    align();

    // look and steer...
    On(LEFT+RIGHT);
    while(true)
    {
        scan();
        steer();
    }
}
```

A similar program can be construction in RCX Code. The blocks for aligning the head are shown in Figure 10-15. The only difference between the RCX Code and NQC approaches is that the NQC function uses a do-while loop, which is always guaranteed to execute at least one iteration of the loop (it only checks the condition *after* executing the body). RCX Code just has a **Repeat While** loop, which checks the condition *before* executing the body. This means that if the condition is not met initially, the body will never get executed. Since the condition depends on the value of **previous**, it is therefore important to set it before the loop starts. By setting **previous** to 999.0, the loop will always run at least once.

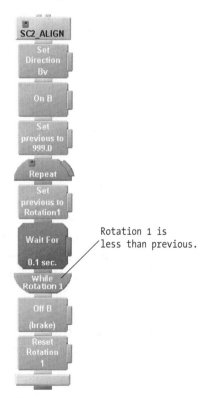

Rotation 1 is less than previous.

Figure 10-15.
Improved head alignment in RCX Code

The **My Blocks** used for looking around (**SC2_SCAN** and **SC2_CHECK**) are shown in Figure 10-16. These blocks function identically to their counterparts in the NQC program (functions scan and check).

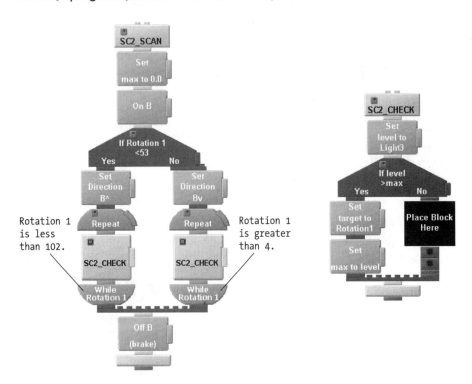

Figure 10-16.
Looking around in RCX Code

Steering is accomplished by the **SC2_STEER** block (which calls **SC2_SPIN**). Both blocks are shown in Figure 10-17. The calculation of **spinTime** is slightly different in RCX Code. First of all, it uses the **Make Positive** block, which simply converts negative numbers into positive ones. By using this block, the rest of the calculation is the same regardless of whether the target was found to the left or the right of center. The second difference is that **spinTime** is computed by division rather than multiplication. In NQC wait times are represented as hundredths of a second (so a value of 100 would mean a 1 second delay). In RCX Code, wait times are represented in seconds (1.0 for 1 second). Since we want to turn for 0.02 seconds per unit of target rotation, the RCX Code program needs to divide **target** by 50.

All of the blocks can then be pulled together in the program shown in Figure 10-18.

Figure 10-17.
Proportional steering in RCX Code

Figure 10-18.
Improved Scanbot program in RCX Code

USING SCANBOT WHEN SPACE IS LIMITED

Scanbot tends to need a lot of floor space when running the previous program. With some modification we can adapt Scanbot to operate better in crowded environments. There are two basic modifications we need to make. First of all, since Scanbot picks the brightest light source as its target, there is always *some* target available. We can make Scanbot more selective by introducing an *ambient light threshold*. This is just a fancy name for the lowest light sensor reading that Scanbot will consider a valid target. It is very similar to the threshold used in the very first Scanbot program, but rather than programming in a specific value, we'll have Scanbot look around a little bit and pick the value itself. Once this threshold is set, Scanbot will be able to stop if no suitable target is found, rather than simply choosing the next brightest object in the room and homing in on it.

Second, Scanbot is always moving—even when not zeroed in on a light source. We'll change the program so that Scanbot moves forward only when it is locked on target. Assuming that an ambient threshold has already been established (and stored in the variable named ambient), the new steer function in Listing 10-7 will do nicely.

Listing 10-7. Steering and Stopping in NQC

```
void steer()
{
    int spinTime;

    if (max <= ambient)
    {
        Off(LEFT + RIGHT);
        return;
    }

    target -= CENTER;

    if (target > SLOP)
    {
        OnFwd(LEFT);
        OnRev(RIGHT);
        spinTime = TURN * target;
    }
    else if (target < -SLOP)
    {
        OnFwd(RIGHT);
        OnRev(LEFT);
        spinTime = -TURN * target;
    }
    else
    {
        // we're on target...go straight
        OnFwd(LEFT+RIGHT);
        return;   // no need to steer, just return now
    }

    Wait(spinTime);
    Off(LEFT+RIGHT);
}
```

Note how the function first checks to see if the maximum light value exceeded the ambient light threshold. If it didn't, then the motors are turned off and the function returns immediately. In this case, Scanbot will sit still and continue scanning until a bright light appears.

In the case of a turn (either right or left), the drive motors are turned on in opposite directions. The function will then wait the appropriate amount of time and stop the motors.

The last case is when Scanbot is heading directly toward the target. In this case the motors are turned on and the function returns immediately. This allows Scanbot to make its next scanning pass while driving toward the target.

The ambient light threshold can be computed by looking from one side to the other and recording the brightest light sensor reading. For a little extra safety, this value should be padded a bit to ensure that Scanbot will pay attention only to lights that are noticeably brighter than the normal background lighting. Coincidentally, the scan function already looks from one side to the other and remembers the brightest value it has seen. We can just call scan early on in the program and compute the ambient threshold from the maximum value it found. Another minor change is that the drive motors should not be turned on initially. A suitable main task is shown in Listing 10-8.

Listing 10-8. Ambient Threshold Main Task in NQC

```
#define AMBIENT_MARGIN 2  // a little extra range for ambient light

task main()
{
    // configure sensors
    SetSensor(EYE, SENSOR_LIGHT);
    SetSensor(ANGLE, SENSOR_ROTATION);

    align();
    scan();
    ambient = max + AMBIENT_MARGIN;

    // look and steer...
    while(true)
    {
        scan();
        steer();
    }
}
```

We now have everything we need for a new Scanbot program. Starting with the `scanbot2.nqc` program from the previous section, simply replace the `steer` function and `main` task with the code shown in Listings 10-7 and 10-8. Don't forget to declare the new `ambient` variable somewhere near the top of the program:

```
int ambient;
```

Similar changes can also be made to the RCX Code program. Starting with the **Scanbot2** program, replace the steering blocks with those shown in Figure 10-19, and alter the program stack to appear like the one shown in Figure 10-20.

Figure 10-19.
Steering and stopping in RCX Code

Figure 10-20.
Scanbot3 program
in RCX Code

This program performs rather well in homing in on a flashlight or other bright light source. The only caveat is that the target light needs to be turned off when the program is first started and is determining the ambient light threshold. Once the head makes a complete sweep from left to right, it is then safe to turn on the flashlight (or other light) and let Scanbot home in on it. If you then turn off the light, Scanbot will stop and wait for the light to reappear.

CONCLUSION

Scanbot is a fun robot to play with. Unlike the previous ones, which wandered about randomly, Scanbot seems to have a more directed purpose. The construction of Scanbot required a few new elements: the worm gear and pulley-and-belt drive. It also introduced the rotation sensor, which is perhaps the most versatile MINDSTORMS sensor. With it, a robot can measure speed, distance, position, and other quantities. Because the rotation sensor is not part of the Robotics Invention System, use of it has been minimized in this book. However, once you own a rotation sensor you will certainly find new uses for it in your own robots.

Scanbot is also the last of our robots based on Tankbot. This versatile chassis has served us well for the last several chapters, but it is now time to move on to other vehicle designs such as three-wheeled vehicles and rack and pinion steering. The Tankbot chassis (in the guise of Dumpbot) will make one final appearance in Chapter 17.

Chapter 11
Tribot

So far, all the robots have been based on the Tankbot chassis, using caterpillar treads for both motion and steering. Tread-based vehicles are compact, able to traverse a variety of terrain, and easy to maneuver. However, treads also have a few disadvantages. First of all, LEGO treads come in only one size, which puts some restrictions on the size and speed of tread-based robots. Second, the treads are a compromise between providing enough traction to propel the vehicle forward and having enough slip to allow turning. Last, the process of the treads moving around the hubs involves a significant amount of friction; hence some of the motors' energy is wasted, thus limiting the speed and power of such robots even more.

This chapter introduces a three-wheeled robot that steers in the same way as the previous tread-based designs, but uses wheels rather than treads. A simple bumper is added to this chassis, and the resulting robot can be thought of as a variation of Bumpbot. Of course, the three-wheeled chassis may also be adapted for other purposes.

THE SWIVEL WHEEL

Tribot is powered by two rear wheels, each driven by its own motor. Steering is accomplished in much the same manner as with the tread-based designs. When both wheels turn at the same speed and in the same direction, the vehicle will be propelled in a straight line forward (or backward). Turning one wheel faster than the other will force Tribot to turn. Very tight turns can be made by running the wheels in opposite directions.

The two wheels alone, however, are not sufficient to balance Tribot—it requires a third support. Attaching this wheel can cause a bit of a problem. When Tribot is moving straight ahead, the wheel should point forward. When turning, this wheel must point in the direction of the turn, otherwise the friction of the skidding wheel would interfere with the turn. However, we don't have to aim the wheel ourselves—all we need to do is allow it to pivot freely, and it will align itself in whichever direction is required.

The key to making this work is to ensure that the pivot axis is offset from the wheel's axle, as shown in Figure 11-1. In such an arrangement, the wheel will always trail slightly behind the pivot axis and tend to line up with the direction of travel. This sort of wheel mechanism can be found on everything from grocery carts to bed frames in the real world.

Figure 11-1.
Swivel wheel

CONSTRUCTION

Tribot's wheels are attached directly to their respective motors without any intervening gears, so, as with Tankbot, the wheels spin at the rate of the motors themselves. However, since the wheels have a larger diameter and do not suffer from the same internal friction as treads, Tribot moves significantly faster than Tankbot. A pair of wheels are mounted on their hubs and then attached to a pair of motors in Figures 11-2 and 11-3. Be sure to use the correct-size wheels—they should be slightly larger than the motor so that they will be able to touch the ground and propel Tribot. The motor assembly can then be set aside for later.

Figure 11-2.
Tribot step 1

Figure 11-3.
Tribot step 2

Figures 11-4 and 11-5 illustrate the mounting used to hold the swivel wheel in place. The structure is built around a pair of liftarms, a #8 axle, and a #6 axle. The crossblock provides the actual mounting hole for the swivel wheel, and four bushings are used as spacers. Since all of the pieces involved use cross-shaped holes, the entire structure is quite rigid.

Figure 11-4.
Tribot step 3

Figure 11-5.
Tribot step 4

The mounting is held between two beams, as shown in Figure 11-6, and the structure continues to be built up in Figures 11-7 and 11-8. The oval-shaped pieces added in Figure 11-7 are another kind of liftarm: a 1×3 liftarm. They provide a very compact way to add vertical bracing to a structure. In Figure 11-8 a pair of #3 axles are inserted through beams into the tops of the 1×3 liftarms, thus completing the vertical bracing.

Figure 11-6.
Tribot step 5

Figure 11-7.
Tribot step 6

Figure 11-8.
Tribot step 7

The swivel wheel is started in Figure 11-9. The new piece here is called a #1 *angle brick*. When we combine it with the #5 angle brick in Figure 11-10, we get a very compact swivel wheel. The #6 axle extending upward serves as the swivel's axis, and it is inserted as shown in Figure 11-11. The swivel-wheel portion of our robot is now complete, but we still need to build a bumper on the front end.

Figure 11-9.
Tribot step 8

Figure 11-10.
Tribot step 9

Figure 11-11.
Tribot step 10

The bumper, constructed in Figures 11-12 and 11-13, consists of a pair of angle beams and a pair of #8 axles, joined in the center by an *axle extender*. The axle extender is often used to construct a long axle out of two shorter ones. In this case, we effectively get a #16 axle by combining two #8 axles. The bushings, as usual, are used as spacers. In order to operate smoothly, the bumper needs to be "square" (the axles must be perpendicular to the angle beam). Without the spacers, manual adjustment would be required to keep things square. A small black rubber band is used to give the bumper the proper tension. One minor detail is the addition of a friction peg on the bumper's angle beam (just above where the rubber band hooks on). When the bumper hits an obstacle, it pivots such that one end of the angle beam comes into contact with the touch sensor. The friction peg helps keep the touch sensor pressed while the angle beam continues to pivot past the sensor. Overall, this bumper design extends a little farther forward than previous designs, which is a good thing since Tribot moves faster than our other robots and needs more time to react.

Figure 11-12.
Tribot step 11

Figure 11-13.
Tribot step 12

The swivel wheel's axle is secured in place by a series of bushings and the 2×6 Technic plate. This plate may seem like overkill, but its function is actually quite important. Part of Tribot's weight must be supported by the swivel wheel. In the orientation shown here, the axle is in front of the actual wheels. This means that the downward force of Tribot's weight will make the axle tilt; the top will be pushed forward while the bottom is pushed backward. This tilting creates additional friction between the axle and the crossblock it is mounted through, thus hampering its swivel ability. Adding the top plate solves this problem quite nicely.

The bumper, motor assembly, and RCX are put together in Figure 11-14. The RCX is secured to the bumper assembly with a pair of 1×6 beams, and the motors are mounted at the back of the RCX. Finally, the wiring for the motors and touch sensor may be completed.

Figure 11-14.
Tribot step 13

PROGRAMMING

To test out Tribot, we will write a simple program to drive forward until it hits something, then back up a little, turn a little, and resume. A sample program in NQC appears in Listing 11-1. By now, its structure should be familiar. Sensors, motors, and constants are defined at the top, and the main task has an infinite loop that waits for a condition to be true (the bumper being hit), then reacts accordingly (back up for 0.50 second, spin around for 0.20 second).

A similar program written using RCX Code is shown in Figure 11-15.

Listing 11-1. Tribot Program in NQC

```
// tribot.nqc
//    three wheeled robot

// motors and sensors
#define LEFT   OUT_A
#define RIGHT OUT_C
#define BUMP   SENSOR_1

// constants
#define REV_TIME    50
#define TURN_TIME   20

task main()
{
    SetSensor(BUMP, SENSOR_TOUCH);

    On(LEFT+RIGHT);

    while(true)
    {
        until(BUMP==1);

        // back up a litle
        Rev(LEFT+RIGHT);
        Wait(REV_TIME);

        // spin a little
        Off(LEFT);
        Wait(TURN_TIME);

        // resume going forward
        OnFwd(LEFT+RIGHT);
    }
}
```

Figure 11-15.
Tribot program in RCX Code

VARIATIONS

The Tribot chassis can be adapted for any of the previous Tankbot-based robots. The bumper itself can be easily modified to provide separate left and right bumpers, each with its own touch sensors. The resulting vehicle could then be programmed much the same way as Bugbot.

For some tasks, such as line following, a slower robot is required. The three-wheeled design can still be used, but some gear reduction between the motors and the wheels is required. A 3:1 gear reduction will result in a very powerful robot that still moves at a reasonable speed.

If a faster robot is needed, the wheels can be replaced by larger ones, such as the large motorcycle-style wheels included in the Robotics Invention System set. The motors will have to work rather hard in such a design, and they may even stall on rough surfaces such as carpet. Top speed on a smooth floor, however, is quite impressive.

A variation of Tribot that uses only a single motor for driving and turning is presented in the next chapter.

Both the three-wheeled and tread designs rely on evenly matched motors for straight travel. If the motors (or the wheels or treads) vary slightly between the left and the right sides, there will be a tendency for the vehicle to curve slightly instead of traveling in a straight line. An alternative drive mechanism that avoids this problem is presented in Chapter 14.

Chapter 12
Onebot

The RCX has only three outputs, and this can become a serious limitation when designing a robot. In our examples so far, two motors have been used just for movement, leaving only a single output free for other functions. What if those other functions need two independent motors? Onebot is a variation of Tribot that uses a single motor to move around. Although Onebot itself is only a simple bumper car, its design can serve as the basis for more complicated robots.

DRIVING WITH ONE MOTOR

The previous robots were very flexible in their driving and steering. They could go forward or backward, turn left or right (in forward and reverse), or even spin in place. Although convenient, not all of these operations are needed for most tasks. For example, the combination of driving straight ahead and turning in reverse is sufficient for many tasks.

Forward motion in Tribot was accomplished by turning both motors on in the forward direction. Turning was accomplished by stopping the left motor and running the right motor in the reverse direction. (Tribot also traveled straight backward, but we are ignoring that mode for Onebot.) As you can see, the right motor must be able to turn in both directions, but the left motor only needs to turn forward. The ratchet mechanism discussed in Chapter 4 is perfect for allowing motion in one direction while preventing motion in the other direction.

The most obvious way of using a single motor to power both wheels would be to put both wheels on a single axle, then use the motor to turn that axle (via gears or pulleys). Unfortunately, if a ratchet is then used to prevent the left wheel from reversing, it will also prevent the right wheel from reversing. The wheels must therefore both have their own axle, but the problem remains of how to transfer power from the motor to both axles. If gears are used, the ratchet will still prevent the right wheel from turning, since it will "lock up" the entire gearing mechanism (including the motor itself). Pulleys and belts can be used instead to allow one side of the drive mechanism to slip while the other side still turns. Although functional, the use of belts limits the amount of power that can be delivered to the wheels, as well as the overall efficiency of the drive mechanism.

A more elegant solution is to use the differential. As discussed in Chapter 4, the differential consists of a shell and two independent axles. One axle may turn faster or slower than the other (they may even turn in opposite directions), but their average will always equal the speed of the shell itself. If we use the motor to turn the shell, then the default case is for both axles to turn at the same speed. Reversing the motor will result in trying to reverse both axles. Stopping one of the axles with a ratchet will result in the other wheel's turning twice as fast (so that the average still equals the speed of the shell).

This is the mechanism that is used to power Onebot. It is like the ratchet splitter presented in Chapter 4, with one important difference. The ratchet splitter uses ratchets on both axles, while Onebot only has a single ratchet. This is because the ratchet splitter was designed to turn one axle or the other, but never both at the same time. In contrast, Onebot always needs to turn one axle; it is only the second one that is sometimes powered and sometimes stopped.

CONSTRUCTION

Onebot uses the same swivel-wheel and bumper assembly as Tribot. If you still have Tribot around, remove the RCX and rear motors. Otherwise, follow the instructions in Chapter 11, steps 3 through 12. The resulting assembly is shown in Figure 12-1.

Figure 12-1.
Onebot step 1

The previous section outlined the principles behind Onebot's drive mechanism, but there are also a few implementation details of its construction that are worth pointing out. The differential and related gears are built in Figures 12-2 through 12-5. Note that each side has its own #6 axle, which is attached to a bevel gear within the differential shell. A third bevel gear inside the differential transfers power between these two axles.

Figure 12-2.
Onebot step 2

Figure 12-3.
Onebot step 3

Figure 12-4.
Onebot step 4

Figure 12-5.
Onebot step 5

A stack of 1×1 plates is placed behind the crown gear (a 1×1 brick could have been used instead, but the Robotics Invention System set does not include any). This construction provides firm support behind the crown gear. Without it, the crown gear would have a tendency to flex slightly and not mesh properly when under strain. The result would be an annoying clicking sound and a robot that doesn't move very well.

The motor and ratchet are added in Figures 12-6 through 12-8. An 8-tooth gear is placed on the motor, which then meshes with the crown gear (24 teeth), resulting in a 3:1 gear reduction. Tribot was able to propel itself effectively without the use of gear reduction, but it was also using two motors. In Onebot, the power from a single motor must be divided between both wheels. A gear reduction is thus used to increase the power to the wheels (at the expense of speed).

Figure 12-6.
Onebot step 6

Figure 12-7.
Onebot step 7

Figure 12-8.
Onebot step 8

The motor itself is mounted on special mounting brackets. The brackets are attached above and below the 1×12 beams. The motor is then slid into place and secured by a 1×4 plate. This results in a compact yet robust mounting for the motor. There are quite a few situations where these brackets can be used to position motors in places where traditional building techniques would fail.

The ratchet design is fairly simple: gravity pulls the crossblock down such that it engages with the teeth of the 16-tooth gear. Try turning the axle clockwise; the gear's teeth catch the crossblock at an angle and get locked in place. Now try turning the axle slowly in the counterclockwise direction; the teeth are now able to push the crossblock up and out of the way. If you give the axle a quick turn counterclockwise, you'll notice that the crossblock gets "kicked up" a bit. If you turn it quickly enough, the crossblock will flip all the way around to the other side. This potential problem will be solved later on by placing the RCX so that it prevents the crossblock from getting kicked up too high.

The final steps for Onebot, shown in Figures 12-9 and 12-10, involve attaching the front bumper assembly to the drive mechanism, then adding the RCX and wires.

Figure 12-9.
Onebot step 9

Figure 12-10.
Onebot step 10

PROGRAMMING

The program for Onebot is similar to Tribot's program. The differences are that only a single motor is controlled and that there is no reverse mode—just forward and reverse/turn. A sample NQC program is shown in Listing 12-1.

A similar program for RCX Code is shown in Figure 12-11.

Listing 12-1. Onebot Program in NQC

```
// onebot.nqc
//   robot driven by a single motor

// motor and sensor
#define DRIVE OUT_A
#define BUMP SENSOR_1

// constant
#define REV_TIME     40

task main()
{
    SetSensor(BUMP, SENSOR_TOUCH);

    On(DRIVE);

    while(true)
    {
        until(BUMP==1);

        // back up / turn a little
        Rev(DRIVE);
        Wait(REV_TIME);

        // resume going forward
        Fwd(DRIVE);
    }
}
```

Figure 12-11.
Onebot program in RCX Code

CONCLUSION

Although somewhat limited in overall movement, the single-motor design behind Onebot can be useful when both other motors are required for auxiliary functions. The drive mechanism can also be adapted to use different wheels or even treads.

Chapter 13
Steerbot

Many of the previous robots have been based on the tread-driven chassis introduced with Tankbot. Although such designs are easy to build and program, they are limited by the size and traction of the treads themselves. This puts a practical limitation on the size and speed of robots that can be built with the standard LEGO treads. In this chapter, we will construct a faster robot using a new steering mechanism. In addition, proximity detection will be used (instead of physical bumpers) to avoid obstacles.

RACK AND PINION STEERING

In the real world a different steering mechanism, known as *rack and pinion steering*, is much more common. In fact, it is the same mechanism used in virtually all automobiles. Rack and pinion steering provides complete flexibility on the shape and size of tires, thus it is often a good choice for vehicles that do not perform adequately with tracks. In the case of Steerbot, the steering will be done by the front wheels, and the drive train will power the rear wheels. Other combinations are also possible—forklifts often steer the rear wheels, sport utility vehicles power all four wheels, and some cars even provide four-wheel steering—however, the basic principles are the same.

When driving straight, a vehicle's wheels are parallel to one another. In order to turn, the front wheels are angled slightly. In a sense, this angle aims the front of the vehicle to the right or left. As long as the wheels remain angled, the vehicle will continue to turn.

In order for the wheels not to slide, the outside wheels must turn slightly faster than the inside wheels. This is the same effect that we exploited in the track-based designs, but this time cause and effect are reversed. Whereas before we changed the speed of one side in order to cause a turn, now the turn (which is caused by the angle of the wheels) will cause a difference in speed to be required. Even if we were willing to use two motors (one for the right-rear wheel, and one for the left-rear wheel), the required difference in speed depends on the sharpness of the turn and is rather complicated.

The solution involves using a *differential*, which was described in Chapter 4. We can use a motor to turn the shell of the differential. The differential functions by distributing power to both wheels in such a way as to minimize the overall friction. When driving straight, this means that both wheels will turn at the same speed. When turning, however, the inside wheel will turn slightly slower than the differential shell, and the outside wheel will turn slightly faster. This variation in speed will happen without any direct intervention—the only thing we need to do is spin the differential itself.

CHASSIS CONSTRUCTION

Steerbot is mechanically the most complicated robot so far, but if you look carefully you will see the same familiar techniques employed on earlier robots. The only truly unique portion of Steerbot is the rack and pinion steering. LEGO manufactures several specialized pieces that can be used to easily build a compact rack and pinion mechanism. Unfortunately, the RIS set does not include all of the necessary pieces, so we will have to use a little creativity and build the mechanism from scratch.

Figures 13-1 and 13-2 show the initial construction of the chassis, including a differential and the special brackets used to mount a motor. The new pieces near the front of the frame (left side of the illustration) are something of a "hack." This is the area where the rack will need to slide back and forth; thus a smooth surface is required. Ideally, a couple of *tiles* (plates without studs on top) would be used. Since the Robotics Invention System doesn't include any regular tiles, these odd pieces are used instead.

Figure 13-1.
Steerbot step 1

Figure 13-2.
Steerbot step 2

The motor (with a crown gear attached) is shown in Figure 13-3, slid into position in Figure 13-4, then locked in place in Figure 13-5. The crown gear is a 24-tooth gear with curved teeth that allows it to mesh at a right angle with another gear (see Chapter 4 for a more detailed explanation of the crown gear). The gearing between the motor and differential may appear a bit odd. The motor turns a crown gear (24 teeth), which meshes with an 8-tooth gear for a 3:1 reduction. This 8-tooth gear then meshes with the 24-tooth side of the differential for a 1:3 gear ratio. The resulting ratio is simply 1:1. So why not skip the 8-tooth gear and mesh the crown gear directly with the differential? In order to do this, the crown gear would need to be moved closer to the differential. Unfortunately, at such close proximity, the center of the crown gear would collide with the shell of the differential. By introducing the 8-tooth gear, space is added between the crown gear and the differential without altering the overall speed and power (aside from a minor amount of friction).

Figure 13-3.
Steerbot step 3

A light sensor, which will be used for proximity detection, is also added in Figure 13-4. The touch sensor added in Figure 13-5 will be used to detect when the steering is centered.

Figure 13-4.
Steerbot step 4

Figure 13-5.
Steerbot step 5

Figures 13-6, 13-7, and 13-8 show the construction of the steering rack. The small #2 axle underneath the rack will press against the touch sensor when the rack is centered.

Figure 13-6.
Steerbot step 6

Figure 13-7.
Steerbot step 7

Figure 13-8.
Steerbot step 8

The steering rack is added to the chassis in Figure 13-9. It should rest lightly on the smooth pieces and slide back and forth easily. The #10 axle added in this step will eventually be the point of support between Steerbot and its front wheels. Because of this, it is important that it be properly braced, hence the 1×3 liftarms that anchor it firmly to the 1×16 beams of the chassis itself. The axle and gear added in Figure 13-10 will be used to control the steering.

Figure 13-9.
Steerbot step 9

Figure 13-10.
Steerbot step 10

The axles for the front wheels are constructed in Figures 13-11 and 13-12. The wheels need two degrees of freedom—they must be able to both spin and pivot. This is similar to building the swivel wheel for Tribot, except that this time it is all right if the wheel is a little off center from the pivot point.

Figure 13-11.
Steerbot step 11

Figure 13-12.
Steerbot step 12

Once the two pivot assemblies are completed, they are added to the rest of the model. The rack and pinion mechanism is completed by the addition of two 1×4 liftarms that link the steering rack to the wheel pivots as shown in Figure 13-13. Be sure to leave a small gap when attaching these liftarms to the axle pegs at the ends of the steering rack. This gap is necessary to make the liftarms level and allow the steering mechanism to move freely. Observe how the wheels rotate right and left as the rack is moved back and forth and how the touch sensor gets pressed only when the wheels are centered (or very close to center). If the touch sensor is not getting pressed in firmly enough, you may have to adjust the #2 axle.

Figure 13-13.
Steerbot step 13

A few odds and ends are added in Figure 13-14, then in Figure 13-15 (which shows the view from the back of Steerbot), a pair of pulleys and a blue rubber belt are used to transfer power from a motor to the steering mechanism. The difference in size between the pulleys provides a reduction of approximately 7:2, which constitutes a good compromise between power and speed. A belt was intentionally used (as opposed to gears) in order to allow slippage when the steering has been turned completely to the left or right. As usual, support for the motor must take into account the rather unusual shape of its bottom.

Figure 13-14.
Steerbot step 14

Figure 13-15.
Steerbot step 15

Steerbot is completed by adding the RCX and wheels to the chassis as shown in Figure 13-16.

Figure 13-16.
Steerbot step 16

PROGRAMMING

We will first introduce three operations to manage the steering. The RCX Code versions of these functions are shown in Figure 13-17, and the NQC version appears in Listing 13-1. To turn the wheels left, we run the steering motor backward for a little while—$1/2$ second to be exact. This number was chosen because it provides ample time for the steering to be moved from the far right extreme to the far left extreme. Turning the wheels right is the same, except the motor is run in the forward direction.

Touch 1
Release

Figure 13-17.
Steering blocks in RCX Code

Listing 13-1. Steering Functions in NQC

```
#define CENTER    SENSOR_1
#define STEER     OUT_A
#define FULL_TURN_TIME   50

void right()
{
    Fwd(STEER);
    OnFor(STEER, FULL_TURN_TIME);
}


void left()
{
    Rev(STEER);
    OnFor(STEER, FULL_TURN_TIME);
}


void center()
{
    Toggle(STEER);
    On(STEER);
    until(CENTER==1);
    Off(STEER);
}
```

Centering the steering is a little different. The centering operation assumes that the steering had previously been moved to the right or left. As a result, switching the motor's direction will get the steering moving back toward center. The motor remains on until the centering touch sensor is triggered. If you find that the centering operation is turning either too little or too much, then it may be adjusted by either adding a delay after the sensor is triggered (turning too little), or reversing the motor's direction for a bit (turning too much). Examples of this in NQC are shown in Listing 13-2.

Listing 13-2. Adjusted Steering Functions in NQC

```
// version of center () that turns a little extra
void center()
{
    Toggle(STEER);
    On(STEER);
    until(CENTER==1);
    Wait(10);
    Off(STEER);
}

// version of center() that turns a little less
void center()
{
    Toggle(STEER);
    On(STEER);
    until(CENTER==1);
    Toggle(STEER);
    Wait(10);
    Off(STEER);
}
```

Steerbot also needs a way to detect obstacles. Unlike previous robots, which used a physical bumper, Steerbot will look for obstacles with a light sensor using a technique that is commonly called *proximity detection*. The light sensor detects incoming light, so all we need to do is shine a lot of light in front of Steerbot, and as it nears an obstacle, some portion of that light will bounce back and be detected by the sensor. Unfortunately, the red LED built into the sensor itself does not emit enough light to work at a distance. However, the RCX has its own infrared LED that is normally used for communication. Even though you can't see its light (because it is infrared), the light sensor has no trouble detecting it.

The RCX's communication LED can operate at two different power levels. The lower level is good for short range communication, while the higher level emits more light. Since we want as much light as possible, it is important to tell the RCX to use the high power mode. If you are using the RIS software, this is controlled from the Settings screen. From the Main Menu screen press the **Settings** button, and then select **high** in the **Communication** box. If you are using NQC, the program itself can specify that the RCX use the high power mode, as you will see a bit later in the chapter.

If we instruct the RCX to send a message, it will emit some pulses of infrared light. By repeatedly sending messages within a loop, we will ensure that pulses are continually being generated, and if we get close to an obstacle one of these pulses will bounce back and be detected by the light sensor. An RCX Code program that uses proximity detection along with the steering functions introduced earlier is shown in Figure 13-18.

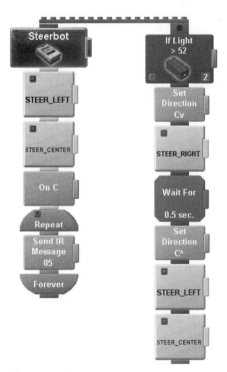

Figure 13-18.
Proximity detection in RCX Code

By placing the **Send IR Message** block in the program stack and using a sensor watcher for the light sensor, we ensure that the pulses of infrared light will be sent concurrently with checking the light sensor. If instead we had a single loop that sequentially sent the message and then checked the sensor, the pulses of light would have stopped by the time the sensor was read.

Listing 13-3 shows the new code that must be combined with Listing 13-1 to program Steerbot in NQC. While most of our previous NQC programs used condition-based tests, this one uses events. Since event checking is done "in the background," using events allows the light sensor to be monitored at the same time the messages are being sent. Another option would be to use two separate tasks, but then we would have a potential risk of missing one of the pulses being reflected back if the light sensor wasn't checked frequently enough. One other item of note is the SetTxPower function, which allows a program to control whether communication uses low or high power.

Listing 13-3. Proximity Detection in NQC

```
#define EYE          SENSOR_2
#define DRIVE        OUT_C
#define STRAIGHT_TIME    50

#define PROX_EVENT 1
#define PROX_THRESHOLD 52

task main()
{
    // set up sensors and event
    SetSensor(CENTER, SENSOR_TOUCH);
    SetSensor(EYE, SENSOR_LIGHT);
    SetEvent(PROX_EVENT, EYE, EVENT_TYPE_HIGH);
    SetUpperLimit(PROX_EVENT, PROX_THRESHOLD);

    // align wheels and drive forward
    left();
    center();
    On(DRIVE);

    // use high power communication
    SetTxPower(TX_POWER_HI);

    while(true)
    {
        monitor(EVENT_MASK(PROX_EVENT))
        {
            while(true)
            {
                SendMessage(85);
            }
        }
```

```
        catch
        {
            // back up while turning
            Rev(DRIVE);
            right();
            Wait(STRAIGHT_TIME);

            // forward while turning other direction
            Fwd(DRIVE);
            left();

            // center steer
            center();
        }
    }
}
```

The message number to send is somewhat arbitrary. I used 85 because it gets transmitted as alternating pulses of light. Another option is message 255, which will "clump" the pulses of light together more (longer periods of light, but also longer periods of dark), but generally doesn't make much difference.

Both the RCX Code and NQC programs use a constant threshold to detect obstacles (the light sensor watcher in RCX Code, and PROX_THRESHOLD in NQC). This value must be adjusted for the environment that Steerbot will be driving around in. Run the program, use the **View** button to monitor sensor 2, and hold Steerbot about 1' from an obstacle. The values shown on the RCX will probably bounce around quite a bit. This is because sometimes the RCX reads the sensor when a pulse of light is being emitted, and sometimes it reads the sensor when no pulse is present. Take note of the highest value shown on the RCX's display, and use that as a starting point for the light sensor threshold.

If Steerbot is having trouble detecting obstacles, try lowering the threshold value. If you are using RCX Code, you should check the Settings screen and make sure that the RCX is configured for high power. Proximity detection will work better in darker rooms since there will be more range between the ambient light of the room and the pulses of light emitted from the RCX.

Another common problem is that the #2 axle underneath the rack isn't sticking out far enough to activate the touch sensor. If this is case, then the program will get stuck during its initial centering operation and Steerbot won't go anywhere. To correct this, adjust the #2 axle such that it makes good contact with the touch sensor.

ASYNCHRONOUS STEERING

This section presents a more advanced programming technique that can be used with Steerbot. Although it is possible to apply this technique with RCX Code, the resulting program becomes quite cumbersome. Since NQC lends itself more easily to this style of programming, all of the sample code will be in NQC.

In the previous example, when the program wanted to turn right it called a function or My Block, which didn't return until the wheels had turned completely to the right. This sort of behavior, where an operation does not return until some external activity is complete, is known as *synchronous* behavior. Sometimes it is desirable to be able to start an operation, then continue doing other processing while the operation completes. This execution model is called *asynchronous* behavior.

Consider the process of cooking a "bacon and eggs" breakfast. One way to do this would be first to cook the bacon, and only when it was finished move on to preparing the eggs. In this case the bacon is being cooked synchronously. Another option would be to start cooking the bacon, then begin preparing the eggs while the bacon was still cooking. In this case the bacon is being cooked asynchronously. Preparing the eggs while still keeping an eye on the bacon is a bit more difficult than simply cooking one then the other, but overall it takes less time. This tradeoff often applies to software as well. Synchronous behavior is often the simplest to implement, but in some cases asynchronous behavior is worth the extra effort.

Since turning the wheels completely to the right or left can take up to $1/2$ second, steering control is a good candidate for asynchronous operation.

The key to asynchronous behavior (at least in the RCX) is to use multiple tasks. We will create a separate task whose sole function is to turn the wheels to a desired position. Of course, other tasks (known as *clients*) will need some way of interacting with the steering task in order to specify which position the steering mechanism should be set to. It is also desirable for these clients to be able to determine when the steering task has completed its work.

This is starting to sound pretty complicated, and one of the techniques programmers use to make complicated systems easier to understand is called *abstraction*. The key to abstraction is to take some feature of the system and separate "how to use it" from "how it works." The "how to use it" portion is called the *interface* to the feature, and "how it works" is the *implementation*.

We make such abstractions in our everyday lives as well. We constantly use devices—televisions, microwave ovens, automobiles—without completely understanding how they actually work. In many cases the internal operation of these devices has changed considerably over the years, yet the way they are used remains relatively unchanged. Of course, new features are added over time, but typically in a way that is compatible with the old features. Abstracting and designing good programming interfaces, which can grow to accommodate new features while still remaining compatible with existing clients, is one of the most challenging tasks a programmer must face.

Returning to asynchronous steering, the way a client interacts with the steering task is the *interface* to the steering feature. As mentioned previously, the interface must allow a client to specify which position to set the steering to and then determine when the operation has been completed. In NQC we build this interface using several constants and a pair of variables as shown in Listing 13-4.

Listing 13-4. Interface to Steering Task

```
// interface for steering task
#define STEER_LEFT      -1
#define STEER_CENTER     0
#define STEER_RIGHT      1

int steer_goal; // set this to steer
int steer_current = -999; // check this
```

A client may indicate its desired steering position by setting the value of steer_goal to one of the three position constants (such as STEER_LEFT). The task may check to see what the current steering position is by reading the value of steer_current. Initially, steer_current is set to an invalid number (-999) to indicate that the steering task has not been initialized. Once the steering task completes its initialization, this variable will contain a valid steering position.

Note that a client does not need to know anything about how the steering task works (i.e., its implementation). It is sufficient to understand only the interface to the task.

The implementation of our steering task is a bit more complicated than its interface. A complete listing is shown in Listing 13-5.

Listing 13-5. Implementation of Steering Task

```
// implementation of steering task
#define CENTER    SENSOR_1
#define STEER     OUT_A
#define FULL_TURN_TIME    50

task steer_task()
{
    SetSensor(CENTER, SENSOR_TOUCH);
```

```
    // align
    OnFwd(STEER);
    Wait(FULL_TURN_TIME);
    Toggle(STEER);
    until(CENTER==1);
    Off(STEER);

    steer_goal = 0;
    steer_current = 0;

    while(true)
    {
        int goal;

        goal = steer_goal;
        if (goal != steer_current)
        {
            if (goal == STEER_LEFT)
            {
                // turn left
                Fwd(STEER);
                OnFor(STEER, FULL_TURN_TIME);
            }
            else if (goal == STEER_RIGHT)
            {
                // turn right
                Rev(STEER);
                OnFor(STEER, FULL_TURN_TIME);
            }
            else
            {
                Toggle(STEER);
                On(STEER);
                until(CENTER==1);
                Off(STEER);
            }

            steer_current = goal;
        }
    }
}
```

As usual, the code begins with some defines for the motor, sensor, and constants. The task itself starts by configuring the sensor, then centering the wheels using code that is almost identical to that from our earlier synchronous example. After the wheels are centered, the two interface variables, steer_goal and steer_current, are set to indicate that the wheels are centered.

The task then enters an infinite loop which checks to see if steer_goal differs from steer_current. The actual value of steer_goal is copied into the local variable goal, prior to this test. This is because the steering task must make a number of decisions, and a change of goal in the midst of these decisions could lead to unpredictable behavior. Since a client may change steer_goal at any time, the steering task must read it once, then make all decisions from that single reading. Each time through the loop, this copy is refreshed with the latest value from steer_goal.

When steer_goal does not match steer_current, the task then takes the appropriate action (turning the wheels to the left, right, or center), then updates steer_current with the new location. Although the steering happens asynchronously with respect to the clients, each steering operation must run to completion before another one can be acted upon. For example, if steer_goal is set to STEER_RIGHT, the steering task will begin to move the wheels to the right. This may not complete for another $1/2$ second. Meanwhile a client may set steer_goal to STEER_LEFT. The steering task will continue moving the wheels all the way to the right before checking steer_goal again and determining that the wheels must be moved back to the left. In short, once a steering operation has started, it cannot be canceled.

Before the steering task may be used, the client program must start it. In addition, it is often desirable for the client to wait until the steering task has finished its initialization before moving on to other things. These two steps can be done with the following code:

```
start steer_task;
until(steer_current == 0);
```

Using the asynchronous steering task, we can write a new version of our bumper car program. In this version we will add a new behavior: the robot will beep as it backs up. The following code snippet will spend 1 $1/2$ seconds beeping every $1/2$ second.

```
repeat (3)
{
    PlayTone(880, 30);
    Wait(50);
}
```

If we used this code with the previous synchronous steering functions, then the beeps wouldn't start until the steering had been completed. Now that we have asynchronous steering, the beeps can start immediately. The main task for such a program is shown in Listing 13-6 (combine with Listings 13-4 and 13-5 for the complete program).

Listing 13-6. Main Program for Asynchronous Steering

```
#define EYE      SENSOR_2
#define DRIVE     OUT_C
#define STRAIGHT_TIME      50

#define PROX_EVENT 1
#define PROX_THRESHOLD 52

task main()
{
    SetSensor(EYE, SENSOR_LIGHT);
    SetEvent(PROX_EVENT, EYE, EVENT_TYPE_HIGH);
    SetUpperLimit(PROX_EVENT, PROX_THRESHOLD);

    start steer_task;
    until(steer_current == 0);

    On(DRIVE);

    // use "far" messages
    SetTxPower(TX_POWER_HI);

    while(true)
    {
        monitor(EVENT_MASK(PROX_EVENT))
        {
            while(true)
            {
                SendMessage(85);
            }
        }
        catch
        {
            Rev(DRIVE);
            steer_goal = STEER_RIGHT;
            repeat (3)
            {
                PlayTone(880, 30);
```

```
            Wait(50);
        }

        steer_goal = STEER_CENTER;
        Fwd(DRIVE);
    }
  }
}
```

If synchronous behavior is desired while using the steering task, then the client needs to wait for `steer_current` to equal the desired setting before moving on. For example, in the program shown in Listing 13-6, the operation of centering the wheels before driving forward could be made synchronous by replacing

```
steer_goal = STEER_CENTER;
Fwd(DRIVE);
```

with

```
steer_goal = STEER_CENTER;
until(steer_current == STEER_CENTER);
Fwd(DRIVE);
```

CONCLUSION

Rack and pinion steering is not limited to bumper cars. In general, it can be used with the sensor mechanisms from the previous robots to make faster versions of Bugbot, Scanbot, and others. Proximity detection is also applicable to a wide variety of robots; it is much more friendly than ramming into everything with a bumper.

The touch sensor isn't a very reliable way to determine when the wheels are centered, and as a result Steerbot tends to drift a little to the left or right. A more precise steering mechanism can be constructed by using a rotation sensor. For improved accuracy, there should be a gear reduction between the rotation sensor and the 8-tooth gear that turns the rack. That way the rotation sensor will be able to measure smaller amounts of movement of the rack. A belt drive, if used, should be between the motor and the rotation sensor, and not between the rotation sensor and the rack. If a rotation sensor is used, then the value of the sensor itself can replace the `steer_current` variable in the asynchronous steering task.

Even with its challenges, rack and pinion steering can be an interesting choice for almost any robot.

Chapter 14
Diffbot

Many of the robots so far have been powered by two independent motors, each driving one side of the robot. Whether treads (Tankbot) or wheels (Tribot) are used, the principle remains the same: drive both sides at the same speed to go straight, and drive one side faster than the other to turn. Since driving straight requires both motors to be turning at the exact same speed, slight variations in the motors can cause the robot to drift quite a bit to the left or right.

Diffbot is still driven by treads, but it avoids the drifting problem through the use of two differentials. Instead of operating autonomously, Diffbot will be controlled directly by a remote control that is built from the RCX and sensors. Both the drive mechanism and the remote control may be incorporated into other robot designs.

NOTE

Extra Pieces Required:

2 16-Tooth Gears   **1 Differential**   **1 Bevel Gear (not needed for RIS 1.0)**

See Appendix B for information on obtaining extra pieces.

DUAL-DIFFERENTIAL DRIVE

Diffbot uses a special drive mechanism constructed from two differentials. The easiest way to understand how it works is to start building it as shown in Figures 14-1 through 14-4.

Figure 14-1.
Diffbot step 1

Figure 14-2.
Diffbot step 2

Figure 14-3.
Diffbot step 3

Figure 14-4.
Diffbot step 4

The rear differential, hereafter referred to as the *primary* differential, drives axles that will eventually power the treads. This is the traditional application of a differential: Power is applied to the shell, and the axles will then turn so that their average speed is that of the shell itself. This gives us an easy way to power both axles from a single motor, thus avoiding the drift associated with slight variations in drive systems with two motors. The secondary differential (roughly in the middle of the chassis) is the key to turning. The far axles of both differentials are joined by a series of 16-tooth gears. Since there is an even number of gears (an odd number of meshes) on that side, the axle for the secondary differential will always turn in the opposite direction of the axle turning the far tread. The near axles of the differentials are also linked together, but this time using three gears. Since this is an odd number of gears, both axles will turn in the same direction. Ideally, all three of these gears would be ordinary 24-tooth gears; however, the Robotics Invention System only includes four such gears and we would need a total of five for Diffbot. As a workaround, a crown gear (which also has 24 teeth) is used as the middle gear. If you have an extra 24-tooth gear (perhaps from service pack #5229), it may be used instead.

Consider the case of both treads turning at the same speed. Both axles of the primary differential will turn at the same speed as the shell itself. The axles of the secondary differential will also be spinning. The near axle will turn in the same direction as the primary differential, while the far axle will turn in the opposite direction. Since these axles are turning at the same speed but in opposite directions, the shell of the second differential will remain motionless. In effect, the shell of the second differential turns at a speed that is *one half of the difference* between the speeds of the right and left treads. The rotation of the differentials can be summarized as follows:

If the primary differential is stopped, then the treads will turn at the speed of the secondary differential, but in opposite directions. This results in the vehicle turning in place.

$$Primary = \frac{left + right}{2}$$

$$Secondary = \frac{left - right}{2}$$

If both differentials are turned at the same speed in the same direction, then the right tread will be stopped while the left one turns at twice the speed of the differentials. The reverse case happens when the differentials are turned at the same speed, but in opposite directions. This can be used for very sharp turns, but since turning in place is already possible, perhaps we can arrange for more gentle turning.

If the second differential is turned at a fraction of the speed of the primary, then both treads will still turn in the same direction, but one will be turning slightly faster than the other. The greater the ratio between the two differentials, the more gradual the turn will be. For Diffbot, a 9:1 gear reduction will be used. Figures 14-5 through 14-8 show the gearing used to turn the secondary differential.

Figure 14-5.
Diffbot step 5

Figure 14-6.
Diffbot step 6

Figure 14-7.
Diffbot step 7

Figure 14-8.
Diffbot step 8

In Figures 14-9 through 14-11, the primary motor is suspended above the differential using motor brackets, without which such a placement would be impossible.

Figure 14-9.
Diffbot step 9

Figure 14-10.
Diffbot step 10

Figure 14-11.
Diffbot step 11

In Figures 14-12 and 14-13, the secondary motor and treads are added. The secondary drive uses a crown gear, which is well supported from behind in order to prevent slipping. A long wire should be connected to each motor as shown. In the next section, these wires will be connected to the remote control for Diffbot.

Figure 14-12.
Diffbot step 12

Figure 14-13.
Diffbot step 13

CONSTRUCTING THE REMOTE

The remote must be able to control two motors. Furthermore, it is desirable for each motor to be independently run forward, reverse, or turned off. Using two touch sensors to control a single motor is simple. The first touch sensor, while pressed, can be used to run the motor in the forward direction. The second touch sensor can be used to run it in the reverse direction.

It is a little more difficult to use a light sensor to control a motor. Since the motor may be in one of three states (forward, off, reverse), we need three discernable colors that can be placed in front of the light sensor: yellow, green, and black work well. A simple control stick is constructed that moves one of the three colors in front of the light sensor. A rubber band is used to keep the control stick centered when not in use.

Since the controls are built directly above the RCX input connectors, the first step is to attach the sensor wires to the RCX itself as shown in Figure 14-14. Use short wires for ports 1 and 2, and the light sensor for port 3. Figures 14-15 and 14-16 show how the light sensor is attached to the remote.

Figure 14-14.
Remote step 1

Figure 14-15.
Remote step 2

Figure 14-16.
Remote step 3

The two touch sensors are added and connected to the RCX as shown in Figure 14-17. A double peg is also inserted into the 1×6 beam. This double peg will be used later to anchor the rubber band that centers the control stick.

Figure 14-17.
Remote step 4

As mentioned before, the control stick uses different colors to trigger a response from the light sensor. In Figure 14-18, a yellow brick, green cross beam, and black brick are used as the foundation for the control stick. A black rubber band should also be placed around the #2 axle protruding from the cross beam. The control stick is completed in Figure 14-19.

Figure 14-18.
Remote step 5

Figure 14-19.
Remote step 6

The completed control stick is attached to the rest of the control in Figure 14-20. The rubber band is used to provide tension so that the control stick centers itself when not in use. For the right amount of tension, the band should be wrapped a second time around the double peg. The wires connected to the RCX's outputs are the other ends of the wires used in Diffbot. The wire from the primary motor (the one with the 24-tooth gear) should be connected to output A, and the secondary motor should be connected to output C.

Figure 14-20.
Remote step 7

PROGRAMMING THE REMOTE

The remote has two touch sensors and a light sensor, each of which requires its own sensor watcher in RCX Code or task in NQC. For the touch sensors, operation is simple: turn on the primary motor (either forward or backward) when the button is pressed, and then wait until it is released to turn off the motor. RCX Code program stacks for this appear in Figure 14-21.

Figure 14-21.
Motor control with touch sensors in RCX Code

The light sensor must control both forward and reverse directions of the secondary motor. The RCX Code for using the light sensor is shown in Figure 14-22. As usual, the first thing we need to do is determine appropriate thresholds for the light sensor. The program assumes that when it starts, the green brick is in front of the light sensor. It then sets the variable **tooDark** to a little darker than the green brick, and **tooBright** to a value slightly brighter than the green brick. Three sensor watchers are then used to detect the black brick (too dark) and yellow brick (too bright). In both cases the secondary motor is turned on (albeit in different directions). When the light sensor sees the green brick, it turns off the secondary motor.

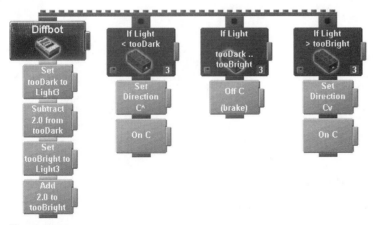

Figure 14-22.
Motor control with a light sensor in RCX Code

A similar program can be written in NQC, as shown in Listing 14-1. Unlike previous programs, which did most of their work within the main task, this one has three auxiliary tasks (fwd_task, rev_task, and steer_task) that do all of the work. As a result, the main task only has to configure the sensors and start the tasks. The resulting code is very similar in structure to the RCX Code program presented in Figure 14-22.

Listing 14-1. Diffbot Program in NQC

```
// diffbot.nqc
//  remote control for DIFFBOT

// motors and sensors
#define DRIVE        OUT_A
#define TURN         OUT_C
#define FWD_BUTTON   SENSOR_1
#define REV_BUTTON   SENSOR_2
#define STEER        SENSOR_3


task main()
{
    // configure sensors
    SetSensor(FWD_BUTTON, SENSOR_TOUCH);
    SetSensor(REV_BUTTON, SENSOR_TOUCH);
    SetSensor(STEER, SENSOR_LIGHT);

    // start all tasks
    start steer_task;
    start fwd_task;
    start rev_task;

    // this task is done now...
}


task fwd_task()
{
    while(true)
    {
        // drive forward while button is pressed
        until(FWD_BUTTON == 1);
        OnFwd(DRIVE);
        until(FWD_BUTTON == 0);
        Off(DRIVE);
```

```
    }
}


task rev_task()
{
    while(true)
    {
        // drive backward while button is pressed
        until(REV_BUTTON == 1);
        OnRev(DRIVE);
        until(REV_BUTTON == 0);
        Off(DRIVE);
    }
}


task steer_task()
{
    // calibrate
    int tooDark = STEER - 2;
    int tooBright = STEER + 2;

    while(true)
    {
        // should we turn left?
        if (STEER < tooDark)
        {
            OnFwd(TURN);
        }
        else if (STEER > tooBright)
        {
            OnRev(TURN);
        }
        else
        {
            Off(TURN);
        }
    }
}
```

Once the remote control is programmed, you're ready to take Diffbot for a spin. Run the program, then start playing with the controls. The touch sensors can be used to drive forward or backward, and the control stick can be used to turn in place. Experiment with turning in place (control stick only) and gradual turns (touch sensor + control stick).

CONCLUSION

The dual-differential drive mechanism used in Diffbot is a good substitute for the Tankbot chassis used in many of the previous robots. Although it is a little larger and more complex to build, the elimination of drift and addition of gradual turning make this drive mechanism a good overall choice as long as space isn't at a premium.

The remote control itself is also a useful construction. The programming can be adapted for other drive mechanisms, and provides a convenient way to control two motors during construction and experimentation with new robots.

Chapter 15
Brick Sorter

Brick Sorter is a robot that sorts LEGO bricks by color. It was designed to accommodate the green and yellow 1×2 bricks included in the original Robotics Invention System 1.0. If you are using RIS 1.5 or 2.0, then green 1×2 cross beams may be substituted for the green 1×2 bricks. The design could easily be adapted for other brick sizes or colors.

Brick Sorter consists of a chute with a light sensor at the bottom. The bricks to be sorted are lined up within the chute. The light sensor determines the color of a brick, and then an ejector arm pushes the brick to either the left or the right. The next brick slides into place and the process is repeated. A touch sensor is used to determine the position of the ejector arm and thus control when it should change direction or stop.

CONSTRUCTION

In order for the bricks to slide down the chute, a smooth surface is required. In many LEGO designs, this is accomplished by using tiles (plates with a smooth top). The Robotics Invention System does not include any tiles, so we need a different approach. Turning a pair of beams upside down solves this problem nicely. Friction pegs and double-pegs attach these inverted beams to the rest of the chute, as shown in Figures 15-1 through 15-4.

Figure 15-1.
Brick Sorter step 1

Figure 15-2.
Brick Sorter step 2

Figure 15-3.
Brick Sorter step 3

Figure 15-4.
Brick Sorter step 4

The chute is also designed to minimize the amount of stray light that can enter it and hit the light sensor. This is important because the light sensor not only determines what color brick is in front of it, but also must decide when the chute is empty. This means that the sensor must be able to distinguish between a green brick and no bricks, which in turn means that the chute should be very dark when empty. Figure 15-5 shows how the upper portion of the chute is enclosed in solid bricks (rather than beams).

Figure 15-5.
Brick Sorter step 5

The light sensor needs to be mounted at the end of the chute. It would be easiest to turn the light sensor upside down and attach it directly to the inverted beams. Unfortunately, this would place the sensing portion of the sensor too high to detect the bricks in the chute. Instead, plates are attached to the sensor, as shown in Figure 15-6. Then, the plates are attached to the sides of the chute in Figure 15-7, thus suspending the light sensor from above. The ejector arm needs to slide back and forth so that, just as in Steerbot, a pair of odd hinge pieces are used as substitutes for actual tiles.

Figure 15-6.
Brick Sorter step 6

Figure 15-7.
Brick Sorter step 7

The ejector arm is 16 units long. A beam would be a little too thick, so plates are used instead. Since there are no 1×16 plates, 1×6 and 1×10 plates are combined, as shown in Figures 15-8 and 15-9. Note how the seam in the second layer of plates is offset from the seam in the first layer. This is a common construction technique in both the real world and the LEGO world, and it results in stronger structures because there is never a single seam through more than one layer. The arm is completed in Figure 15-10. The three 10-tooth racks combine to make a single long rack.

Figure 15-8.
Brick Sorter step 8

Figure 15-9.
Brick Sorter step 9

Figure 15-10.
Brick Sorter step 10

The ejector arm is added to the chute, along with a motor and a touch sensor, in Figure 15-11. Note how the touch sensor detects the spaces between the 1×2 bricks on the ejector arm. This allows the brick sorter to determine the position of the arm.

Figure 15-11.
Brick Sorter step 11

The base for the Brick Sorter is constructed in Figures 15-12 through 15-14. Its "T" shape is the key to its stability. Equally important is the fact that there is a layer of plates below the beams making up the base. Later on, vertical beams will be added as legs for the chute. When beams are attached to one another this way, the end of the vertical beam extends slightly below the bottom of the horizontal beam. Without the bottom layer of plates, the brick sorter would rest on the ends of the legs rather than on the base itself. Note that you will need to use yellow 2×4 plates when building the base, since there are not enough of the gray plates.

Figure 15-12.
Brick Sorter step 12

Figure 15-13.
Brick Sorter step 13

Figure 15-14.
Brick Sorter step 14

The chute is mounted on a support frame that holds it at just the right angle. If the angle is not steep enough, the bricks will not slide down reliably. If it is too steep, the bricks may fall over as they slide, and the sorter will become jammed. A pair of 1×8 beams are used in front, and 1×12 beams are used in the rear. The resulting angle isn't a natural right triangle (such as 3-4-5), so the vertical "legs" are not quite parallel, and only the front pair of legs uses vertical bracing to assure that they are perpendicular to the floor. The finished model is shown in Figure 15-15.

Figure 15-15.
Brick Sorter step 15

PROGRAMMING

The theory behind Brick Sorter's operation is use of the light sensor to determine if there are bricks in the chute and, if so, the color of the next brick. Depending on the color of the brick (yellow or green), the motor is set to the forward or backward direction. The motor is then run until the touch sensor detects the gap at either end of the arm. At that point, the arm will have already pushed the brick out to one side or the other. The motor's direction is then reversed. Once the center gap is detected, the motor is turned off. After a slight delay (to allow the next brick to fall into place), the process is repeated. An NQC program for running the sorter is shown in Listing 15-1.

Listing 15-1. Brick Sorter Program in NQC

```
// sorter.nqc
//  program for Brick Sorter

#define EYE     SENSOR_1
#define NOTCH   SENSOR_3

#define ARM     OUT_A

// you may need to adjust these
#define NO_BRICKS      35
#define BRIGHT_BRICK   45
#define BRICK_DELAY    10

task main()
{
    // configure sensors
    SetSensor(EYE, SENSOR_LIGHT);
    SetSensor(NOTCH, SENSOR_TOUCH);

    // run until no more bricks
    while(EYE >= NO_BRICKS)
    {
        // check color of brick
        if (EYE > BRIGHT_BRICK)
            Fwd(ARM);
        else
            Rev(ARM);
```

```
    // wait until arm has moved to end
    On(ARM);
    until(NOTCH==1);
    until(NOTCH==0);

    // reverse direction arm and wait until centered
    Toggle(ARM);
    until(NOTCH==1);
    until(NOTCH==0);

    // stop arm
    Off(ARM);

    // wait a little while for next brick to slide down
    Wait(BRICK_DELAY);
  }
}
```

As you can see, the bulk of the program is contained within a loop that uses the light sensor to determine if more bricks remain to be sorted. A pair of until statements are used to detect the gaps. The first until waits until the touch sensor is pressed, which means it is no longer in the current gap. The second until waits until the sensor is released, which means the next gap has been reached. Note how the Toggle command is used to reverse the direction of the motor regardless of its current direction.

There are two thresholds that need to be determined in the program: BRIGHT_BRICK and NO_BRICKS. To determine the BRIGHT_BRICK threshold, view the light sensor's values when a yellow brick and when a green brick are in front of it. The BRIGHT_BRICK threshold should be about halfway between these two values. The NO_BRICKS threshold should be halfway between the value for a green brick and the value when the chute is empty. If the empty chute's value is too bright, try turning the sorter so that no outside light shines directly into the chute.

The sorter program can also be written in RCX Code, as shown in Figure 15-16. The program's structure is nearly identical to the NQC version except that the event-based **Wait Until** blocks were used to detect notches (compared to the condition-based tests in the NQC program). The threshold values discussed previously become the values in the **Repeat While** and **If** blocks.

Figure 15-16.
Brick sorting in RCX Code

SORTING

The sorter is now ready to be used. Carefully slide a few green and yellow 1×2 bricks or cross beams into the chute (if a brick falls on its side, the sorter will become jammed). Make sure the ejector arm is centered, then run the program. If the bricks are not lined up straight or the ejector arm isn't properly centered, Brick Sorter will tend to self-destruct as it attempts to sort the bricks. Special care should be taken to ensure that the ejector arm itself is solidly assembled and that its ends can slide freely in and out of the chute.

If the thresholds are set properly, the robot will stop after a few moments with a pile of green bricks on one side, and a pile of yellow bricks on the other. If it cannot tell green from yellow, then the BRIGHT_BRICK threshold (or the value in the RCX Code **If** block) needs to be adjusted. If the sorter fails to stop when the chute is empty, then you need either to position it so that no external light is shining into the chute, or perhaps to adjust the NO_BRICKS threshold (or the value in the RCX Code **Repeat While** block).

CONCLUSION

Many of the previous robots were general-purpose vehicles that could be used as building blocks for a variety of other robots, just the way Linebot was used as a starting point for Dumpbot. By contrast, Brick Sorter is a special purpose robot suitable for little besides sorting some 1×2 bricks. Adapting it for bricks of other sizes or colors would be simple enough, but otherwise its use is fairly limited. The construction and programming techniques, however, are very reusable. For example, using inverted beams to provide a smooth surface is utilized in the next chapter.

Chapter 16
Vending Machine

Vending Machine dispenses small candies, such as M&M's. It is composed of two mechanisms: a card reader and a candy dispenser. Special cards are inserted into the card reader, and the appropriate number of candies is then pushed out of the dispenser.

CONSTRUCTION

The cards for Vending Machine, shown in Figure 16-1, are based on a 2×10 plate, with 1×1 plates representing the value of the card. The front-right corner of the card must always have a 1×1 plate. Up to three more 1×1 plates may be placed along the right edge subject to the following conditions: no two 1×1s may be placed adjacent to one another, and the back two rows must be left blank. Two cards (with values 4 and 2) are shown in the figure. The front of the cards is toward the top-left corner of the illustration.

Figure 16-1.
Vending Machine cards

The candy dispenser is similar to the chute constructed for Brick Sorter. Once again inverted beams are used to provide a smooth surface, and double pegs are used to join these beams to the rest of the assembly. Figures 16-2 through 16-6 show the construction of the bottom portion of the dispenser. The candy will slide down the dispenser until it hits the 1×2 beam at the end. The 1×10 plates serve as guardrails to keep the candy from accidentally rolling off the side until the dispenser pushes them out.

Figure 16-2.
Vending Machine step 1

Figure 16-3.
Vending Machine step 2

Figure 16-4.
Vending Machine step 3

Figure 16-5.
Vending Machine step 4

Figure 16-6.
Vending Machine step 5

The dispenser must be able to push the candy out one at a time. For this, a small arm is turned by a motor—each revolution of the arm will push a single candy out of the dispenser. A touch sensor is used to determine the position of the arm, thus allowing Vending Machine to count how many candies have been dispensed. The beams added in Figure 16-7 provide support for the motor and touch sensor. The arm is added to a #12 axle in Figure 16-8. Note how a crossblock has been placed at the other end of the axle. When the arm is pointed straight down, the crossblock will point up and brush against the touch sensor.

Figure 16-7.
Vending Machine step 6

Figure 16-8.
Vending Machine step 7

The dispenser is completed by adding the motor and touch sensor in Figure 16-9. The arm is turned using a 3:1 gear reduction. Without a gear reduction, the arm would turn much faster, shooting the candies out rather than pushing them. It would also be more difficult for the RCX to respond to the touch sensor if the arm was moving that fast.

Figure 16-9.
Vending Machine step 8

The base of Vending Machine is started in Figures 16-10 and 16-11. The base has three functions: reading a card, supporting the RCX, and supporting the dispenser. In Figure 16-12 the base is starting to take shape. The 2×2 bricks and 2×4 plates near the back of the base will eventually support the RCX. The inverted beam provides a smooth surface for the cards to slide in on, and the 1×16 beam near the front of the base will eventually support one side of the dispenser.

Figure 16-10.
Vending Machine step 9

Figure 16-11.
Vending Machine step 10

Figure 16-12.
Vending Machine step 11

Figures 16-13 through 16-15 continue to develop the base. A light sensor will be used to detect the card's position near the back of the reader. In order to minimize interference from stray light, the rear portion of the reader is enclosed in bricks rather than beams. Note the two 1×2 beams near the back of the base. As usual, two plates separate these beams from the 1×16 beams below, thus providing the correct spacing for vertical bracing.

Figure 16-13.
Vending Machine step 12

Figure 16-14.
Vending Machine step 13

Figure 16-15.
Vending Machine step 14

All of the card reader's electronics are added in Figure 16-16. When a card is placed at the front of the reader, it will activate the touch sensor. The motor can then be used to pull the card in while the touch sensor counts how many 1×1 plates are on the card. This use of a tire is something new. In previous robots, tires were used as a way of moving the robot. Being made of rubber, they have much better grip than a smooth LEGO piece. In addition, their "sponginess" allows them to grip uneven surfaces (such as the top of a 2×10 plate). As a result, they are ideal for grabbing and pulling items through a machine. There are several different tires that will fit on the hub; be sure to use the smallest size. The light sensor detects when the card has been fully inserted, after which the motor can be reversed to eject the card.

Figure 16-16.
Vending Machine step 15

Figures 16-17 through 16-19 complete the base. Note how the motor is held in place by the 2×4 plates above it. The 1×6 and 1×8 beams serve as two legs to hold the dispenser at the proper angle. As with Brick Sorter, the angles required do not quite work out to a natural right triangle, so one pair of legs is not quite perpendicular to the base.

Figure 16-17.
Vending Machine step 16

Figure 16-18.
Vending Machine step 17

Figure 16-19.
Vending Machine step 18

Vending Machine is completed in Figure 16-20 by adding the dispenser and two more support legs. As usual, the orientation of motor wires is particularly important. Figure 16-19 shows the ends of motor A's wire, while Figure 16-20 shows the ends of motor C's wire. These orientations provide the most obvious path for the wire to reach its motor and they also ensure that forward rotation of the motors corresponds to what the programs expect. Specifically, the forward rotation of the reader motor should pull the card in and the forward rotation of the dispenser motor should turn the arm counterclockwise.

Figure 16-20.
Vending Machine step 19

The dispenser was designed to accommodate M&M's Crispy Candies. Other candies may require slight adjustments. Possible adjustments include the size and position of the rotating arm, the size of the opening at the bottom of the chute, the height of the guardrails, or even the size and angle of the chute itself. For example, adding a bushing on the end of the rotating arm makes it more suitable for working with smaller candies.

THEORY OF OPERATION

Card reading is triggered by the reader's touch sensor (which will become pressed if a card is placed at the opening of the reader). At this point, the program needs to turn on the reader's motor in order to pull the card into the reader. The light sensor is used to determine when the card is fully inserted, and the motor must be stopped at this point. While the card is being pulled in, the number of times the touch sensor is pressed must be counted, since this determines how many candies should be dispensed.

Once the card has been read, candies can be dispensed by running the dispenser's motor. If set up properly, each rotation of the arm will result in a single candy being pushed out of the dispenser. The exact number of rotations can be monitored by counting the number of times the dispenser's touch sensor is released. Waiting for the sensor to be released (rather than pressed) ensures that the arm has pushed the candy out of the dispenser before we stop the motor.

Once the candy has been dispensed, the card may be ejected from the reader. This can be accomplished by running the reader motor in the reverse direction for a little while (1 second is plenty of time). Just to be safe, the motor should continue running until the reader's touch sensor becomes released.

PROGRAMMING IN RCX CODE

Vending Machine's program involves three different actions: reading a card, dispensing candy, and ejecting the card. Each one of these actions will be implemented in a separate My Block, then the main program will simply call those blocks in order.

The **VM_READ** block shown in Figure 16-21 handles card reading. First, it waits for the touch sensor to be pressed (indicating that a card has been placed at the reader opening), then it sets **count** to 1 and turns on the card-grabbing motor. The tricky part is that it now has to respond to two different stimuli: the touch sensor being pressed (which should cause **count** to be incremented), and the light sensor detecting that the card is fully inserted. RCX Code's event-based blocks make this relatively easy to do. Button presses can be counted by using a **Wait Until** block for the touch sensor, and an enclosing **Repeat Until** block ensures that this process will be stopped as soon as the card is fully inserted. If the light sensor instead used a **Repeat While** block, which is condition based, then it would not be able to interrupt the block waiting for a touch sensor press.

Touch 1 Press

Touch 1 Press

Light 2 is brighter than threshold.

Figure 16-21.
RCX Code for card reading

The rest of the program is shown in Figure 16-22. The **VM_DISPENSE** block turns on the dispensing motor, then waits for **count** presses of the dispensing sensor. **VM_EJECT** turns on the card motor for at least one second, and continues to wait for the touch sensor to be released before stopping the motor. The program itself starts by setting **threshold** (which is used in **VM_READ** to determine when the card is fully inserted) to a value slightly larger than the light sensor's first reading.

Figure 16-22.
Vending Machine program in RCX Code

PROGRAMMING IN NQC

The NQC program , like the RCX Code version, can be broken into separate functions for the different phases of operation: reading the card, dispensing candy, and ejecting the card. The process of reading the card must monitor both the touch sensor and light sensor while the card is being inserted. A first attempt at programming this in NQC might look something like Listing 16-1.

Listing 16-1. Faulty Approach for Reading the Card

```
#define CARD_COUNT   SENSOR_1
#define CARD_STOP    SENSOR_2
#define CARD_GRAB    OUT_A

int count;
int threshold;

void readCard()
{
```

```
    // wait for card to be inserted, then grab it
    until(CARD_COUNT == 1);
    OnFwd(CARD_GRAB);

    count = 0;
    while(CARD_STOP <= threshold)
    {
        // count number of presses
        if (CARD_COUNT == 1)
        count++;
    }

    Off(CARD_GRAB);
}
```

Unfortunately, this doesn't quite work. The while loop may execute several times during the time it takes a single 1×1 plate to pass by the sensor. In order to count the actual presses, we must somehow keep track of whether the button was previously pressed or not, and only count new presses. One such solution is shown in Listing 16-2.

Listing 16-2. Using a Variable to Check for State Changes

```
int lastValue, currentValue;
lastValue = 0;
while(CARD_STOP <= threshold)
{
    currentValue = CARD_COUNT;
    if (lastValue != currentValue)
    {
        if (currentValue == 1) count++;
        lastValue = currentValue;
    }
}
```

Two variables are introduced: lastvalue is used to remember the previous touch sensor value, and currentvalue is used to latch in the sensor's value. Setting lastvalue to 0 initially ensures that the first 1×1 plate will be counted. In effect, a small state machine has been constructed inside of the while loop. A state machine can be described as a set of states and a set of transitions between states. In addition, one or more actions may be associated with a transition between states. In our example, there are two possible states (0 and 1), which are stored in lastvalue. A transition occurs when the current sensor reading is different from the state. If the transition is from state 0 to state 1, an action is performed (count is incremented). In either case, lastvalue is updated to reflect the new state. Although our example was rather simple, state machines provide a powerful way to describe complex systems and are used quite extensively in programming.

The RCX's multitasking capability can be exploited to solve this same problem as shown in Listing 16-3.

Listing 16-3. Using Multitasking to Read the Card

```
void readCard()
{
    // wait for card to be inserted, then grab it
    until(CARD_COUNT == 1);
    OnFwd(CARD_GRAB);
    // start the card counting task
    start countTask;

    // continue grabbing until completely inserted
    until(CARD_STOP > THRESHOLD);
    Off(CARD_GRAB);

    // stop the counting task
    stop countTask;
}

task countTask()
{
    count = 0;

    while(true)
    {
        until(CARD_COUNT == 1);
        count++;
        until(CARD_COUNT == 0);
    }
}
```

In this case, a separate task waits for the sensor to read 1, then increments and waits for the sensor to return to 0. This task is explicitly started and stopped as needed by the readCard function. Since this task runs in parallel with the main task, the readCard function needs only to watch the light sensor and determine when to stop reading.

A third approach to the problem is to use the RCX's event handling capability. Assuming that the event has been set up properly to trigger when the card is fully inserted, reading the card could be done with the code shown in Listing 16-4. Note that the inner loop increments count whenever the touch sensor changes from 0 to 1. Since we also want to count the initial bump at the front of the card, count is set to 1 prior to this loop.

Listing 16-4. Using an Event to Read the Card

```
#define CARD_EVENT 1

void readCard()
{

    // wait for card to be inserted, then grab it
    until(CARD_COUNT == 1);
    OnFwd(CARD_GRAB);
    count = 1;

    monitor(EVENT_MASK(CARD_EVENT))
    {
        while(true)
        {
            until(CARD_COUNT == 0);
            until(CARD_COUNT == 1);
            count++;
        }
    }

    Off(CARD_GRAB);
}
```

Each of the approaches have their advantages, although in such a simple example there aren't compelling reasons to prefer one to the others. The remainder of this chapter will continue to use the event monitoring version, since it is similar to how programs in RCX Code are constructed and is slightly more efficient.

Our second function must dispense the candy. As mentioned previously, the dispenser's touch sensor allows the RCX to monitor the number of revolutions of the rotating arm. As with the card reader, the program waits for the sensor to be pressed then released. The dispensing function is shown in Listing 16-5.

Listing 16-5. Dispensing Candy in NQC

```
#define CANDY_COUNT   SENSOR_3
#define CANDY_MOTOR   OUT_C

void dispenseCandy(const int &n)
{
    // dispense the candy
    On(CANDY_MOTOR);
    repeat (n)
    {
        until(CANDY_COUNT == 1);
        until(CANDY_COUNT == 0);
    }
    Off(CANDY_MOTOR);
}
```

Although previous programs have used functions, this is the first time a nonempty *argument* list is present. When a function is defined, one or more *formal arguments* may be declared. In this case, the formal argument n is declared. Each formal argument must have its type specified as well—in this case const int &. This rather strange type is just a terse way of saying that the value is passed by reference but never changed within the function.

When a function is called, it must be provided with the appropriate *actual arguments* that are substituted for the formal arguments during the execution of the function. Here are a few examples of calling the dispenseCandy function:

```
dispenseCandy(2);   // dispense 2 candies

int x;
dispenseCandy(x);   // dispense "x" candies

dispenseCandy(SENSOR_1);   // dispense based on sensor value
```

The details of substituting the actual arguments for the formal ones are called *argument passing semantics*, and depend on the declared types of the arguments. In fact, since all values in NQC are 16-bit integers, the only information truly specified in the type are the argument passing semantics. There are four possible types for arguments: int, int &, const int, and const int &, shown in Table 16-1. Complete descriptions of the semantics of each of these types can be found in Chapter 3. Additional information is also available in the *NQC Programmer's Guide*, which can be downloaded from the NQC web site.

Table 16-1. Function Argument Types

TYPE	SEMANTICS	COMMENTS
int	by value	uses up a variable, actual argument is not altered
int &	by reference	efficient, actual argument must be a variable
const int	n/a	efficient, actual argument must be constant
const int &	by reference	efficient, argument cannot be modified

Since dispenseCandy does not need to modify the argument, using const int & gives us flexibility in calling the function while still generating a very efficient code. Using a type of int would latch the actual argument into a temporary variable, which is often helpful when dynamic quantities are being used. However, in the case of dispenseCandy, the formal argument is only accessed a single time (setting the repeat count), thus latching has little advantage.

At this point argument passing may seem overkill. After all, why not just let dispenseCandy directly use the global variable count? The answer is that using arguments can make a function much easier to reuse later on. Right now we want to dispense a number of candies based on a global variable count, but later on perhaps we'll want to use the function some other way. Perhaps the variable will be named candy, or perhaps we'll want to call it several times with a different variable each time. In fact, in the next chapter, we'll reuse dispenseCandy and call it with something that isn't even a variable.

Our third function is used to eject the card. It turns on the card reader's motor for a little while, then waits for the card to be removed before shutting off the motor. The code for this is shown in Listing 16-6.

Listing 16-6. Ejecting the Card

```
void ejectCard()
{
    // eject card
    OnRev(CARD_GRAB);
    Wait(100);
    until(CARD_COUNT == 0);
    Off(CARD_GRAB);
}
```

All that remains is to add a suitable `main` task that initializes the event and sensors, and then calls `readCard`, `dispenseCandy`, and `ejectCard` in order. The complete program is shown in Listing 16-7. Note that `SetEvent()` is used to define an event for whenever the light sensor reads a high value, and `SetUpperLimit()` is used to set the threshold for that high value. The threshold is set to be slightly larger than the light sensor's initial reading.

Listing 16-7. Vending Machine Program in NQC

```
// vending.nqc
//  program for the Vending Machine using card reader

#define CARD_COUNT    SENSOR_1
#define CARD_STOP     SENSOR_2
#define CARD_GRAB     OUT_A

#define CANDY_COUNT   SENSOR_3
#define CANDY_MOTOR   OUT_C

#define CARD_EVENT 1

int count;

task main()
{
    // set up sensors
    SetSensor(CARD_STOP, SENSOR_LIGHT);
    SetEvent(CARD_EVENT, CARD_STOP, EVENT_TYPE_HIGH);
    SetUpperLimit(CARD_EVENT, CARD_STOP + 2);

    SetSensor(CARD_COUNT, SENSOR_TOUCH);
    SetSensor(CANDY_COUNT, SENSOR_TOUCH);

    while(true)
    {
        readCard();
        dispenseCandy(count);
        ejectCard();
    }
}
```

```
void readCard()
{

    // wait for card to be inserted, then grab it
    until(CARD_COUNT == 1);
    OnFwd(CARD_GRAB);
    count = 1;

    monitor(EVENT_MASK(CARD_EVENT))
    {
        while(true)
        {
            until(CARD_COUNT == 0);
            until(CARD_COUNT == 1);
            count++;
        }
    }

    Off(CARD_GRAB);
}


void dispenseCandy(const int &n)
{
    // dispense the candy
    On(CANDY_MOTOR);
    repeat (n)
    {
        until(CANDY_COUNT == 1);
        until(CANDY_COUNT == 0);
    }
    Off(CANDY_MOTOR);
}


void ejectCard()
{
    // eject card
    OnRev(CARD_GRAB);
    Wait(100);
    until(CARD_COUNT == 0);
    Off(CARD_GRAB);
}
```

TESTING

Vending Machine is now ready for use. Start with the arm pointing up and load some candy into the dispenser. Run the program and place a card at the front of the reader.

The reader motor should immediately start pulling in the card. If the motor pushes out the card, then the orientation of one of the wire's ends need to be changed. If the motor does not turn on at all, then verify that the card is constructed properly and activates the touch sensor. Assuming the card has been pulled in, the motor should stop when the card is fully inserted.

Arranging things so that a single candy is dispensed with each rotation of the arm may require some adjustments depending on the specific details (weight, shape, and size) of the candy. If the candy is relatively heavy, then when the dispenser is full the weight of all of the candy may be sufficient to push the bottom one out of the dispenser. If this is the case, then the angle of the dispenser can be made less steep or the guardrails can be enlarged. If the candy is not sliding down into position fast enough, then the angle of the dispenser may need to be increased. A slightly smaller or larger arm may also be needed to ensure that a single candy is pushed out each time. The existing arm can be enlarged by adding one or more bushings. For a smaller arm, a 1×3 liftarm can be used.

If a single candy is being ejected with each rotation of the arm and Vending Machine is still dispensing the wrong number of candies, then the touch sensor isn't being activated reliably. The crossblock that presses against the touch sensor may require some slight adjustment so that it activates the touch sensor exactly once per rotation.

CONCLUSION

Vending Machine is my personal favorite of the robots in this book. It combines some familiar techniques (inverted beams, etc.) with a few new twists such as using a tire to "grab" an object and using a touch sensor to count rotations. Granted, the idea of dispensing M&M's in exchange for inserting a LEGO card is a bit contrived, but the robot is still fun to play with.

There are several obvious enhancements that can be built; perhaps a hopper to catch the candies as they are dispensed, or a large loading bin at the top of the chute for added capacity. The card reader itself works quite smoothly and could be easily integrated into other machines.

Vending Machine is used again in the next two chapters. In Chapter 17, Vending Machine is reprogrammed to accept orders from either a computer or another RCX via infrared messages. In Chapter 18, Vending Machine is programmed to maintain a record of all of its "transactions."

Chapter 17
Communication

The RCX is able to send and receive simple messages via infrared light. These messages can be exchanged with another RCX, or even a computer. This chapter presents two different projects that illustrate how to incorporate such communication into a robot.

In the first project, Vending Machine from Chapter 16 will be reprogrammed to use messages instead of the card reader for determining when to dispense candy. Vending Machine can then be controlled remotely from a computer. Although this project can be programmed in RCX Code, the Robotics Invention System software itself cannot send a message from the computer to the RCX. Therefore some other means of sending messages to the RCX is required for testing the modified Vending Machine. There are several ways of doing this: using NQC to send the message from a computer, programming a second RCX to send it, or using the LEGO Remote Control (#9738) to send it directly.

In the second project, things get even more interesting as multiple RCXs communicate with one another. A robotic vehicle, Delivery Truck, will be created from Dumpbot, and Vending Machine will be rebuilt as the stand-alone Candy Dispenser. Delivery Truck can accept an order from the user (via a touch sensor), drive to the dispenser, request the appropriate number of candies, then return and deliver its cargo. In order to build both robots at the same time, a few extra pieces are required, most notably, a second RCX.

Extra Pieces Required for Dual-RCX Example:

3 1×12 Beams   **2 Motors**   **1 RCX**   **1 2×4 Brick**
(only required when using set #9747)

See Appendix B for information on obtaining extra pieces.

This is a great project to work on with a friend who owns their own MINDSTORMS Robotics Invention System set. However, even if you are not able to complete the second project, reading through the material can still be instructive.

REPROGRAMMED VENDING MACHINE

Our first project is a modified Vending Machine that accepts orders via an infrared message instead of the card reader. If you still have Vending Machine built from the last chapter, you may use it as is. However, if you have not built Vending Machine, you may find it easier to build Candy Dispenser as described in the next section, rather than building the entire Vending Machine. Both Vending Machine and Candy Dispenser use the same dispensing motor and sensor arrangement, which is the important point from a programming perspective.

Before delving into the program itself, we need to understand how the RCX uses messages. Each message has a value between 0 and 255. The RCX is always listening for new messages and will remember the value of the most recent message it received (the value is 0 if no message has been received). This value can be used just like a sensor's value. For example, an RCX Code program can have a sensor watcher that responds to a specific message value, or an NQC program can use the value of the message in an if statement. It is also important for the RCX to be able to respond to another message once the current one has been handled. For this, commands to reset the message value back to 0 are provided (**Clear IR Message** in RCX Code, and ClearMessage in NQC).

We are now ready to make Vending Machine respond to messages. In RCX Code all we need is a sensor watcher for the message (called the **IR** watcher). The watcher is set to respond to any message greater than 0 and will then set **count** to the value of the message, use **VM_DISPENSE** to dispense the appropriate number of candies, and finally use **Clear IR Message** so that the RCX will be ready for another message. The program is shown in Figure 17-1. If you have previously created the Vending Machine program, **VM_DISPENSE** should already be available in the **My Blocks** tray. If not, then refer to Figure 16-22 for the definition of **VM_DISPENSE**.

Figure 17-1.
Message-based Vending Machine in RCX Code

A similar program, written in NQC, is shown in Listing 17-1. Message always returns the value of the most recently received message, and it remains 0 until a message is received. The program then calls dispenseCandy (copied directly from the original Vending Machine program), using Message as the argument. Finally, ClearMessage is called to set the message value back to 0 and get ready for another message.

Listing 17-1. Message-Based Vending Machine in NQC

```
// vending2.nqc
//  program for message-based Vending Machine

#define CANDY_COUNT   SENSOR_3
#define CANDY_MOTOR   OUT_C
```

```
task main()
{
    // set up sensors
    SetSensor(CANDY_COUNT, SENSOR_TOUCH);

    while(true)
    {
        // wait for message
        until(Message() != 0);

        // dispense candy
        dispenseCandy(Message());

        // get ready for next message
        ClearMessage();
    }
}


void dispenseCandy(const int &n)
{
    // dispense the candy
    On(CANDY_MOTOR);
    repeat (n)
    {
        until(CANDY_COUNT == 1);
        until(CANDY_COUNT == 0);
    }
    Off(CANDY_MOTOR);
}
```

Regardless of whether NQC or RCX Code was used to program Vending Machine, we still need one more thing before we can test the program: a way to send a message to the RCX. The specifics of doing this depend greatly on the programming tools you are using. For example, if you are using the command line version of NQC, simply enter the following command line, substituting the desired message value for *value:*

```
nqc -msg value
```

If you are using BricxCC, select **Send Messages** from the **Tools** menu. This will bring up a window from which you can send messages. Click on the appropriate number button, or use the arrows to enter a number at the bottom of the window and press the **Send** button.

In MacNQC, select **Miscellaneous Panel** from the **RCX** menu. In the Message section of the window enter the appropriate number and press the **Send** button.

If you are using the Robotics Invention System software, then things are a bit more difficult. RCX Code allows you to write RCX programs that send and receive messages, but sending a message from the computer to the RCX is not supported. If you happen to have an extra RCX lying about, the following program shown in Figure 17-2 will turn it into a message sender.

Figure 17-2.
Sending a message in RCX Code

Hook a touch sensor up to sensor port 1, run the program, and press the touch sensor to send a message. A second option is to use the LEGO Remote Control, which can be used to send three different messages. The buttons labeled "1," "2," and "3" on the remote control correspond to sending messages of values 1, 2, and 3, respectively.

A final option is to use one of the NQC programming tools (NQC, BricxCC, or MacNQC) to send the message. Inside the RCX, both NQC and RCX Code use the same messages, so programs written in NQC can communicate with programs written in RCX Code and vice versa. Furthermore, the NQC tools can be used to send a message from the computer to an RCX Code program. For this you'll need to install the appropriate tools (see Chapter 1) and follow the instructions given earlier for sending messages.

CANDY DISPENSER

Our second communication example uses two robots: Candy Dispenser and Delivery Truck. Candy Dispenser is really just a stripped-down version of Vending Machine with the dispenser raised high enough to extend over Delivery Truck. The dispenser portion of Vending Machine, shown in Figure 17-3, can be used with only one minor modification: both of the short wires used in Vending Machine should be replaced with long wires.

Figure 17-3.
Dispenser step 1

A new base for the dispenser must then be built as shown in Figures 17-4 through 17-7. The bottom 2×8 plate gives the base a slight "T" shape, which increases its side-to-side stability. The only other subtle detail is the 2×4 plate on top of the 1×2 beams. It provides little structural value, but it does make assembly a little easier by holding the 1×2 beams in place when it is time to add vertical beams. Sometimes good design is just as much about the assembly process as the final product.

Figure 17-4.
Dispenser step 2

Figure 17-5.
Dispenser step 3

Figure 17-6.
Dispenser step 4

Figure 17-7.
Dispenser step 5

The dispenser is attached to the base using a pair of 1×10 beams and a pair of 1×12 beams, as shown in Figure 17-8. As in our previous examples, one pair of beams (1×12s) is kept perpendicular while the other pair (1×10s) is allowed to form a slightly different angle. The RCX sits off to the side and is connected to the dispenser by two long wires. This allows the RCX to be positioned so that it can receive messages, and the dispenser positioned to drop candy into Delivery Truck.

Figure 17-8.
Dispenser step 6

The program for Candy Dispenser is nearly identical to the message-based vending machine program presented earlier, with one slight modification. In our scenario Delivery Truck will send a message to Candy Dispenser, then wait for the candy before turning around and returning home. How long should Delivery Truck wait? The solution is to have Candy Dispenser tell Delivery Truck when it is done by sending a message back. The RCX Code version of the program is shown in Figure 17-9, while the NQC version appears in Listing 17-2.

Figure 17-9.
Candy Dispenser program in RCX Code

Listing 17-2. Candy Dispenser Program in NQC

```
// dispense.nqc
//   program for Candy Dispenser

#define CANDY_COUNT     SENSOR_3
#define CANDY_MOTOR     OUT_C

task main()
{
    // set up sensors
    SetSensor(CANDY_COUNT, SENSOR_TOUCH);

    while(true)
    {
        // wait for message
        until(Message() != 0);

        // dispense candy
        dispenseCandy(Message());

        // get ready for next message
        ClearMessage();

        // tell Delivery Truck we are done
        SendMessage(1);
    }
}
```

288

```
void dispenseCandy(const int &n)
{
    // dispense the candy
    On(CANDY_MOTOR);
    repeat (n)
    {
        until(CANDY_COUNT == 1);
        until(CANDY_COUNT == 0);
    }
    Off(CANDY_MOTOR);
}
```

DELIVERY TRUCK

Delivery Truck requires a trivial extension to Dumpbot: the only thing added is a touch sensor connected to sensor port 3, shown in Figure 17-10. This touch sensor is how orders are given to Delivery Truck.

Figure 17-10.
Delivery Truck

Delivery Truck's mission is to accept an order from the user, follow a line until it reaches Candy Dispenser, request the desired number of candies, turn around and return home, and dump its cargo. Most of these functions were previously developed for Dumpbot in Chapter 9. The new requirements are to accept an order and communicate with Candy Dispenser.

A touch sensor is used to input orders to Delivery Truck—the "order" is simply the number of times the button is pressed. Counting button presses is easy, but how will the program know when to stop counting and start driving? We will use a *timeout*, which means that if the program does not detect a new button press after a certain amount of time, it will assume that the order is complete.

PROGRAMMING DELIVERY TRUCK IN RCX CODE

The easiest way to create the RCX Code program is to start with the program for Dumpbot from Chapter 9. Figure 17-11 shows the new RCX code stacks for taking an order and picking up the candy. The button presses for an order are counted using a sensor watcher. Each time the touch sensor is pressed, the RCX will play a sound (as feedback to the user), increment **count**, and reset the timer. The **DEL_ORDER** block is used to take an order. It first clears **count** (to get rid of a previous order), waits for the first button press (which will increment **count** to 1), then waits until the timer reaches 2 seconds. Since each button press will reset the timer, this effectively waits until 2 seconds have gone by without a button press.

Figure 17-11.
Taking an order in RCX Code

Figure 17-12.
Delivery Truck
program in RCX Code

The **DEL_PICKUP** block is used by Delivery Truck to request the appropriate number of candies from Candy Dispenser. Note how **Clear IR Message** is called before sending the message to Candy Dispenser. The call to **Clear IR Message** is required so that an old message doesn't cause the program to think a reply has been sent before Candy Dispenser is really done. After receiving its cargo, Delivery Truck backs up a little (0.8 second). This gets Delivery Truck clear of Candy Dispenser before it starts turning around.

The main program stack for Delivery Truck is shown in Figure 17-12. Although it is a large stack, its operation is straightforward. It starts by using **LB3_SETUP** to prepare the light sensor thresholds for line following. **DEL_ORDER** is then used to wait for the user to place an order. **LB3_FOLLOW** causes the robot to follow the line until it reaches a stopper, at which point **DEL_PICKUP** is used to request the desired number of candies from Candy Dispenser. When dispensing is complete, the robot will back away from Candy Dispenser, then **DB_TURN** is used to turn the robot around, **LB3_FOLLOW** is again used to follow the line (back to the beginning), and **DB_DUMP** causes Delivery Truck to dump its cargo.

PROGRAMMING DELIVERY TRUCK IN NQC

Delivery Truck's program is an adaptation of the Dumpbot program presented in Chapter 9 (which in turn was based on linebot3.nqc from Chapter 8). Starting with the dumpbot.nqc program, you only need to replace the main task and add the new code shown in Listing 17-3.

Listing 17-3. New NQC Code for Delivery Truck

```
int count;
#define REVERSE_TIME 80
#define TIMEOUT 20
#define BUTTON    SENSOR_3

task counting_task()
{
    // count the number of button presses
    while(true)
    {
        until(BUTTON == 1);
```

```
            ClearTimer(0);
            PlaySound(SOUND_CLICK);
            count++;
            until(BUTTON == 0);
    }
}

void get_order()
{
    // start with a clean order
    count = 0;

    // start counting
    start counting_task;

    // wait until at least 1 press and then a timeout
    until(count == 1);
    until(Timer(0) >= TIMEOUT);

    // no more counting
    stop counting_task;
}


task main()
{
    setup();
    SetSensor(BUTTON, SENSOR_TOUCH);

    get_order();

    follow();

    // send request, wait for response
    ClearMessage();
    SendMessage(count);
    until(Message() != 0);

    // turn around
    Rev(LEFT+RIGHT);
    OnFor(LEFT+RIGHT, REVERSE_TIME);
    turn_around();

    // return to starting place and dump
    follow();
    dump();
}
```

Most of the new code is associated with taking the order. This requires that the RCX respond to two different stimuli—the touch sensor being pressed, and a timeout expiring. In Chapter 16, we used events as a way of working with multiple stimuli. We could use a similar approach for this program, but it can also be instructive to try a new approach. In this case we will use multitasking. The code in `counting_task` waits for the touch sensor to be pressed, then it plays a sound, increments `count`, and clears the timer. Once started, this task will constantly monitor the touch sensor, keeping track of the total number of presses.

The `get_order` function is used to wait for the user's order. First it clears `count`, then it starts `counting_task`. It waits for the first button press, and then for a timeout to occur, after which it stops `counting_task`. Actually, it would usually be okay to leave `counting_task` running all the time, but by stopping it we prevent any inadvertent changes to `count`.

Note the similarities between this code and the RCX Code program presented earlier. The `counting_task` responds to button presses the same way the sensor watcher does in the RCX Code program. The `get_order` function is also similar to **DEL_ORDER** in the RCX Code program. The major difference is that while RCX Code implicitly uses multiple tasks, NQC requires the programmer to explicitly create each task. Furthermore, an NQC program has control over starting and stopping each task.

The `main` task is straightforward, and should be quite reminiscent of the previous RCX Code program. Note how `ClearMessage` is called before sending the message to Candy Dispenser. The call to `ClearMessage` is required so that an old message doesn't cause the program to think a reply has been sent before Candy Dispenser is really done. Before turning around, Delivery Truck backs up a little (0.80 second). This gets Delivery Truck clear of Candy Dispenser before it starts turning around. Finally, the program follows the line back to the other stopper and dumps its cargo.

TESTING

Testing Delivery Truck requires some sort of line to follow, with stoppers at either end. As with Dumpbot (and Linebot before it), the line should be $3/4$" thick and colored gray or green on a white surface. Curves should have a 6" or larger radius, and stoppers (which are black) should be at least $3/4$" long. If Delivery Truck is having trouble following the line, refer to Chapter 8.

Candy Dispenser needs to be positioned at one end of the line. For best results, a short, straight section of line (at least 12") should precede this end. This will ensure that Delivery Truck always approaches Candy Dispenser straight on. Run Delivery Truck and make sure it stops at the end of the line. Now set Candy Dispenser's RCX so that it is a few inches away and facing Delivery Truck. The dispenser itself should be positioned as close as possible to Delivery Truck, so that the candies will fall into the cargo bin. I created a simple test mat on a piece of 22"×28" poster board as shown in Figure 17-13.

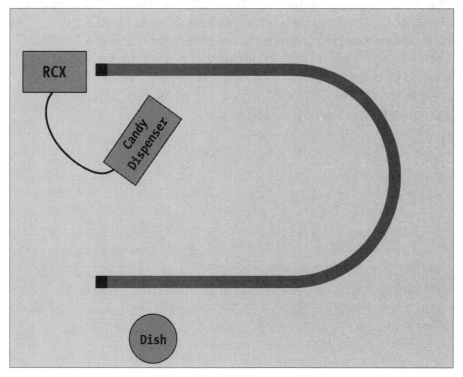

Figure 17-13.
Test mat for Delivery Truck

A small dish was also placed on the mat to catch the candies as they were dumped from Delivery Truck's cargo bin. It may take a few rounds of adjustment to get Candy Dispenser placed just right. If it is too close, Delivery Truck may bump into it. If it is too far away, some candy may miss the dish.

CONCLUSION

Communication is perhaps the most powerful feature of the RCX. It allows the RCX to accept commands from a computer, or multiple RCXs to cooperate to accomplish a joint mission. In either case, messages provide a way to overcome some of the RCX's inherent limitations. For example, the RCX normally can only control three motors and use three sensors. If a certain mission requires more motors and/or sensors, multiple RCXs can be used, coordinating their activities via messages.

Communication with a computer can be used to overcome limitations in the RCX's own computational power. Data can be sent from the RCX to the computer for processing, which can then relay commands back down to the RCX via messages. At one extreme, the computer can even take over "primitive" control of the robot—turning on and off each motor individually. A more sophisticated approach would be to have the robot performing semi-autonomously: an order could be sent to the RCX, which would then execute a complete sequence of actions and report back to the host computer.

Chapter 18
Using the Datalog

The *datalog* allows the RCX to record data that can later be uploaded to a computer. Using the datalog, it is possible to turn the RCX into a data collection device. Existing robots can be adapted to log information about their operation, or new devices can be built specifically for detecting and recording information.

In this chapter, three uses for the datalog will be explored. In the first example, the message-based Vending Machine from Chapter 17 (or Candy Dispenser) will be augmented to keep track of each candy request. This transaction list can then be uploaded to a computer for analysis (perhaps to figure out how much more candy to buy). This example illustrates how the datalog can be used to supplement an existing robot's functionality.

In the second example, the RCX will keep track of how often and for how long a television is turned on. In this case, the RCX is being used merely as a data collection device. The third example takes the data collection a step further. In it, a temperature sensor is used to watch the temperature of water as it is being frozen. This example illustrates how the datalog can be used to assist in performing experiments. The temperature sensor is not part of the MINDSTORMS Robotics Invention System, and must be purchased separately. The temperature sensor isn't nearly as versatile as the other sensors, so you should only get one if you are really interested in building some temperature-based robots. See Appendix B for more information on how to obtain a temperature sensor.

Unfortunately, RCX Code does not provide access to the datalog. Therefore, only NQC versions of the sample programs will be shown in this chapter.

DATALOG BASICS

The datalog must be initialized before any data can be added to it. Initialization consists of telling the RCX how many entries the datalog should hold. The datalog is shared across all programs and retained even when the RCX is turned off. The datalog requires 3 bytes of memory per entry, and this memory comes from the same pool used to store programs (about 6000 bytes total). If several large programs are loaded into the RCX, then there may not be enough room for the desired datalog. Conversely, a large datalog may prevent certain programs from being loaded. The largest possible datalog would hold over 2000 entries, but such a large datalog would leave almost no room for programs.

The NQC function to initialize the datalog is `CreateDatalog`, which takes a single argument, the desired size (number of entries). The RCX may only hold a single datalog at any given time, so each call to `CreateDatalog` erases the previous datalog and then creates a new datalog of the specified size. The following statement initializes the datalog to hold 100 entries:

```
CreateDatalog(100);  // create datalog to hold 100 entries
```

A size of 0 indicates that no datalog should be created. This is a good way to get rid of the previous datalog when memory is getting tight.

```
CreateDatalog(0);  // eliminate datalog
```

Initialization of the datalog reserves enough memory to hold the specified number of entries. The datalog itself is empty after initialization. Data can be added using the `AddToDatalog` command. A sensor reading is the most obvious thing to add, but any other value (such as a timer or variable) may be added as well.

```
AddToDatalog(SENSOR_1);   // add the value of sensor 1
AddToDatalog(Timer(0));   // add the current timer value
AddToDatalog(Watch());    // add the system watch
AddToDatalog(7);          // add a constant
```

Data can continue to be added until the datalog is full, after which any additional calls to `AddToDatalog` will be ignored. When data is added, the datalog records the source of the data as well as the data value itself. There are four data sources that the datalog understands directly: variables, timers, sensors, and the system watch. Any other type of value (such as a constant) is first moved into a variable, then the variable is added to the datalog. The NQC compiler takes care of this detail for you, but you need to be aware of it when you look at the datalog later, since logging a constant (or other nonsupported type) will appear in the datalog as a variable.

The RCX's display contains a datalog indicator, which shows if a datalog is currently in use, and if so how much data has been added. The indicator is a small circle divided into four sections, which appears at the right side of the display. When no datalog exists, all four sections are turned off. When the datalog is in use, each section represents approximately one quarter of the datalog. As each quarter of the datalog is filled, the appropriate section is shown. In addition, the quarter where the next entry will be added is indicated by a flashing section. For example, if a datalog for 100 entries was created and 60 entries have been added, two sections will be solid, and a third section will be flashing. Once the datalog is completely full, all four sections will be solid.

The datalog can be uploaded to a computer at any time, even if it is not yet full. The upload is typically initiated from the computer, and the specifics depend on the programming tool being used. When using the command line version of NQC, the following command will upload the current datalog and print it on screen:

```
nqc -datalog
```

Each line will contain a single datalog entry value, formatted as a signed decimal integer. In order to view the sources for the entries as well as their values, use the following command:

```
nqc -datalog_full
```

To upload the datalog from BricxCC, select **Datalog** from the **Tools** menu and press the **Upload Datalog** button. The datalog will be uploaded and the sources and values of the entries will appear within the datalog window.

In MacNQC, the datalog can be uploaded by selecting **Upload Datalog** from the **RCX** menu. The datalog will be uploaded and displayed in its own window. If the **Verbose Datalog** preference is set, then both the sources and values will be displayed; otherwise only the values will be shown. The preferences can be edited by selecting **Preferences** under the **Edit** menu.

LOGGING TRANSACTIONS

The first datalog example adds a transaction record to the message-based Vending Machine from the last chapter. However, since the dispensing mechanisms and programming are so similar, the same changes could also be made to either the previous chapter's Candy Dispenser, or even the original Vending Machine (Chapter 16).

Two features need to be added to the program: initialization of the datalog, and the capability to add entries to the datalog. Initialization of the datalog can be very simple—adding a single line to the main task should do the trick:

```
CreateDatalog(100);
```

However, this has two disadvantages. The first is that we will have no way of knowing if the call is successful. The RCX does not provide a way for a program to detect if the datalog initialization was successful, but the user can always check by looking for the datalog indicator on the LCD display. Unfortunately, if a previous (and smaller) datalog already exists, it is possible that initialization could fail but the display still indicate a datalog is present (the old one). This would mislead the user into thinking the proper size datalog was created when in fact it wasn't. We can work around this by first erasing the old one, then creating the new one:

```
CreateDatalog(0);
CreateDatalog(100);
```

This code will still fail in the same situations as the first one (namely, not enough memory). The difference is that when the code fails, the previous datalog will have already been deleted so the display will indicate no datalog present. Therefore the user can tell immediately from the LCD display if the desired datalog has been created or not.

The second disadvantage of such an initialization is that a new datalog is created every time the program is run. What if we want the log to span several different runs of the program? One way to do this is to have a completely separate program initialize the datalog. The user could then run this other program whenever a new datalog was desired. A better solution is to let the program figure out if the user wants a new datalog. Consider the following function:

```
#define CANDY_COUNT    SENSOR_3
#define DATALOG_SIZE   100
void init_datalog()
{
    // if not pressed, don't init datalog
    if (CANDY_COUNT == 0) return;

    CreateDatalog(0);
    CreateDatalog(DATALOG_SIZE);
    PlaySound(SOUND_FAST_UP);

    // wait for button to be released
    until(CANDY_COUNT == 0);
}
```

The function first checks to see if the CANDY_COUNT sensor (the touch sensor on the dispenser portion of Vending Machine) is released. Under normal operation, Vending Machine will always stop with this sensor released, so the only way it would be pressed is if the user is intentionally holding it in. If it is released, then the function simply returns, doing nothing. However, if the sensor is pressed, then a new datalog is created, a sound is played (to provide some feedback to the user), and the function waits for the sensor to be released. Assuming that init_datalog is called fairly early from within the main task, the user can cause a new datalog to be created by pressing and holding the touch sensor before running the program. Once the sound is played, it is safe to release the touch sensor.

So much for initialization of the datalog. We also need to add data to it. We'll keep it simple and only add the number of candies dispensed for each request. A good place to do this is within the dispenseCandy function:

```
void dispenseCandy(const int &n)
{
    // log the request
    AddToDatalog(n);
    // dispense the candy
    On(CANDY_MOTOR);
    repeat (n)
    {
        until(CANDY_COUNT == 1);
        until(CANDY_COUNT == 0);
    }
    Off(CANDY_MOTOR);
}
```

This has one potential problem. In certain situations it is possible that the value of n will change between the AddToDatalog command and the repeat state- ment. For example, in the case where dispenseCandy is called using Message as the argument (as in Chapter 17), it is possible that a new message would be received at just the wrong moment. This problem is very unlikely, and could probably be ignored, but I like to be on the safe side. The best way to combat this problem is to latch the value of n. We could do this explicitly by creating another variable and copying n to the new variable. Another option is to change the type of n so that dispenseCandy is called by value (which means the compiler will create a variable and do the copying for us).

```
void dispenseCandy(int n)
{
    // log the request
    AddToDatalog(n);

    // dispense the candy
    On(CANDY_MOTOR);
    repeat (n)
    {
        until(CANDY_COUNT == 1);
        until(CANDY_COUNT == 0);
    }
    Off(CANDY_MOTOR);
}
```

The complete program for a message-based Vending Machine with datalog support is shown in Listing 18-1. The choice of using a datalog size of 100 is arbitrary. It is large enough to do plenty of experimenting, but small enough not to cause any severe memory shortages. Feel free to use another size if it suits your needs better.

Listing 18-1. Candy Dispensing with a Datalog

```
// vending3.nqc
//  program for message-based Vending Machine with data logging

#define CANDY_COUNT     SENSOR_3
#define CANDY_MOTOR     OUT_C

#define DATALOG_SIZE    100

task main()
{
    // set up sensors
    SetSensor(CANDY_COUNT, SENSOR_TOUCH);

    init_datalog();

    while(true)
    {
        // wait for message
        until(Message() != 0);

        // dispense candy
        dispenseCandy(Message());
```

```
        // get ready for next message
        ClearMessage();
    }
}

void init_datalog()
{
    // if not pressed, don't init datalog
    if (CANDY_COUNT == 0) return;

    CreateDatalog(0);
    CreateDatalog(DATALOG_SIZE);
    PlaySound(SOUND_FAST_UP);

    // wait for button to be released
    until(CANDY_COUNT == 0);
}

void dispenseCandy(int n)
{
    // log the request
    AddToDatalog(n);

    // dispense the candy
    On(CANDY_MOTOR);
    repeat (n)
    {
        until(CANDY_COUNT == 1);
        until(CANDY_COUNT == 0);
    }
    Off(CANDY_MOTOR);
}
```

Be sure to press and hold the dispenser's touch sensor (the one attached to input 3) when running the program for the first time. If all goes well, you should hear the sound being played and the datalog will be initialized. If the sound was not played, then the program is not trying to initialize the datalog. Check the LCD display. It should show a single flashing datalog section. If the sound was played, but the LCD display does not show any datalog indicators, then there isn't enough memory for the datalog. Try using a smaller value for DATALOG_SIZE in the program and/or freeing up memory by removing unwanted programs.

The most thorough way to clear out memory is to erase everything, then reload whichever program (or programs) are needed. To clear memory using the command line version of NQC, use the following command:

```
nqc -clear
```

In BricxCC, the same function can be accomplished by selecting **Clear Memory** from the **Tools** menu. In MacNQC, select **Clear Memory** from the **RCX** menu.

Be aware that clearing memory using any of these methods will erase all programs in the RCX as well as any previous datalog.

Assuming that the datalog was initialized properly, use Vending Machine (or Candy Dispenser) a few times, then upload the datalog. You should see a list of all the requests processed since the datalog was created. For example, a transcript using the command line version of NQC is shown here:

```
> nqc -msg 2
> nqc -msg 4
> nqc -msg 1
> nqc -datalog
2
4
1
> nqc -msg 3
> nqc -datalog
2
4
1
3
```

KEEPING TRACK OF THE TELEVISION

Our second example shows how the datalog enables the RCX to be used as a data collection device. The first thing to determine is what data should be collected. It just so happens that my television has a small red LED that lights up whenever the television is turned on. By placing a light sensor up against this LED, the RCX will be able to use the light sensor to determine when the television is on. We could record the light sensor's value periodically (e.g., once a minute), but this would lead to a large amount of data—much of which has little value.

A more efficient way of keeping track of the television is to just record those instances when the television's state changes: going from off to on, and vice versa. For each of these events, the time at which the event occurred will be recorded in the datalog. There are two different ways of measuring time in the RCX: the timers and the system watch. The timers provide resolution of 10 ticks per second, and have a maximum value of 54.6 minutes. The watch has a resolution of 1 minute and a maximum value of 23 hours and 59 minutes. The watch is a good match for our application, so we'll use it (see Listing 18-2).

Listing 18-2. Keeping a TV Log

```
// tvlog.nqc
//   program that logs television usage

// some constants
#define TV_SENSOR       SENSOR_1
#define THRESHOLD       40
#define DATALOG_SIZE    100

task main()
{
    // set up sensors
    SetSensor(TV_SENSOR, SENSOR_LIGHT);

    // create the datalog
    CreateDatalog(0);
    CreateDatalog(DATALOG_SIZE);

    while(true)
    {
        // wait for TV to be turned on and log it...
        until(TV_SENSOR > THRESHOLD);
        AddToDatalog(Watch());
        PlaySound(SOUND_CLICK);

        // now wait for TV to be turned off...
        until(TV_SENSOR < THRESHOLD);
        AddToDatalog(Watch());
        PlaySound(SOUND_CLICK);
    }
}
```

For each transition from off to on, or on to off, the program will add the current time (according to the system watch) to the datalog. The threshold for the light sensor can be adjusted by changing the value of THRESHOLD. Similarly, the capacity of the datalog can be adjusted by changing DATALOG_SIZE.

The system watch resets to 00.00 (0 hours and 0 minutes) each time the RCX is turned on. The watch may be set to some other, perhaps more meaningful, value. When using the command line version of NQC, use the following command, substituting the desired time for *hhmm*.

```
nqc -watch hhmm
```

For example, to set the watch to 1:30, you would use the following command:

```
nqc -watch 130
```

Note that in this case a leading 0 is optional when specifying a value for the time.

Another option is to automatically set the watch to the current time (at least the current time according to the computer).

```
nqc -watch now
```

To set the watch when using BricxCC, select **Diagnostics** from the **Tools** menu. You can either enter a new value for the watch manually, or press the **Set Current** button to set it to the current time. In MacNQC, the watch can be set from the Miscellaneous Panel (select **Miscellaneous Panel** from the **RCX** menu). Enter the desired value under **Watch**, then press **Set** to send the new value to the RCX.

In order to conserve batteries, the RCX will automatically shut off after a certain period of inactivity (known as the *power down time*). Curiously enough, running a program is not enough "activity" to keep the RCX from turning itself off, therefore the power down time will need to be changed from its initial setting of 15 minutes if any significant amount of logging is to be done. To change the power down time using the command line version of NQC, use the following command, substituting the desired number of minutes:

```
nqc -sleep minutes
```

Setting the power down time to 0 disables the feature.

```
nqc -sleep 0
```

If you are using BricxCC, the power down time can be changed by selecting **Diagnostics** from the **Tools** menu and entering the appropriate time in the dialog box. In MacNQC, the power down time can be set from the Miscellaneous Panel (select **Miscellaneous Panel** from the **RCX** menu). Enter the desired value under **Sleep** and press the **Set** button to send the new value to the RCX. In all cases, a time of 0 minutes indicates that the RCX should never turn itself off.

Speaking of batteries, the RCX consumes batteries the fastest when it has to power motors. In this experiment, no motors are involved, so power consumption is relatively small. Even so, running an RCX program for 20 or 30 hours is likely to drain batteries completely. If you plan on running a data logging program for extended periods of time, consider using an AC adapter (if available for your RCX). LEGO makes an appropriate adapter (see Appendix A for more information).

After setting up the RCX such that the light sensor was directly in front of my television's power indicator, I let the program run for a while. Here's a sample datalog:

```
1110
1140
1260
1320
```

The watch records time in minutes using a 24-hour clock. For example, 1:00 A.M. would be 60, 2:00 A.M. would be 120, and 1:00 P.M. would be 780. The preceding log entries correspond to the following times:

6:30 P.M.

7:00 P.M.

9:00 P.M.

10:00 P.M.

This indicates that the television was turned on twice: the first time at 6:30 P.M. for 30 minutes, and the second time at 9:00 P.M. for 60 minutes.

This program could also be used in other situations, perhaps for monitoring how much time a room's lights are turned on, or how often a refrigerator is opened.

WATCHING WATER FREEZE

The next example makes use of the temperature sensor to observe the process of water freezing. Before digging into the specifics of the experiment, it is important to understand some of the limitations of this particular sensor. The temperature sensor reacts much slower than the other sensors. This is because the sensor is really measuring the temperature of the sensor itself, which is not necessarily the same temperature as whatever environment it is in. It always takes some amount of time for the sensor to reach the same temperature as its environment. Consider what happens if the sensor is suddenly put in the freezer. Although the temperature of the freezer is quite cold, the sensor will initially still be at room temperature. Over time, the sensor will cool off until it reaches the ambient temperature of the freezer itself.

The time it takes for the sensor to equalize to a new environment depends on many factors, including the change in temperature and the properties of the material the sensor is in contact with. The graph in Figure 18-1 shows temperature readings taken at 1-minute intervals as the sensor was moved from room temperature into a refrigerator. In the first case, the sensor was simply placed inside the refrigerator and was thus in contact only with air. In the second case, the sensor was immersed in a small dish of water that had already been in the refrigerator for some period of time.

Figure 18-1.
Cooling effects of air and water

Both cases reached different final temperatures, but this is not very significant. The reason is that only one touch sensor was used and the experiments were thus done at slightly different times. The temperature inside a refrigerator is not constant; it continually moves up and down a few degrees as it gradually warms up, then turns on the compressor and cools down. Therefore, the refrigerator was not at the same exact temperature for both tests.

The significant point is that water caused a much faster change in temperature. This is because water conducts heat much better than air. That is the reason that swimming in 70-degree water feels much colder than walking around in a 70-degree room. The water does a much better job of conducting your body heat away, thus making you feel colder.

The lesson here is that it can take quite a while, upwards of 15 minutes in this example, for the temperature sensor to settle in on close to the right value after a drastic temperature change. Good conductors, such as water, can lower this time to a couple of minutes, but this is still a far cry from the nearly instantaneous reactions of the touch, light, and rotation sensors.

In order to observe what happens as water freezes, we need a program that will collect temperature readings regularly over a large period of time. I chose to read the sensor every 15 seconds over a 6-hour period. By clearing out all other programs, the resulting 1440 data entries, which use up over two-thirds of the RCX's memory, should all fit. Collecting exactly 1440 data points can be a bit tricky. One attempt might be

```
repeat(1440)
{
    // collect a data point
}
```

The problem with this is that repeat only works with numbers up to 255. Anything larger is an error that will be caught by the compiler. You can fool the compiler like this:

```
int x = 1440;
repeat(x)
{
    // collect a data point
}
```

But the RCX still won't repeat 1440 times. This is because the RCX only supports repeats up to 255, and will ignore the "overflow" when a larger value is supplied. You just can't use repeat loops for iterations of more than 255.

When large (greater than 255) repeat counts are used, the actual number of repeats is a consequence of how the RCX stores numbers. Most values in the RCX are stored as 2 bytes. However, the repeat count is only stored as a single byte, so the second byte is discarded. The resulting count is equal to the remainder of the initial value divided by 256. For example, a repeat count of 257 becomes a repeat of 1. The repeat count of 1440 in the example becomes a repeat of 160.

What about nesting the loops?

```
repeat(6)
{
    repeat(240)
    {
        // collect a data point
    }
}
```

This would appear to make sense. We still have a total of 1440 data points, but never a repeat over 255. The problem is that the RCX just can't handle it— repeat loops cannot be nested at all. We need to abandon the idea of using a repeat loop.

The solution is to use a variable to keep track of the iterations and manually check it ourselves using a for loop. The complete program is shown in Listing 18-3.

Listing 18-3. Creating a Temperature Log

```
// templog.nqc
//     log temperature every 15 seconds for 6 hours

#define SAMPLE_TIME    1500  // 15 seconds
#define DATALOG_SIZE   1440  // 6 hours of data

task main()
{
    SetSensor(SENSOR_1, SENSOR_FAHRENHEIT);
    SelectDisplay(1);

    CreateDatalog(0);
    CreateDatalog(DATALOG_SIZE);
```

```
    int i;
    for(i=0; i<DATALOG_SIZE; ++i)
    {
        AddToDatalog(SENSOR_1);
        Wait(SAMPLE_TIME);
    }
}
```

Strictly speaking, the samples won't be exactly 15 seconds apart. Each iteration of the loop will take slightly longer than 15 seconds due to the time spent adding to the datalog and the overhead of the loop itself. This variation in timing is known as *drift*. In this case, the amount of drift is nearly insignificant compared to the time between samples (a few milliseconds every 15 seconds), so we can safely ignore it.

We're now ready to perform the experiment. Put some fresh batteries in the RCX (or use an AC adapter if your RCX can be used with one), get a small dish of water ready, and immerse the tip of the temperature sensor in the water. I used a quarter cup of distilled water and heated it up to about 100 degrees first. Tap water at room temperature (or any other temperature for that matter) could also be used. I placed the water (and temperature sensor) inside the freezer and left the RCX outside, then let the program run. The display will show the current temperature reading, which can tell you at a glance how things are going inside the freezer.

Water and electronics generally don't mix. Ice can be even worse. I arranged things such that only the tip of the sensor got wet and the rest of it remained dry. I haven't noticed any ill effects yet, but you can never be sure. If you are concerned about potential damage to the sensor, then consider "sealing" it in a lightweight plastic bag. The plastic is an insulator and will obscure the readings a bit, but the general experiment can still be performed.

After 6 hours, the datalog was ready to be uploaded to a computer. The first thing that you will notice about the datalog is that it contains rather large numbers.

995
977
955
937
917
901
. . .

This is because the RCX always uses integers. Since the temperature sensor measures with 0.1 degree of precision, the RCX internally works with the temperature multiplied by 10. Therefore, 99.5 degrees is represented as 995, hence the absurdly high datalog numbers.

The other problem with the datalog is that 1440 data points is a lot of data. Graphs with that many data points can be unwieldy. Thinning out the data to a sample every 5 minutes and dividing the temperatures by 10, we see the graph shown in Figure 18-2.

Figure 18-2.
From water to ice

Several things are evident from this graph. During approximately the first 25 minutes the water was rapidly being cooled down to roughly 30 degrees. At this point something interesting happened. Rather than continuing to cool, the water remained around 30 degrees for nearly 100 minutes. This was the period of time that the water was gradually turning to ice. In general, a mixture of water and ice will remain at the freezing point until all of the water has been frozen. This property of freezing lets us "see" just how long it took for the water to freeze.

Notice that it took about four times as long to freeze the water as it did to cool it 70 degrees. This is because *phase changes* such as going from water to ice (or water to steam) involve significantly more energy than just raising or lowering temperature.

Another interesting point is that the graph shows the freezing point at 30 degrees rather than 32 degrees. Does my freezer make ice at a different temperature than everywhere else in the world? No. This is because the temperature sensor is really not accurate to more than a few degrees. It is quite reliable in terms of relative temperature (hence the shape of the graph), but cannot be used to accurately establish an absolute temperature.

NOTE *If you duplicate this experiment yourself, it is very possible that your water will freeze at a temperature lower than 32 degrees. Salts and other impurities that are present in water will lower its freezing point. Using distilled water, however, ensures a minimum of impurities.*

After the water turned completely to ice, the temperature of the ice continued to drop until it reached about 2 degrees, then oscillated between 2 and 5 degrees. This oscillation gives us some insight into how the freezer itself is working. The compressor (which cools the freezer) turns on at 5 degrees, then turns off at 2 degrees. Remember the discussion on feedback in Chapter 8? The 3-degree difference between the on and off temperatures provides enough hysteresis so that the compressor turns on about every 50 minutes.

If we "zoom-in" to the period of time just before ice started forming, we can observe another interesting phenomenon. The graph in Figure 18-3 shows all of the samples (every 15 seconds) between 15 and 35 minutes into the experiment.

Notice how the temperature of the water dips several degrees too low, then snaps up to the freezing point. During this time the water was still in liquid form at a temperature below the freezing point. This is known as *supercooling*. Ice crystals don't spontaneously form as soon as water reaches the freezing point. Some other factor, such as an impurity in the water, or a rough surface, is the impetus for starting the crystallization. When fewer impurities are present, it may take the water molecules a little longer to start forming, thus allowing for supercooling.

Once the first crystal forms, additional ones form quite rapidly around the first one. The result of this is that once the ice starts forming, the temperature of the mixture will quickly rise back up to the freezing point. In fact, the temperature probably rose faster than the graph indicated because the temperature sensor itself is somewhat slow to respond to changes.

Figure 18-3.
Supercooling

CONCLUSION

Three different applications for the datalog were presented. In the first example, the datalog was used to record transactions in a robot. A variation of this approach can be useful in debugging a robot's program. At various points in the program, information can be added to the datalog. Later on, the datalog can then serve as a record of what bits of the program were being executed and in what order.

The second example showed how events could be logged over a long period of time. This technique can also be adapted for a variety of purposes. The third example probably sounded more like a physics lesson than a discussion of robotics, but it is another good illustration of how the RCX can be used for data collection purposes.

Many robots won't have any use for the datalog. However, for those few situations where data needs to be collected, the datalog is an indispensable feature of the RCX.

Chapter 19
Roboarm

Roboarm is mechanically the most complex robot presented in this book. Its three motors allow it to spin around looking for objects, grab and release them, and lift them up and down. Two touch sensors are used to determine the position of the arm, and a light sensor allows Roboarm to "see" objects to pick up.

Roboarm also uses more pieces than any of the other robots. Therefore it is especially important to use the correct pieces in each step; otherwise you may run out of a critical piece later on. Pay particular attention to using regular yellow 2×4 plates (rather than the gray ones with holes) wherever appropriate. Also note the difference between 1×2 bricks (each without a hole) and 1×2 beams (each with a hole).

THE BASE

Roboarm needs a stable base underneath it. In order for Roboarm to be able to turn freely, the base must have a smooth top. By contrast, the bottom of the base needs to grip well, so that it will remain firmly planted as the arm itself rotates. In order to meet these requirements, the base is built in a slightly unorthodox manner. The sides of bricks become the top of the base, and wheels are placed facedown on the bottom of the base to provide a grip. In addition, beams are used within the base itself for increased strength.

The base was designed such that it could be built from any of the RIS sets with a minimum of extra parts. RIS 1.0 (set #9719) includes a number of 2×8 bricks that may be substituted for the combinations of bricks in the bottom and top layers of the base. Using these longer bricks will result in a more sturdy base. Similarly, if you are using RIS 1.5 or RIS 2.0 and have some other LEGO bricks on hand, feel free to substitute larger bricks for combinations of smaller ones wherever feasible.

Figures 19-1 through 19-3 show the initial construction of the base. Note how two 1×2 beams with friction pegs are embedded near the bottom of the base. In later steps, another pair of beams and pegs will also be embedded near the top. Long beams will then be attached between these pegs as a way of reinforcing the structure. The center bricks are narrower than the ones on the side; this will result in a recessed area within the center of the base.

Figure 19-1.
Roboarm base step 1

Figure 19-2.
Roboarm base step 1

Figure 19-3.
Roboarm base step 3

So far, the base has been symmetrical, but in Figure 19-4 a small gap is created on one side. This will eventually be used to allow the robot to detect its current position with respect to the base. This gap is extended into the next layer in Figure 19-5.

Figure 19-4.
Roboarm base step 4

Figure 19-5.
Roboarm base step 5

The upper half of the base, constructed in Figures 19-6 through 19-8, is like the bottom half, with the exception that there is no gap and a layer of plates has been added. The reason for the plates is that 1×12 beams will be used to brace the structure. The distance between the end holes of a 1×12 beam is 10 LEGO units. Since a brick is 1.2 LEGO units high, it will take a stack of 8.33 bricks to fill this same distance—in other words we need 8 bricks and 1 plate.

Figure 19-6.
Roboarm base step 6

Figure 19-7.
Roboarm base step 7

Figure 19-8.
Roboarm base step 8

The 1×12 beams added in Figure 19-9 brace the structure and provide a way to attach the wheels shown in Figure 19-10.

Figure 19-9.
Roboarm base step 9

Figure 19-10.
Roboarm base step 10

For the final step, shown in Figure 19-11, the base is placed facedown. The #6 axle will become the axis of rotation for Roboarm. Note how the 40-tooth gear is locked into position by the pair of axle pegs. During assembly it may be easier to remove these pegs, insert them into the gear, and attach the combined gear and pegs to the base. Roboarm's body will later use an 8-tooth gear meshed with the base's 40-tooth gear to rotate itself. One other detail is the small alcove that resulted from the gaps introduced back in Figures 19-4 and 19-5. This alcove is used by Roboarm's body to determine a home position while spinning.

Figure 19-11.
Roboarm base step 11

The base is now complete and can be set aside for later.

THE ARM

As its name implies, Roboarm needs an arm. The arm has three basic design requirements. First of all, it must be capable of being raised and lowered. Second, it must be able to grasp and release objects. Third, it needs to be able to "see" objects within its grasp.

Raising and lowering an arm can be a lot of work. In fact, the longer the arm the more torque required to lift it. This is because the arm is actually a lever, and the torque required to lift a given weight is proportional to the weight's distance from the axis of rotation. In other words, a 2' arm will require twice as much torque as a 1' arm (assuming all other factors are the same).

Generating a lot of torque is not too difficult. The output of a standard motor can be put through a gear train of some sort to reduce speed and increase torque. Transferring the resultant torque to the arm is another matter. Torque is the product of force and distance from the axis. Thus, the amount of torque generated by a given force increases the farther away from the axis the force is applied. This is the reason that long wrenches and screwdrivers with fat handles are better at loosening tight nuts and bolts. The simplest way to lift the arm is to attach a gear to one end and then rotate the gear. There is a practical limitation, however, to the total amount of force that can be applied to the teeth of a standard LEGO gear. For this reason, it would be wholly inadequate to use a small 8-tooth gear. The large 40-tooth gear is a much better choice because it has a much larger diameter, and thus can generate much more torque given the same force on its teeth.

Figures 19-12 through 19-15 show how the rear portion of the arm is constructed, including how a pair of 40-tooth gears are anchored to the beams that form the arm's structure. The #6 axle serves as the axis of rotation for the arm, and the #4 axle is used to lock the gears to the beams. Although a single 40-tooth gear would probably be sufficient in most cases, sharing the load between a pair of gears provides a more robust design capable of lifting larger weights. Two other important details are the 1×2 brick and half peg added to the near side of the arm in Figure 19-15. These will be used later on by Roboarm to detect the position of the arm.

Figure 19-12.
Roboarm arm step 1

Figure 19-13.
Roboarm arm step 2

Figure 19-14.
Roboarm arm step 3

Figure 19-15.
Roboarm arm step 4

The arm must be able to grab objects, and this function requires its own motor, which is added in Figures 19-16 through 19-18. Although the grabbers will be at the far end of the arm, the motor itself will be placed closer to the axis used to lift the arm. Once again, we need to think in terms of torque. The motor's weight is actually quite significant relative to other LEGO pieces. Placing this motor farther out on the arm increases the torque required to lift it. Keeping the motor close to the axis minimizes its effect on the arm, and it is an easy enough matter to connect it to the grabbers by using a #8 axle (shown in Figure 19-17) and a #12 axle (introduced later). The motor is coupled to this axle using a white rubber belt and two friction pulleys. This does not affect the speed or torque (apart from the effect of friction), but it does allow the motor to slip once the grabbers have closed around an object. Attach one end of a long wire to the motor as shown. This wire will be attached to the RCX later.

Figure 19-16.
Roboarm arm step 5

Figure 19-17.
Roboarm arm step 6

Figure 19-18.
Roboarm arm step 7

The remaining length of arm is constructed in Figures 19-19 and 19-20, along with the grabbers. One grabber uses a pair of crossblocks at its end, but the other uses a pair of cross catches. The difference is not significant other than the fact that a total of four parts is required and the Robotics Invention System only includes two each of the crossblock and the cross catch.

Figure 19-19.
Roboarm arm step 8

Figure 19-20.
Roboarm arm step 9

The pair of 16-tooth gears added in Figure 19-20 keep the two sides of the grabber aligned with one another. It is important to position the grabbers properly before locking both gears into place. A good way to do this is to start by placing only one of the gears. Close the grabbers so that they meet at a point directly below the axle for the rear grabber (closer to the motor). Then, slip the second gear into place, adjusting the grabbers slightly in order to get the two gears to mesh. Turning the 24-tooth gear should now result in opening and closing both grabbers, and they should be roughly centered. Note that it is impossible to get the grabbers to be perfectly symmetrical. This is due to the fact that the gears have an even number of teeth, and, in order to mesh, the axles must be at slightly different angles.

To give the grabbers a better grip, tires are stretched around the crossblocks and cross catches at the ends of the grabbers, as shown in Figure 19-21. Be sure to use the smallest tires; otherwise the grabbers will not be able to close properly. The grabbers are powered by a worm gear meshed with the 24-tooth gear, shown in Figure 19-22. This results in a 24:1 gear reduction, which provides the grabbers with a reasonable amount of force before the rubber belt starts to slip. The worm gear also operates as a one-way transfer of power. The motor can easily spin the worm gear, which will result in a rotation of the 24-tooth gear. The reverse, however, is impossible. No amount of force applied to the 24-tooth gear will cause the worm gear to spin. This means that the motor can be used to open and close the grabbers, but that, once closed, the motor is no longer required for the grabber to maintain its grip.

Figure 19-21.
Roboarm arm step 10

Figure 19-22.
Roboarm arm step 11

Only one design requirement remains: "seeing" objects within the arm's grasp. This can be accomplished by mounting the light sensor on the side of the arm such that it is aimed roughly between the grabbers, as shown in Figures 19-23 through 19-25. The light sensor is attached to a pair of 1×2 cross beams (the green ones), which in turn are connected to a 1×3 liftarm. Ideally, a #3 axle would be used to join the cross beams and the liftarm; however, all of the available #3 axles are needed elsewhere, so a #2 axle is used instead. This means that it will only be partially inserted into the first cross beam shown in Figure 19-23.

Figure 19-23.
Roboarm arm step 12

Figure 19-24.
Roboarm arm step 13

Figure 19-25.
Roboarm arm step 14

The arm is now complete and can be set aside until we are ready to attach it to the rest of Roboarm.

THE BODY

Roboarm's body is where most of the action takes place. The motors for spinning and lifting are with the body, along with suitable gear reduction. A touch sensor is mounted flush with the bottom of the body to detect the home position when rotating on the base. A second touch sensor is used to determine when the arm has been lowered to a level position. Construction begins with the relatively straightforward design of a frame for the rest of the body as shown in Figures 19-26 through 19-28.

Figure 19-26.
Roboarm body step 1

Figure 19-27.
Roboarm body step 2

Figure 19-28.
Roboarm body step 3

The motor to be used for rotating the arm is added in Figure 19-29. Eventually, the body will sit on top of the base, and it will rotate itself via an 8-tooth gear that meshes with the 40-tooth gear embedded in the base. The 8-tooth gear must therefore be below the body itself. In a later step, the #6 axle added in Figure 19-29 (hereafter called the *spinner axle*) will be pushed through to extend below the frame, and the 8-tooth gear will be added. For now, however, it is convenient for the frame to sit level on a table, so everything will be built as if the axle did not need to extend below the frame. It is also worth noting that when the body is mounted on the base, the main axle of the base will extend up through the center hole of the 2×4 plate just added.

Figure 19-29.
Roboarm body step 4

The next few steps, shown in Figures 19-30 through 19-33, build up several features in parallel. A number of gears are used to transfer power from the motor to a 40-tooth gear on the spinner axle. First the 8-tooth gear on the motor meshes with a 24-tooth gear (3:1 gear reduction). This gear is on the same axle as a crown gear (24-teeth) that meshes with the 40-tooth gear (3:5 reduction). This results in a 5:1 overall gear reduction between the motor and the spinner axle.

Figure 19-30.
Roboarm body step 5

Figure 19-31.
Roboarm body step 6

Figure 19-32.
Roboarm body step 7

Figure 19-33.
Roboarm body step 8

The touch sensor for detecting the rotational position of the body is mounted flush with the bottom of the frame. Its position is such that once the body is placed on the base, the touch sensor will be pressed except when it is directly over the alcove in the base. This allows Roboarm to detect its home position. A second motor for lifting the arm is also added. For now, this motor simply turns a worm gear.

Attach one end of a short wire to each of the motors and the touch sensor as shown. Later on, these three wires will be attached to the RCX.

The next step, shown in Figure 19-34, is to place the body on top of the base. First, the spinner axle must be pushed downward enough that an 8-tooth gear can be added below the body. The body is now ready to be placed on the base. Carefully align the body so that the axle from the base fits through the vacant hole in the body's 2×4 plate. The 8-tooth gear underneath the body must mesh with the base's 40-tooth gear. This 5:1 gear reduction combines with the 5:1 reduction between the motor and spinner axle for a total reduction of 25:1. Getting everything aligned may require the body to be turned slightly as it is lowered onto the base. If completed properly, the bottom of the body should be level and flush with the top of the base.

Figure 19-34.
Roboarm body step 9

This rotation mechanism is a little unusual. Previously, in order to turn something (such as a wheel), a series of gears was used to transfer power from the motor to the item to be turned. In this case, the motor powers the 8-tooth gear beneath the body, which is meshed to the 40-tooth gear in the base. If the base gear were free to spin, activating the motor would cause the base gear to turn. In this case, however, the base gear is not free to spin (it is anchored to the base); thus the entire base must rotate relative to the body. This can happen in one of three ways: the base can spin, the body can spin, or some combination of both can spin. From a design perspective, we need to make sure that the body spins and the base remains motionless. This is why rubber tires were used on the bottom of the base—they ensure that the friction between the base and the table is great enough to keep the base firmly in position.

It can be instructive to manually turn the motor (or at least the 24-tooth gear it meshes with) and observe how the overall mechanism works.

A more traditional design could have used a motor in the base to turn a gear that was attached to the body, but this would cause an eventual wiring problem. Most of the motors and sensors are required to be part of the body and/or arm, which means they will be rotating with respect to the base. The RCX must be part of either the base (nonrotating) or the body (rotating). If one motor were contained in the base, then either RCX location would require at least one wire to go from the rotating portion to the nonrotating portion. To prevent the wire from becoming extremely twisted, software would need to ensure that the arm never completed too many revolutions in one direction before reversing direction. Since this is a somewhat annoying restriction to place on the operation of the arm, a design that allowed all of the motors to be on the rotating portion was used instead.

We are now ready to attach the arm to the body. Figures 19-35 through 19-37 show how the arm is mounted to a simple frame. A pair of 8-tooth gears mesh with the arm's 40-tooth gears (5:1 reduction).

Figure 19-35.
Roboarm body step 10

Figure 19-36.
Roboarm body step 11

Figure 19-37.
Roboarm body step 12

The frame is then mounted to the body in Figure 19-38 and secured in place with two 1×6 beams used for vertical bracing. The worm gear in the body now meshes with a 24-tooth gear (24:1 reduction), which combines with the previous 5:1 reduction for a total of 120:1 between the motor and the arm itself. This is more than enough torque to raise and lower the arm smoothly. Once again the one-way property of a worm gear is exploited; in this case it means that the angle of the arm is maintained even when the lifting motor is turned off.

Figure 19-38.
Roboarm body step 13

A touch sensor and wire are also added on top of the lifting motor. This sensor is used to determine when the arm is level. The half peg and 1×2 brick previously added to the arm ensure that the sensor remains pressed whenever the arm is in a lifted position. Only when it is nearly level will the touch sensor be released.

The final step, shown in Figure 19-39, is to attach the RCX and wires. Position the RCX so that it is centered above the 1×6 and 1×4 beams near the back of the body. The wire on the light sensor is not long enough to reach to the RCX, so it must be extended by connecting it to a long wire.

Figure 19-39.
Roboarm body step 14

Pay careful attention to the orientation of motor wires. On the RCX, all of the motor wires are attached such that the wire points to the front of the RCX (toward the LCD display). For sensor wires, orientation is not important. The sensor and motor assignments are shown in Tables 19-1 and 19-2.

Table 19-1. Roboarm Sensor Wires

INPUT	SENSOR	WIRE
1	lifting touch sensor	short wire
2	light sensor	extend with long wire
3	rotation touch sensor	short wire

Table 19-2. Roboarm Motor Wires

OUTPUT	MOTOR	WIRE
A	lifting motor	short wire
B	grabber motor	long wire
C	rotation motor	short wire

In order to prevent the long wires from becoming tangled during operation of the arm, it is a good idea to coil up the excess length and secure it with a rubber band. The construction of Roboarm is now complete.

BASIC OPERATIONS

Just as Roboarm is constructed from several simpler subassemblies, its programs are constructed from several basic operations, or programming "building blocks." Each operation performs a specific action such as closing the grabbers or lifting the arm. There are a total of five operations: *home*, *up*, *down*, *grab*, and *release*. *Home* spins the arm until the touch sensor indicates that it is in the home position. *Up* raises the arm a fixed amount by running the lifting motor for a short period of time. *Down* lowers the arm by running the lifting motor until the other touch sensor indicates the arm is approximately level. *Grab* and *release* close and open the grabbers by running a motor for a fixed amount of time. The time for grabbing is slightly longer than releasing to ensure that the grabbers will always close firmly. The RCX Code stacks for these operations are shown in Figure 19-40.

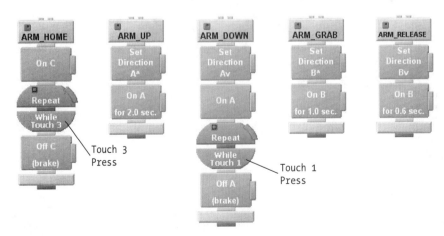

Figure 19-40.
Basic operations in RCX Code

When using NQC, these basic operations will be placed in their own file named roboarm.nqh (see Listing 19-1). This file will later be *included* by the actual programs. Keeping commonly used operations in their own separate file allows multiple programs to use them without having to write the same function repeatedly. It is a long-standing tradition in C programs to use the extension ".h" for included files (as opposed to ".c" for actual program files). We will emulate this tradition by using the ".nqh" extension for included files (instead of the more typical ".nqc" for programs).

Listing 19-1. Basic Operations in NQC

```
// roboarm.nqh
//      basic operations for RoboArm

// motors and sensors
#define LIFTER    OUT_A
#define GRABBER   OUT_B
#define SPINNER   OUT_C
#define LEVEL     SENSOR_1
#define EYE       SENSOR_2
#define HOME      SENSOR_3

// various timing parameters
#define UP_TIME      200
#define DOWN_DELAY    10
#define GRAB_TIME    100
#define RELEASE_TIME  60


void up()
{
    // raise arm
    Fwd(LIFTER);
    OnFor(LIFTER,UP_TIME);
}


void down()
{
    // lower arm until level
    OnRev(LIFTER);
    until(LEVEL == 0);
    Wait(DOWN_DELAY);
    Off(LIFTER);
}
```

```
void grab()
{
    // close the grabbers
    Fwd(GRABBER);
    OnFor(GRABBER, GRAB_TIME);
}


void release()
{
    // open the grabbers
    Rev(GRABBER);
    OnFor(GRABBER, RELEASE_TIME);
}


void home()
{
    // spin until home
    On(SPINNER);
    until(HOME == 0);
    Off(SPINNER);
}
```

The RCX Code and the NQC versions of the commands are similar. The only difference is that the NQC version of *down* leaves the motor running for a short time (DOWN_DELAY) after the sensor condition is met. This is because the touch sensor gets triggered slightly before the arm is level, and the NQC program reacts a little quicker than the RCX Code version. Thus the extra delay gets the arm closer to level.

If the arm raises up but never moves down, perhaps it is missing either the 1×2 brick or the half peg shown in step 4 of the arm's construction (Figure 19-15).

STARTING POSITION

It is a bit easier to program the arm if it is already in a known starting position. A good choice for this position is to have the arm level and in its home position with the grabbers open. It is possible to manually adjust Roboarm by turning the worm gears, but it is more interesting to write a program to do this for us. First we consider the height of the arm. If the touch sensor for the arm height is pressed, then the arm may simply be lowered using the *down* operation. However, if the touch sensor is not pressed, the arm could be too low. In this case, we want to raise it first, then lower it to the level position. In the case of the grabbers, using the *grab* then *release* operations will generally result in their being open the proper amount regardless of their initial position. Rotating the arm into home position is the easiest of all; after all that is the entire purpose of the *home* operation. The NQC program in Listing 19-2 puts everything together in the proper order. Note how the #include statement is used to make everything previously defined in roboarm.nqh available to the program itself.

Listing 19-2. Starting Position in NQC

```
// roboarm1.nqc
//    program put RoboArm in "starting position"

// include the basic operations
#include "roboarm.nqh"

task main()
{
    // configure the sensors
    SetSensor(LEVEL, SENSOR_TOUCH);
    SetSensor(EYE, SENSOR_LIGHT);
    SetSensor(HOME, SENSOR_TOUCH);

    // adjust arm height
    if (LEVEL == 0)
        up();
    down();

    // close and open grabbers
    grab();
    release();

    // spin if not already home...
    home();
}
```

A similar program can be written in RCX Code, as shown in Figure 19-41.

Figure 19-41.
Starting position in RCX Code

In the course of developing more sophisticated programs, mistakes will often leave Roboarm in some unusual position. In these cases, this initial program is a handy utility to have around—simply run it to restore Roboarm to its starting position.

THE TEST MAT

Roboarm is a fairly general-purpose robotic arm capable of grasping a variety of objects. For consistency, however, the remainder of this chapter assumes that the white hubs for treads are being picked up by Roboarm. Although not strictly required, a test mat for Roboarm can also be helpful. The test mat shown in Figure 19-42 indicates the position for Roboarm, the circular path traversed by the arm in its lowered position, and the point on the circle corresponding to home position. The mat should also be a dark color to help the light sensor reliably identify the white hubs. A 22"×28" sheet of black or dark green poster board works well. The actual home position should be determined empirically. Place Roboarm in the box so that the alcove in the base is toward the top of the box. Now run the starting position program and note the final position of the arm (which is its home position).

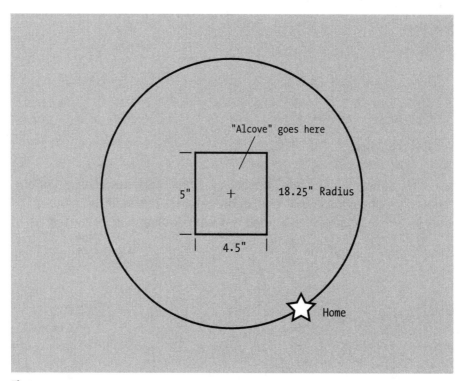

Figure 19-42.
Roboarm test mat

CLEANING UP

Roboarm's first real assignment will be to "clean up its room." The four white hubs will be put at various positions along the circle, and a small container will be placed at the home position. Roboarm must then pick up each of the hubs and deposit them in the container.

For each hub, Roboarm must take the following actions: find the hub, pick it up, and drop it in the container. One way to find a hub is to have Roboarm spin around until the light sensor detects a white-colored object. Then the existing *grab* and *up* operations can be used to pick up the hub. Since the container is in the home location, the *home* and *release* operations can then be used to move the arm over the container and drop the hub. The arm then needs to be lowered (preferably just past the container) in order to proceed onto the next hub. The NQC version of this program is shown in Listing 19-3.

Listing 19-3. Cleaning Up in NQC

```
// roboarm2.nqc
//    program to put 4 hubs away

// include the basic operations
#include "roboarm.nqh"

// threshold to detect a hub
#define THRESHOLD    43

// how far past "home" to spin
#define SPIN_DELAY   50

// number of hubs to put away
#define COUNT        4


void detect()
{
    // spin until a piece is seen
    On(SPINNER);
    until(EYE >= THRESHOLD);
    Off(SPINNER);
}
```

```
task main()
{
    // configure the sensors
    SetSensor(LEVEL, SENSOR_TOUCH);
    SetSensor(EYE, SENSOR_LIGHT);
    SetSensor(HOME, SENSOR_TOUCH);

    // for each piece...
    repeat(COUNT)
    {
        detect();
        grab();
        up();
        home();
        release();
        OnFor(SPINNER, SPIN_DELAY);
        down();
    }

    // we're done
    PlaySound(SOUND_FAST_UP);
}
```

Depending on your lighting conditions, the THRESHOLD value may need to be adjusted. Another constant, SPIN_DELAY, is used to allow the arm to move past the container before being lowered back into position to search for another hub. Depending on the size of your container, this value can be made larger or smaller.

The direction that Roboarm spins while looking for a piece is not arbitrary. The light sensor is slightly offset from the center of the grabber. Because of this, rotation in a counterclockwise direction allows the sensor to detect objects just before they are within Roboarm's grasp. If the arm were rotated in the other direction, the sensor would always be detecting objects a little too late.

A version of the program in RCX Code is shown in Figure 19-43. Like the previous program, it makes use of the basic operations introduced earlier (*home*, *up*, *down*, *grab*, and *release*).

Light 2
is Darker
than 43.

Figure 19-43.
Cleaning up in RCX Code

Before the program is run, the arm should be level with the grabbers open. Since a container will be sitting at the home position, the arm will need to be rotated slightly past home. One way to accomplish all of this is to run the starting position program to get the arm level and open, then manually spin it a bit counterclockwise past home. Manual adjustment of Roboarm is often easier when the RCX is turned off. If all goes well, this adjustment will only be required one time since the "clean up" program leaves the arm in a suitable position after it is completed.

LINING UP

Roboarm's second assignment is to look for the hubs and, instead of dropping them into a container, neatly line them up. In addition, rather than always expecting a fixed number of hubs, it should automatically quit once no more hubs are available.

Many elements of this program, such as the process of grabbing and lifting a hub, are similar to the previous program. However, there are a few new complications. The first issue is how to determine when no more hubs can be picked up. One strategy for dealing with this is to assume that, if the arm ever rotates all the way around to home without spotting a hub, its work is done. As a consequence, the program must be simultaneously checking for two conditions: whether the light sensor has detected a hub and whether the arm has rotated around to home. This sounds like a good candidate for using multiple tasks.

```
task pickup()
{
    while(true)
    {
        until(EYE >= THRESHOLD);
        // pick up and arrange the hub
    }
}

task done()
{
    until(HOME == 0);
    stop pickup;
}
```

Unfortunately, the pickup task may have to rotate past the home position in order to arrange the hub. If this ever happened, the done task would stop the pickup task before its work was done. This implies that some communication between the two tasks should take place to indicate when it is acceptable to stop picking things up. Such communication could take the form of a variable that was set and cleared appropriately.

```
int ok_to_stop = 1;

task pickup()
{
    while(true)
    {
        until(EYE >= THRESHOLD);
        ok_to_stop = 0;
        // pick up and arrange the hub
        ok_to_stop = 1;
    }
}

task done()
{
    while(true)
    {
        until(HOME == 0);
        if (ok_to_stop==1) break;
    }
    stop pickup;
}
```

This is certainly a workable approach, but I find it simpler to abandon multiple tasks and instead use a nested condition within a single task.

```
while(HOME == 1)
{
    if (EYE >= THRESHOLD)
    {
        // do whatever we want with the piece
    }
}
```

Once a hub has been detected, whatever is used to handle the hub will run to completion before another check for home occurs.

The second issue is how to line up the hubs. A good approach is to use a variable to keep track of how many hubs have already been lined up. The position for a new hub is determined by first rotating the arm to its home position, then rotating it for an amount of time proportional to the number of hubs already placed. In effect, this will space the hubs roughly evenly along the circle.

We can put this all together in the program shown in Listing 19-4.

Listing 19-4. Lining Up in NQC

```
// roboarm3.nqc
//     program to line up hubs

// include the basic operations
#include "roboarm.nqh"

// threshold to detect a hub
#define THRESHOLD   43

// how far apart to place pieces
#define SPACING 20

task main()
{
    int count = 0;

    // configure sensors
    SetSensor(LEVEL, SENSOR_TOUCH);
    SetSensor(EYE, SENSOR_LIGHT);
    SetSensor(HOME, SENSOR_TOUCH);

    // spin past "home" position
    On(SPINNER);
    until(HOME == 1);

    while(HOME == 1)
    {
        if (EYE >= THRESHOLD)
        {
            // piece detected - grab it
            Off(SPINNER);
            grab();
            up();
            count++;

            // rotate to next "spot"
            OnRev(SPINNER);
            until(HOME == 0);
            Fwd(SPINNER);
            Wait(count * SPACING);
            Off(SPINNER);
```

```
        // put the piece down
        down();
        release();

        // rotate past the piece
        On(SPINNER);
        Wait(SPACING);
    }
}

// our work is done...
Off(SPINNER);
PlaySound(SOUND_FAST_UP);
}
```

The value for SPACING controls the distance between lined up hubs. A subtle detail is that count is incremented before it is used in the Wait statement. As a result, the first hub isn't placed at home, but is slightly past home. This has the nice side effect of ensuring that after all of the other hubs have been lined up, the first hub won't accidentally be detected and picked up before Roboarm notices it got back to home (and is thus done with its work).

A similar program can be written in RCX Code. Lining up the hubs is accomplished by the **ARRANGE** block, shown in Figure 19-44. Picking up and putting down the hub are straightforward. Getting the arm in the correct position for lining up the hub is a little more involved. The program uses a variable named **position** to keep track of where to put each hub. Each time a hub is picked up, **position** will be increased slightly. The arm will then rotate backward to its home location, then forward for an amount of time determined by **position**. After putting the hub down, the arm continues its forward rotation (the **Wait For** block at the end of **PUTDOWN** ensures that the arm has moved completely past the hub it just put down).

Figure 19-44.
The **ARRANGE** block

The program itself is shown in Figure 19-45. The program starts by clearing the **position** variable, then rotating until it is past the home location. It then enters its main loop, which repeats until the arm has made a complete trip around the circle and returned home. During this loop, if a hub is detected, the **ARRANGE** block is used to pick up the hub and place it in the proper location.

Touch 3
Release

Touch 3
Press

Figure 19-45.
Lining up in RCX Code

CONCLUSION

Roboarm is a fairly general-purpose device that can be programmed for a variety of tasks such as building a small tower or sorting blocks based on their color. Currently, its detection of home and level positions is rather crude. Either of these measurements could be improved by using a rotation sensor instead of a touch sensor. This would allow for more precise positioning in either the rotational or the vertical directions. Other options could include adapting the grabbers for specific objects.

Part Three
Appendixes

Appendix A
MINDSTORMS Sets

This appendix lists the various retail and educational MINDSTORMS sets and accessories available from LEGO. Although the MINDSTORMS sets utilize some new elements (such as the RCX), they are really just extensions of the vast LEGO universe. This means that ordinary LEGO sets, especially those from the Technic line, provide a good means of expanding your MINDSTORMS set.

The MINDSTORMS sets are divided into two groups: retail and educational. The retail sets are intended for the average consumer and can typically be found at toy stores or purchased directly from LEGO via the LEGO Shop At Home service (which provides mail order and online shopping). The educational sets are geared towards classroom use and are marketed by LEGO's educational division, Dacta. In the United States, LEGO Pitsco Dacta is presently the exclusive distributor of Dacta products. They also offer several "bundles" that combine all of the materials necessary to use MINDSTORMS in the classroom.

LEGO also offers MINDSTORMS accessories such as extra sensors and motors. In general the accessories are available directly from LEGO Shop At Home or though LEGO Pitsco Dacta, but not at toy stores and other retail outlets. In some cases, the educational versions have a different part number, but they are all compatible.

The listings that follow contain some price estimates, but these should only be used as a rough guide. Different stores may have different prices, and the prices set by LEGO may change over time. Specifically, there are presently some differences in price between the educational and retail offerings, but these may get equalized over time. The bottom line is that you should shop around a little before buying.

Although every attempt was made to make this list complete, LEGO is constantly introducing new sets and accessories, so don't be surprised if a few new sets are available by the time you read this.

RETAIL BASE SETS

Each of the following sets can serve as a starting point for exploring robotics with LEGO MINDSTORMS. In general, the capabilities of each set are dictated by what kind of programmable brick is included with the set. The RCX is the most powerful programmable brick currently available, but it is also the most expensive. Some of the smaller sets provide a less expensive way to get started with robotics, although the user may outgrow them quite quickly.

#3804–Robotics Invention System 2.0

This set is the cornerstone of the MINDSTORMS lineup. It includes everything needed to get started with MINDSTORMS, including the RCX, 2 touch sensors, 1 light sensor, 2 motors, and about 700 assorted LEGO pieces. An infrared transmitter is also provided that connects to your computer's USB port and allows communication with the RCX.

The bundled CD-ROM contains software that runs on under Microsoft Windows and allows RCX programs to be written in RCX Code—a simple visual programming system created by LEGO. It also includes a number of challenges, which guide the user through the creation of some simple robots. The printed *Constructopedia* provides ideas and hints on solving the challenges.

This set is ideal for getting started with MINDSTORMS. The assortment of LEGO pieces is complete enough to build a reasonable number of interesting robots. In fact, many of the robots in this book can be built completely from the contents of this set. With a list price of $200, the set is also a good value considering the cost of the RCX, motors, and sensors if purchased separately.

For expansion, a third motor and one or two additional sensors (especially a rotation sensor) are recommended.

#9747–Robotics Invention System 1.5 (Discontinued)

This is an older version of the Robotics Invention system, and is no longer in production. Overall, the set is very similar to RIS 2.0 (#3804), with two major differences. First, RIS 1.5 uses an infrared transmitter that connects to a serial port (instead of the USB-based transmitter in RIS 2.0). Second, the RCX Code software in RIS 1.5 is a lot more limited than its RIS 2.0 counterpart.

If you already own RIS 1.5 and are planning on doing a lot of RCX Code programming, then you should consider buying the software upgrade (RIS 2.0 Upgrade Kit, #3805).

#9719–Robotics Invention System 1.0 (Discontinued)

This is the original MINDSTORMS set, and is no longer in production. Overall, this set is similar to the later RIS sets, with a few differences. Like RIS 1.5, the infrared transmitter uses a serial connection (not a USB port like in RIS 2.0). The RCX Code software in version 1.0 is incredibly limited (even more so than in RIS 1.5). The mix of LEGO pieces included in the set is a little different from later RIS sets, but the major components are the same. Lastly, the RCX included in RIS 1.0 featured an external power connector that allows it to be powered by an AC adapter.

If you already own RIS 1.0 and are planning on doing a lot of RCX Code programming, then you should consider buying the software upgrade (RIS 2.0 Upgrade Kit, #3805).

#9735–Robotics Discovery Set (Discontinued)

This MINDSTORMS set is not based on the RCX. Instead, it uses a different programmable brick called "Scout". The Scout is not as flexible as the RCX—it can only power two motors, and it is somewhat restricted in what sensors may be used. The set includes the Scout, two motors, two touch sensors (the Scout has a built-in light sensor), and an assortment of LEGO pieces.

The Scout allows a limited amount of programming directly from its push-buttons and LCD display. As such, this set was originally envisioned as a stand-alone product that would provide an introduction to robotics without requiring a computer. However, at a list price of $150, it did not provide enough value compared to the only slightly more expensive RCX-based sets.

It is possible to program the Scout from a computer (using either LEGO's SDK or NQC), but you need to supply your own infrared tower. Since the Scout can communicate with the RCX, it provides an interesting way to expand an RCX-based system provided you can find the set at a good discount.

#9754–Dark Side Developer Kit,
#9748–Droid Developer Kit

These MINDSTORMS sets are based on the Micro-Scout programmable brick, which is much more limited than the RCX or even the Scout. It has no provision for external connections—just an internal motor and light sensor. Its programmability is extremely limited as well. Overall, both sets should be thought of as *Star Wars* sets with a slight MINDSTORMS flavor. Both sets carried an original list price of $100, although #9748 can now be found for considerably less.

Spybotics (#3806, #3807, #3808, #3809)

Spybotics is a new line of sets from LEGO that use MINDSTORMS technology, but are intended as a completely different kind of toy. The concept is closer to a video game than a construction toy. However, since they are made out of LEGO, they can be combined with any other LEGO set (including MINDSTORMS sets). Additionally, the Spybotics programmable brick can be programmed using NQC and is able to communicate with the RCX, which opens up some interesting possibilities. Given how new the Spybotics sets are, it is still too early to say how useful they may be in terms of expanding an RIS set. Each Spybotics set has a list price of $60.

RETAIL EXPANSION SETS

Each of the following sets is intended as an expansion for a base set (typically for the Robotics Invention System). None of them are very useful on their own. Bear in mind that these sets are not the only way of expanding your MINDSTORMS collection. Other LEGO sets (most notably those from the Technic product line) can also serve as MINDSTORMS expansion sets.

#3805—2.0 Upgrade Kit

This isn't really a set—it's just a CD-ROM that includes the RIS 2.0 software. For owners of RIS 1.0 or RIS 1.5 that program in RCX Code, this CD-ROM is a must-have (list price $20). However, if you do not program much with RCX Code, then there is no point in buying the upgrade.

#3800—Ultimate Builder's Set

This set includes a motor, pneumatic parts, and over 300 LEGO construction pieces. It also includes on-screen instructions for using these new parts with RIS 1.5 or RIS 2.0 to build new projects. A third motor is an essential expansion for an RIS set, and pneumatics add some interesting possibilities. With a list price of $60, it is a relatively expensive expansion set, but certainly worthwhile for the MINDSTORMS enthusiast.

#3801—Ultimate Accessory Set

This set includes a LEGO Remote Control, touch sensor, rotation sensor, light brick, and about 40 assorted LEGO pieces. The remote control can be very useful while building a robot since it allows you to easily control all three motors just by pressing some buttons. The rotation sensor is also very useful, so overall this kit is a good expansion at a list price of $50.

#9731—Vision Command

This set includes a USB-based webcam along with a handful of LEGO pieces and some special vision processing software that runs on your computer and communicates with an RCX. Although the idea of adding vision processing to an RCX robot is incredibly exciting, the fact that the webcam must remain attached to your PC via a USB cable means that the robots need to remain tethered to your computer. This set is currently selling for around $50.

#9736—Exploration Mars

This set includes approximately 150 LEGO pieces and software that provides some new "missions" with a Mars theme. At its current price of $50, it is not a very good value in terms of expanding an RIS set.

#9730—RoboSports (Discontinued)

This expansion set contains 90 LEGO pieces (including a motor), a CD-ROM with additional challenges, and a new *Constructopedia*. The set has a "sports" theme, with challenges such as throwing a ball through a basketball hoop. With a list price of $50, this set is a relatively poor value. Unless you really want to see the challenges and *Constructopedia*, you are much better off purchasing the motor separately and buying LEGO Technic sets for extra pieces.

#9732—Extreme Creatures (Discontinued)

This expansion set includes 149 LEGO pieces. Although no additional motors or sensors are included, the set does contain the LEGO "fiber optic" unit. The set also features a CD-ROM with additional challenges and a *Constructopedia*. As its name suggests, the challenges in this set have a wildlife theme. The "fiber optic" unit is often used as a decorative piece, but it can be coupled with a light sensor to fashion a crude rotation sensor. Some of the other included pieces are useful, but with a list price of $50, this set is a relatively poor value.

EDUCATIONAL SETS

Dacta, the education arm of LEGO, has its own product line of MINDSTORMS sets. In general they are geared towards classroom use, but home users may also find them of interest. Since they use the same pieces as the retail sets, consumers are free to mix and match between retail and educational sets.

#9725—Amusement Park

This set is the entry-level construction set for educational use. It includes 2 touch sensors, 1 light sensor, 2 motors, 1 light brick, and nearly 300 LEGO pieces. The set does not contain an RCX, the infrared transmitter, or any software; these must all be purchased separately. One of the strengths of the Amusement Park is the set of instructions for four models, all within the Amusement Park theme, that provide a framework for introducing MINDSTORMS to a classroom environment. With a list price of $115, this set is an average value.

#9780—ROBOLAB Starter Set

This is a larger educational set with over 1600 pieces. The set does not contain an RCX, infrared transmitter, or any software; these must all be purchased separately. It is designed to be used as four separate individual sets, each of which has its own unique challenges. A large number of resource bricks are also provided. The special elements included are three motors, one micro motor, three light sensors, four touch sensors, and four light bricks. With a list price of $330, this set is an average value.

#9790/9791—Team Challenge Building Set

This set is for the most part an educational version of the retail RIS set. It includes an RCX, 2 motors, 2 touch sensors, 1 light sensor, and about 700 LEGO pieces. Set #9790 includes an infrared transmitter with a serial cable, while #9791 includes the USB version of the transmitter. With a list price of $200, this set is a good value.

#9713–Infrared Transmitter with Serial Cable, #9783–Infrared Transmitter with USB Cable

This is the infrared transmitter that allows a computer to communicate with the RCX. It is a necessity for using the RCX, but you only need one per computer. List price: $29.

#9833–AC Adapter

This is a "wall wart" that allows the RCX to be powered from AC power instead of batteries. This is a good option if most of your creations stand still, but for mobile robots you will want to use batteries (preferably rechargeable ones). This adapter can only be used with RCXs that have an external power connector (from RIS 1.0 or Dacta sets, not RIS 1.5 or RIS 2.0).

ROBOLAB Software

ROBOLAB is the software used to program the RCX in classroom settings. It runs on the Macintosh as well as under Windows, and is in many ways more powerful than the RCX Code environment provided with the Robotics Invention System. Pricing varies depending on the actual package (CD-ROM only, CD-ROM plus user's guide, or site license). A brief description of the ROBOLAB software can be found in Appendix C.

ACCESSORIES

Some MINDSTORMS items are available individually. Selection from LEGO Shop At Home is often quite limited, so Pitsco tends to be a better source for accessories.

#9709–RCX Programmable Brick

This is the brains of any MINDSTORMS creation. An RCX is included in RIS sets, but must be purchased separately when using educational sets #9725 or #9780. Priced between $120 and $130, this is an incredibly expensive piece of LEGO, but it is also the coolest. If you have deep pockets, owning more than one RCX opens up new possibilities with MINDSTORMS.

#9757–Touch Sensor

All of the basic sets already contain at least two touch sensors. Priced around $10, this accessory consists of a touch sensor and connecting wire. A similar accessory (#9911) is available exclusively from Dacta.

#9758–Light Sensor

All of the basic sets already contain at least one light sensor. Additional sensors can be purchased for about $20.

#9756–Rotation Sensor

The rotation sensor (also called an angle sensor) comes with a built-in wire. It is an extremely versatile sensor, and highly recommended. The sensor retails for about $15. Availability from LEGO Shop At Home is limited, but Dacta remains a good source for the sensor. The Dacta number for this sensor is #9891.

#9755–Temperature Sensor

The temperature sensor also includes a built-in wire. It is something of a special purpose sensor and priced at about $25. If you have a specific project in mind that requires a temperature sensor, then by all means get one; otherwise stick with more versatile pieces. Availability from LEGO Shop At Home is limited, but Dacta remains a good source for the sensor. The Dacta number for this sensor is #9889.

#9738–Remote Control

This device is similar to a television remote control, but instead of changing channels it allows you to directly control the RCX. There are buttons to control each of the motors (in either direction) and start or stop programs. In addition, the remote can send three different "messages" to the RCX (similar to how one RCX sends a message to another). The LEGO Remote Control costs about $20.

#5225–9V Motor

This is the same motor included in the various MINDSTORMS sets. If you only have two motors, a third motor is highly recommended (and costs less than $20).

Appendix B
Supplementary Parts

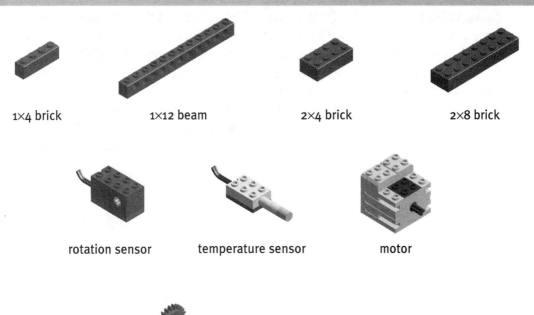

1×4 brick

1×12 beam

2×4 brick

2×8 brick

rotation sensor

temperature sensor

motor

differential

bevel gear

RCX

Many of the projects in the book can be built using only the contents of the MINDSTORMS Robotics Invention System. However, four of the chapters require some supplementary parts, and the projects in two of the advanced chapters can only be partially completed without some extra parts.

There are two basic ways to get extra parts: buy complete LEGO sets, or buy small *service packs* of special parts. In the long run, buying complete sets gives you more parts for your dollar, but the service packs allow you to buy only what you need. In addition, several parts (such as sensors) are only available as service packs. LEGO Shop At Home (http://www.LEGOshop.com or 1-800-453-4652) used to carry a wide variety of service packs, but recently the selection has become quite limited, so some of the packs listed in this appendix may not be available. Pitsco (http://www.pitsco.com or 1-800-362-4308) sells LEGO products for educational use and is another good source for parts.

The supplementary parts required for various chapters are summarized in Tables B-1 and B-2. Since RIS 1.0 includes different pieces from RIS 1.5/RIS 2.0, two different tables are provided. Prices for the service packs are only approximate.

Table B-1. Supplementary Parts for RIS 1.0 by Chapter

CHAPTER	PARTS REQUIRED (QUANTITY)	LEGO SERVICE PACK (PRICE)	PITSCO SERVICE PACK (PRICE)
9, "Dumpbot"	motor (1)	#5225 ($18)	#W775225 ($17)
10, "Scanbot"	motor (1) rotation sensor (1)	#5225 ($18) #9756 ($15)**	#W775225 ($17) #W979891 ($17)
14, "Diffbot"	16-tooth gear (2) differential (1)	#5229 ($5),** in #5229	#W779900 ($7) #W779945 ($6)
17, "Communication"*	1×12 beam (3), motor (2), RCX (1)	see text that follows	see text that follows
18, "Using the Datalog"*	temperature sensor (1)	#9755 ($25)**	#W979889 ($28)*
19, "Roboarm"	motor (1)	#5225 ($25)	#W775225 ($17)

* These chapters may be partially completed without any extra parts.

** Limited availability from LEGO Shop At Home.

Table B-2. Supplementary Parts for RIS 1.5/RIS 2.0 by Chapter

CHAPTER	PARTS REQUIRED (QUANTITY)	LEGO SERVICE PACK (PRICE)	PITSCO SERVICE PACK (PRICE)
9, "Dumpbot"	motor (1)	#5225 ($18)	#W775225 ($17)
10, "Scanbot"	motor (1) rotation sensor (1)	#5225 ($18) #9756 ($15)**	#W775225 ($17) #W979891 ($17)
14, "Diffbot"	16-tooth gear (2) differential (1), bevel gear (1)	#5229 ($5),** in #5229	#W779900 ($7) #W779945 ($6)
17, "Communication"*	1×12 beam (3), motor (2), RCX (1), 2×4 brick (1)	see text that follows	see text that follows
18, "Using the Datalog"*	temperature sensor (1)	#9755 ($25)**	#W979889 ($28)*
19, "Roboarm"	motor (1) 2×4 brick (14), 2×8 brick (1), 1×4 brick (4)	#5225 ($25) #W775225 ($17)	#5144 ($6) n/a

* These chapters may be partially completed without any extra parts.

** Limited availability from LEGO Shop At Home.

The RCX-to-RCX portion of Chapter 17 is intended for people with access to two MINDSTORMS Robotics Invention System sets. It is still possible to purchase the appropriate service packs, although it is not very cost effective since the extra parts would cost almost as much as a second RIS set. In any event, if you don't have (or want) a second RCX, then Chapter 17 can still be partially completed without any of the extra parts. Likewise, Chapter 18 can be partially completed without a temperature sensor.

If you own Robotics Invention System 1.5 or 2.0 and wish to complete Chapter 19, then in addition to an extra motor, seven ordinary LEGO bricks will be needed. These bricks are fairly common and can be obtained from practically any LEGO set. It is even possible to substitute bricks of other sizes if you don't have quite the right combination. A service pack containing these bricks can be purchased (#5114), but you will get a lot more LEGO for your money buying a "bucket" of LEGO at the local toy store.

My personal recommendation is to obtain the motor, rotation sensor, and extra gears. The rotation sensor and extra motor are almost essential expansions to the Robotics Invention System set, and the extra gears are handy to have around (most of the time). If purchased through Pitsco, this will cost about $47. If this sounds a bit too expensive, then consider dropping the differential and gear packs, but strongly consider purchasing the motor and rotation sensor.

If you can afford to spend a bit more money, then the motor and/or rotation sensor can be obtained as part of an expansion set. The Ultimate Builder's Set (#3800, $60) is a great expansion pack that includes a motor and some interesting pneumatic parts. The Ultimate Accessory Set (#3801, $50) includes a rotation sensor as well as the handy LEGO Remote Control.

Don't worry about a second RCX unless your pockets are pretty deep. The problem is that the RCX is only just the start, because once you have two RCXs you then need to have twice as many sensors, motors, gears, and so on. Your best bet may be to just buy another complete Robotics Invention System set. The bottom line is that there is plenty of fun to be had with a single Robotics Invention System set—don't worry about getting a second one until you've exhausted the possibilities of a single RCX.

The temperature sensor is a bit pricey and has a fairly special purpose. If you think you want to do a lot of experiments with it, or you have an interesting temperature-controlled robot in mind, by all means purchase one. Otherwise just read through Chapter 18 without performing the temperature experiment—there are still two other datalog examples in the chapter that don't require any extra parts.

Appendix C
Programming Tools

There are a number of different tools that can be used to program the RCX. Choosing the right tool is largely a matter of personal preference. Some people prefer a graphical approach to programming, and others prefer a more traditional text-based approach. The different tools also provide varying degrees of control over the RCX, so the choice of tool also determines how powerful your programs can be. The operating system you are using also must be taken into account. Although the standard MINDSTORMS software runs only under Windows, some of the other programming tools run under other operating systems including Mac OS and Linux.

RCX CODE

NOTE

RCX Code at a Glance:

Pros: *Included free with MINDSTORMS Robotics Invention System set; easy to use.*

Cons: *User interface can be tedious for experienced programmers; only available for Windows.*

The MINDSTORMS Robotics Invention System includes software that allows users to develop RCX programs using a graphical programming system called RCX Code. This software runs under Microsoft Windows. Its graphical approach and simple block-based programming make it a good choice for those who are completely new to computer programming. Unfortunately, some of this simplicity becomes tedious for experienced users.

Since RCX Code is included with the MINDSTORMS Robotics Invention System, it is the default tool used to program the RCX, and many of the examples in this book are given in RCX Code. If you're just getting started with programming, then RCX Code will probably be sufficient for your needs, and you will find plenty of material in this book to help get you going.

NQC

NQC at a Glance:

Pros: Fast, familiar syntax for C programmers; freely available for Windows, MacOS, Linux, and other platforms.

Cons: More difficult for nonprogrammers to learn.

NQC stands for "Not Quite C," which is a simple language that has a similar syntax to the C programming language. NQC was developed completely independently of LEGO, and is not affiliated with LEGO in any way. It constitutes more of a traditional computer programming approach: A program is written as a text file that is then compiled and downloaded to the RCX. Although this is not as easy to get started with as a graphical tool, for those even moderately familiar with programming, a textual language can be a much more efficient development tool.

NQC is free software—in both price and principle. "Free in price" means that it is available free of charge. "Free in principle" means that the source code itself is also free to anyone who wants it. Official versions exist for Windows, MacOS, and Linux. Because the source code is also freely available, unofficial ports have been made to other systems such as NetBSD, Solaris, LinuxPPC, and OS/2.

There are several wrapper programs for NQC that provide an integrated environment in which to write, compile, and download programs. For Windows, the BricxCC is an excellent environment. MacNQC is a similar program for MacOS users.

One final advantage of NQC is speed. Several of the other tools are awkwardly slow on anything but the fastest computer hardware. NQC runs well even on outdated hardware and can compile and download programs faster than either RCX Code or Robolab.

NQC code is provided for all of the examples in the book.

ROBOLAB

Robolab at a Glance:

Pros: *Easy to use graphical interface; more features than RCX Code; runs under MacOS and Windows.*

Cons: *Must be purchased separately from MINDSTORMS Robotics Invention System.*

Robolab is another LEGO programming tool, but it is a product of Dacta (the educational branch of LEGO) and is aimed at classroom, rather than home, use. Robolab provides an intuitive graphical environment and runs under both Windows and MacOS. The Robolab environment is based on Lab View, by National Instruments, and provides a very different programming paradigm from RCX Code.

Robolab actually provides two different programming environments: one intended for simple introductory use, and the other for more advanced work. Both environments feature multiple levels that facilitate a gradual learning process by introducing new concepts in small steps. At its most advanced level, Robolab provides full access to the features of the RCX's standard firmware. Robolab also provides a full set of tools for capturing and analyzing the datalog. This makes it ideally suited for use in experimentation.

Robolab must be purchased separately from the MINDSTORMS Robotics Invention System. Because of this, Robolab examples are not given in the book, although all of the programs could easily be adapted to run under Robolab.

MINDSCRIPT AND LASM

MindScript and LASM are part of LEGO's Software Development Kit (SDK) 2.0 for the RCX (available from `http://mindstorms.lego.com/sdk2`). MindScript is a structured language, similar to C, but with the addition of special commands and control structures tailored for programming the RCX. RCX Code programs are actually stored as MindScript programs. The RCX Code software in effect provides a graphical way to work with the MindScript commands.

LASM is the assembly language for the RCX. Like any assembly language, LASM works at a very low level—giving the programmer lots of control, but at the expense of ease-of-use. As such, it is really only suitable for advanced programmers.

CUSTOM FIRMWARE

Several people have created custom firmware independently of LEGO in order to enhance the RCX's capabilities. Here are some popular programming environments that use custom firmware:

- **brickOS**—A firmware replacement that provides a complete operating system for the RCX. It was designed to be used with traditional tools such as an assembler and C compiler. BrickOS provides complete control over the RCX.

- **pbFORTH**—A FORTH interpreter that runs on the RCX. Using pbFORTH, the RCX can be programmed using the FORTH language (extended with some special words for accessing the RCX's motors, sensors, etc.).

- **leJOS**—A small Java runtime for the RCX, leJOS allows the RCX to be programmed in Java. This is the most recent, and perhaps most exciting, of the firmware replacements.

Tools based on custom firmware solutions are certainly the most powerful and flexible programming tools around. However, detailed discussion of these alternative programming tools is beyond the scope of this book. For more information, consult some of the resources listed in Appendix E.

Appendix D
NQC Quick Reference

These pages are intended as a quick guide to the most commonly used NQC features. More detailed descriptions of these features (along with several features not presented here) can be found in the *NQC Programmer's Guide*.

THE NQC LANGUAGE

The NQC Language determines the statements and other constructs that can be used to write an NQC program. This includes the statements, operators, and keywords used by NQC.

Statements

Some statements include optional clauses (such as the else clause in an if statement). In the following table, optional clauses are enclosed in square brackets ([and]).

STATEMENT	DESCRIPTION
while (*condition*) *body*	Execute body zero or more times while condition is true.
do *body* while (*condition*)	Execute body one or more times while condition is true.
until (*condition*) *body*	Execute body zero or more times until condition is true.
repeat (*count*) *body*	Repeat body specified number of times.
for(*initial*; *condition*; *iterate*) *body*	Execute initial, then execute body zero or more times while condition is true. After each execution of body, execute iterate.
if (*condition*) *stmt1* [else *stmt2*]	Execute stmt1 if condition is true, otherwise execute stmt2 (if present).
switch (*expression*) *body*	Execute portion of body based on the value of the expression.
monitor (*events*) *body* [*handlers*]	Execute body while monitoring for events. If a monitored event is detected, execution of *body* is stopped and a handler (if present) is executed.
acquire (*resources*) *body* [*handlers*]	Acquire the specified resources then execute body. If resources are lost while body is executing, body is interrupted and a handler (if present) is executed.
start *task_name*	Start the specified task.
stop *task_name*	Stop the specified task.
break	Break out from a while/do/until/for body. Also used in switch statements.
continue	Skip to next iteration of while/do/until/for body.
return	Return from function to the caller.
function(*arguments*)	Call a function using the supplied arguments.
variable = *expression*	Evaluate expression and assign to variable.
expression	Evaluate expression.

Operators

Operators are used in expressions. Several of the operators may be used only in evaluating constant expressions, which means that their operands must be either constants or expressions involving nothing but constants. The operators are listed here in order of precedence (highest to lowest).

OPERATOR	DESCRIPTION	ASSOCIATIVITY	RESTRICTION
abs()	absolute value	n/a	none
sign()	sign of operand	n/a	none
++	increment	left	variables only
--	decrement	left	variables only
-	unary minus	right	none
~	bitwise negation	right	none
!	logical negation	right	none
*	multiplication	left	none
/	division	left	none
%	modulo	left	none
+	addition	left	none
-	subtraction	left	none
<<	left shift	left	constant right argument
>>	right shift	left	constant right argument
<	less than	left	none
>	greater than	left	none
<=	less than or equal	left	none
>=	greater than or equal	left	none
==	equal to	left	none
!=	not equal to	left	none
&	bitwise AND	left	none
^	bitwise XOR	left	none
|	bitwise OR	left	none
&&	logical AND	left	none
||	logical OR	left	none
? :	conditional	n/a	none

Keywords

Keywords are those words reserved by the NQC compiler for the language itself. It is an error to use any of these as the names of functions, tasks, or variables.

__event_src	else
__nolist	for
__sensor	if
__taskid	int
__type	monitor
abs	repeat
acquire	return
asm	sign
break	start
case	stop
catch	sub
const	switch
continue	task
default	void
do	while

THE NQC API

The NQC API consists of functions, values, and constants. A *function* is something that can be called as a statement and generally causes some action to be taken. A *value* is something that gets evaluated by the program and can be used in a calculation, a condition, or an argument to a function. A *constant* is a symbolic name of some number that has a special meaning. In the following example, On() is a function, Timer(0) is a value, and OUT_A is a constant.

```
if (Timer(0) > 10)
    On(OUT_A);
```

The NQC API contains many different functions, values, and constants, which are summarized in the following text by category (such as sensors, outputs, etc.). NQC presently understands four different targets: the original RCX, CyberMaster, Scout, and RCX 2.0 (an RCX running the 2.0 firmware). Since some calls are only available on certain targets, the API reference also includes a column specifying which target(s) the API is valid for. The codes are as follows:

■ **R**—RCX (original or 2.0)

■ **C**—CyberMaster

■ **S**—Scout

■ **R2**—RCX 2.0

Sensors

This portion of the API handles the configuration and reading of sensors. Note that in some cases a sensor's value can be read several different ways (i.e., a raw value, boolean value, or processed value).

FUNCTION	DESCRIPTION	TARGETS
SetSensor(*sensor, config*)	set sensor's type and mode	R
SetSensorType(*sensor, type*)	set sensor's type	R
SetSensorMode(*sensor, mode*)	set sensor's mode	R,C
ClearSensor(*sensor*)	clear a sensor's value	all
CalibrateSensor()	calibrate the light sensor	S
SetSensorHysteresis(*x*)	set light sensor hysteresis	S
SetSensorLowerLimit(*x*)	set light sensor lower limit	S
SetSensorUpperLimit(*x*)	set light sensor upper limit	S

VALUE	DESCRIPTION (RANGE)	TARGETS
SensorValue(*n*)	sensor's current value (n = 0–2)	all
SensorType(*n*)	sensor's type (0–2)	all
SensorMode(*n*)	sensor's mode (0–2)	R,C
SensorValueBool(*n*)	sensor's boolean value (n = 0–2)	R
SensorValueRaw(*n*)	sensor's raw value (n = 0–2)	R,S
SENSOR_1, SENSOR_2, SENSOR_3	alternatives for SensorValue(*n*)	all

CONSTANT	DESCRIPTION	TARGETS
SENSOR_MODE_RAW, SENSOR_MODE_BOOL, SENSOR_MODE_EDGE, SENSOR_MODE_PULSE, SENSOR_MODE_PERCENT	modes for SetSensorMode()	R,C
SENSOR_MODE_CELSIUS, SENSOR_MODE_FAHRENHEIT, SENSOR_MODE_ROTATION	modes for SetSensorMode()	R
SENSOR_TYPE_NONE, SENSOR_TYPE_TOUCH, SENSOR_TYPE_TEMPERATURE, SENSOR_YPE_LIGHT, TSENSOR_TYPE_ROTATION	types for SetSensorType()	R
SENSOR_TOUCH, SENSOR_LIGHT, SENSOR_ROTATION, SENSOR_CELSIUS, SENSOR_PULSE, SENSOR_EDGE	configurations for SetSensor()	R

Outputs

This section of the API handles controlling the outputs, which generally are used for motors, but can also be used for lights. In the case of the Scout, there is an additional function to control its built-in light.

FUNCTION	DESCRIPTION	TARGETS
SetOutput(outputs, mode)	set mode of outputs	all
SetDirection(outputs, dir)	set direction of outputs	all
SetPower(outputs, power)	set power level for outputs	all
On(outputs)	turn outputs on	all
Off(outputs)	turn outputs off	all
Float(outputs)	make outputs float	all
Fwd(outputs)	set outputs to forward direction	all
Rev(outputs)	set outputs to reverse direction	all
Toggle(outputs)	flip direction of outputs	all
OnFwd(outputs)	set outputs to forward and turn on	all
OnRev(outputs)	set outputs to reverse and turn on	all
OnFor(outputs, time)	turn on outputs for specified time	all
SetGlobalOutput(outputs, mode)	set global mode for outputs	R2,S
SetGlobalDirection(outputs, dir)	set global direction for outputs	R2,S
SetMaxPower(outputs, power)	set maximum power for outputs	R2,S

VALUE	DESCRIPTION (RANGE)	TARGETS
OutputStatus(n)	current status of output (n = 0–2)	all
GlobalOutputStatus(n)	global status of output (n = 0–2)	R2,S

CONSTANT	DESCRIPTION	TARGETS
OUT_A, OUT_B, OUT_C	outputs	all
OUT_ON, OUT_OFF, OUT_FLOAT	modes for SetOutput()	all
OUT_FWD, OUT_REV, OUT_TOGGLE	directions for SetDirection()	all
OUT_LOW, OUT_HALF, OUT_FULL	values for SetPower()	all

Sound

This section of the API handles the playing of sounds and notes.

FUNCTION	DESCRIPTION	TARGETS
PlaySound(sound)	play a system sound	all
PlayTone(freq, duration)	play a note of given frequency and duration (Scout and RCX2 can use a variable for frequency)	all
MuteSound()	mute all sounds	R2,S
UnmuteSound()	unmute all sounds	R2,S
ClearSound()	clear any buffered sounds	R2
SelectSounds(group)	select a different group of sounds	S

CONSTANT	DESCRIPTION	TARGETS
SOUND_CLICK, SOUND_DOUBLE_BEEP, SOUND_DOWN, SOUND_UP, SOUND_LOW_BEEP, SOUND_FAST_UP	values for PlaySound()	all

Display

This section of the API manages the LCD display—it is only valid for the RCX.

FUNCTION	DESCRIPTION	TARGETS
SelectDisplay(*mode*)	select a display mode	R
SetUserDisplay(*value, precision*)	display any value	R2

CONSTANT	DESCRIPTION	TARGETS
DISPLAY_WATCH	display mode for system clock	R
DISPLAY_SENSOR_1, DISPLAY_SENSOR_2, DISPLAY_SENSOR_3	display modes for sensors	R
DISPLAY_OUT_A, DISPLAY_OUT_B, DISPLAY_OUT_C	display modes for outputs	R
DISPLAY_USER	mode for SelectDisplay()	R2

Communication

There are a variety of communication mechanisms, including simple IR messages, the Visible Light Link (VLL), and general serial communication.

FUNCTION	DESCRIPTION	TARGETS
SendMessage(*message*)	send an IR message	R,S
ClearMessage()	clear the IR receive buffer	R,S
SetTxPower()	set power level for IR	R,S
SendVLL(*value*)	send value using VLL	S
InternalMessage(*message*)	place message in receive buffer	R2
SetSerialPacket(*value*)	set serial packet format	R2
SetSerialComm(*value*)	set serial communication settings	R2
SetSerialData(*n, value*)	set serial tx data (n = 0–15)	R2
SendSerial(*first, count*)	send specified serial data	R2

VALUE	DESCRIPTION (RANGE)	TARGETS
Message()	check IR receive buffer	R,S
SerialPacket()	serial packet format	R2
SerialComm()	serial communication settings	R2
SerialData(*n*)	serial tx data (n = 0–15)	R2

CONSTANT	DESCRIPTION	TARGETS
TX_POWER_LO, TX_POWER_HI	values for SetTxPower()	R,S
SERIAL_PACKET_DEFAULT	raw packets	R2
SERIAL_PACKET_PREAMBLE	use preamble for packets	R2
SERIAL_PACKET_NEGATED	use negated bytes for packets	R2
SERIAL_PACKET_CHECKSUM	use checksum for packets	R2
SERIAL_PACKET_RCX	RCX-style packets	R2
SERIAL_COMM_DEFAULT	normal comm settings	R2
SERIAL_COMM_4800	use 4800 baud communication	R2
SERIAL_COMM_76KHZ	use 76 KHz carrier	R2
SERIAL_COMM_DUTY25	use 25% duty cycle	R2

Timers and Counters

All of the targets contain timers with 100ms resolution. The Scout features three of these timers, while the other targets all have four. With the RCX 2.0, the timers can also be read with a 10ms resolution. The Scout and RCX 2.0 also counters (the Scout has two while the RCX 2.0 has three). In the case of the RCX 2.0, these counters overlap with global storage locations 0, 1, and 2.

FUNCTION	DESCRIPTION	TARGETS
ClearTimer(timer)	clear a timer (timer = 0–3*)	all
SetTimer(timer, value)	set timer to value	R2
IncCounter(counter)	increment counter by 1	R2,S
DecCounter(counter)	decrement counter by 1	R2,S
ClearCounter(counter)	reset counter to 0	R2,S

* Scout has only three timers (0–2).

VALUE	DESCRIPTION (RANGE)	TARGETS
Timer(n)	value of timer in 100ms (n = 0–3*)	all
FastTimer(n)	value of timer in 10ms (n = 0–3*)	R2
Counter(n)	value of counter (n = 0–2*)	R2,S

* Scout has only three timers (0–2) and two counters (0–1).

Access Control

The Scout and RCX 2.0 provide an access control mechanism, which is supported using NQC's `acquire` statement.

FUNCTION	DESCRIPTION	TARGETS
SetPriority(p)	set a task's priority	R2,S

CONSTANT	DESCRIPTION	TARGETS
ACQUIRE_OUT_A, ACQUIRE_OUT_B, ACQUIRE_OUT_C	acquire codes for outputs	R2,S
ACQUIRE_SOUND	acquire code for sound	R2,S
ACQUIRE_USER_1, ACQUIRE_USER_2, ACQUIRE_USER_3, ACQUIRE_USER_4	user-definable acquire codes	R2

Events

The Scout and RCX 2.0 support event monitoring. In the case of the Scout, the event codes are hard wired to certain stimuli (such as a timer or counter), and constants are provided for each event code. The limits at which the timers or counters should trigger an event are set using specific functions.

In the RCX 2.0, each event can be assigned to any event source and type. Parameters for the event, such as limits and hysteresis, may also be set. When configuring an RCX 2.0 event, its number (between 0 and 15) is used. When specifying lists of events (such as for `Event()` or a `monitor` statement), each event number must be converted into an event mask, and the masks may then be added together. The macro `EVENT_MASK()` takes an event number and computes its event mask.

FUNCTION	DESCRIPTION	TARGETS
SetEvent(event, source, type)	configure event for specified source and type	R2
ClearEvent(event)	clear event configuration	R2
ClearAllEvents()	clear configuration of all events	R2
CalibrateEvent (event, low, high, hyst)	calibrate event	R2
Event(events)	post specified events	R2,S
SetLowerLimit(event, limit)	set lower limit for event	R2
SetUpperLimit(event, limit)	set upper limit for event	R2

continued

FUNCTION	DESCRIPTION	TARGETS
SetHysteresis(*event, hyst*)	set hysteresis for event	R2
SetClickTime(*event, time*)	set click time for event	R2
SetClickCounter(*event, count*)	set event click counter	R2
SetTimerLimit(*timer, limit*)	set limit for timer	S
SetCounterLimit(*counter, limit*)	set limit for counter	S
SetSensorClickTime(*time*)	set click time for light sensor	S

VALUE	DESCRIPTION (RANGE)	TARGETS
ActiveEvents(*task*)	events active for given task	R2,S
EventState(*event*)	state of an event	R2
LowerLimit(*event*)	lower limit for event	R2
UpperLimit(*event*)	upper limit for event	R2
Hysteresis(*event*)	hysteresis for event	R2
ClickTime(*event*)	click time for event	R2
ClickCounter(*event*)	number of clicks for event	R2

CONSTANT	DESCRIPTION	TARGETS
EVENT_TYPE_PRESSED, EVENT_TYPE_RELEASED, EVENT_TYPE_PULSE, EVENT_TYPE_EDGE, EVENT_TYPE_FASTCHANGE	event types for boolean sensors	R2
EVENT_TYPE_LOW, EVENT_TYPE_NORMAL, EVENT_TYPE_HIGH, EVENT_TYPE_CLICK, EVENT_TYPE_DOUBLECLICK	event types for R2 any source	
EVENT_TYPE_MESSAGE	event type for messages	R2
EVENT_1_PRESSED, EVENT_1_RELEASED, EVENT_2_PRESSED, EVENT_2_RELEASED	Scout event codes for touch sensors	S
EVENT_LIGHT_HIGH, EVENT_LIGHT_NORMAL, EVENT_LIGHT_LOW, EVENT_LIGHT_CLICK, EVENT_LIGHT_DOUBLECLICK	Scout event codes for the light sensor	S
EVENT_COUNTER_0, EVENT_COUNTER_1	Scout event codes for counters	S
EVENT_TIMER_0, EVENT_TIMER_1, EVENT_TIMER_2	Scout event codes for timers	S
EVENT_MESSAGE	Scout event code for an IR message	S

Miscellaneous

FUNCTION	DESCRIPTION	TARGETS
Wait(*time*)	wait specified time (in 10ms)	all
StopAllTasks()	stop all tasks	all
SetRandomSeed(*seed*)	set seed for random numbers	R2
SetSleepTime(*minute*)	set minutes before auto-sleep	R,C
SleepNow()	go to sleep	R,C

VALUE	DESCRIPTION (RANGE)	TARGETS
Random(*n*)	random number between 0 and n	all

Special Features—RCX

FUNCTION	DESCRIPTION	TARGETS
CreateDatalog(*size*)	create the datalog	R
AddToDatalog(*value*)	add value to the datalog	R
UploadDatalog(*start, count*)	upload datalog values	R
SetWatch(*hours, minutes*)	set the system clock	R
SelectProgram(*program*)	select and run the specified program	R2

VALUE	DESCRIPTION (RANGE)	TARGETS
Program()	current program number	R
Watch()	value of system clock	R
BatteryLevel()	voltage level of battery	R2
FirmwareVersion()	firmware version number	R2

Special Features—Scout

FUNCTION	DESCRIPTION	TARGETS
SetLight(*x*)	turn light on/off	S
SetScoutRules(*m*,*t*,*l*,*tm*,*fx*)	set the Scout's rules	S
SetScoutMode(*mode*)	set the Scout's mode	S
SetEventFeedback(*x*)	set which events result in audible feedback	S

VALUE	DESCRIPTION (RANGE)	TARGETS
ScoutRules(*n*)	current rules settings (n = 0–4)	S
TimerLimit(*n*)	limit for a timer (n = 0–3)	S
CounterLimit(*n*)	limit for a counter (n = 0–1)	S
EventFeedback()	which events have audio feedback	S

CONSTANT	DESCRIPTION	TARGETS
LIGHT_ON, LIGHT_OFF	values for SetLight()	S
SCOUT_MODE_STANDALONE, SCOUT_MODE_POWER	modes for SetScoutMode()	S

Special Features—CyberMaster

FUNCTION	DESCRIPTION	TARGETS
Drive(*motor0, motor1*)	fully control both motors	C
OnWait(*motors, n, time*)	set direction and speed (n) of motors for specified time	C
OnWaitDifferent (*motors, n0, n1, n2, time*)	set direction and speed (n0–n2) of motors for specified time	C
ClearTachoCounter(*motors*)	reset tacho counters for motors	C

VALUE	DESCRIPTION (RANGE)	TARGETS
SENSOR_L, SENSOR_M, SENSOR_R	alternatives for SensorValue(*n*)	C
TachoCount(*n*)	tacho counter for motor (n = 0–1)	C
TachoSpeed(*n*)	speed for motor (n = 0–1)	C
ExternalMotorRunning()	status of external motor	C
AGC()	value of automatic gain control	C

CONSTANT	DESCRIPTION	TARGETS
OUT_L, OUT_R, OUT_X	alternative names of outputs	C

Appendix E
Online Resources

There is a wealth of online resources for LEGO MINDSTORMS. A brief list of a few such web sites is presented below. Since the printed page moves somewhat more slowly than the Internet does, some of the links below may have changed or moved by the time you read this.

Your first stop should be the official web pages for this book:

- www.apress.com—On this site you can find additional information about the topics and robots in this book, including downloads for all of the programs.

GENERAL INFORMATION

- www.legomindstorms.com—The official MINDSTORMS site. On it you will find tips from LEGO's master builders, product announcements, creations from other MINDSTORMS users, and several discussion groups.

- www.lugnet.com—LUGNET is a fixture in the online LEGO community, combining extensive reference material with discussion groups on a variety of LEGO-related topics. The robotics discussion group (and its subgroups) are of particular interest to MINDSTORMS users.

SHOPPING

- **shop.LEGOshop.com**—LEGO Shop At Home is an online store for purchasing sets directly from LEGO. The store carries a full line of MINDSTORMS sets, including accessories such as sensors and motors.

- **www.pitsco-legodacta.com**—Pitsco LEGO Dacta is the distributor of Dacta products within the United States. This company carries the educational MINDSTORMS sets and ROBOLAB software.

- **www.bricklink.com**—Brick Link is an unofficial LEGO marketplace where people can buy and sell LEGO bricks and sets. This can sometimes be an effective way to purchase a few special pieces, although since you are buying from other sellers, price and availability can be somewhat volatile.

PROGRAMMING TOOLS AND ADVANCED TOPICS

- **www.baumfamily.org/nqc**—The home page for Not Quite C (NQC). Check here for updates to NQC, links to NQC-based robots, and other NQC information.

- **members.aol.com/johnbinder/bricxcc.htm**—The home page for BricxCC, an easy-to-use NQC-based development environment for Windows.

- **homepage.mac.com/rbate/MacNQC**—The home page for MacNQC, an easy-to-use NQC-based development environment for Macintosh.

- **www.lego.com/dacta/robolab**—The official site for ROBOLAB, the educational version of MINDSTORMS software.

- **www.crynwr.com/lego-robotics**—A repository for information and links about the internal operation of the RCX, covering alternative development tools, creating custom sensors, and many other advanced topics.

- **brickos.sourceforge.net**—The home page for BrickOS (formerly known as legOS), a replacement operating system for the RCX that allows programming in assembly language, C, or other languages.

- **www.hempeldesigngroup.com/lego/pbFORTH**—The home page for pbFORTH, an implementation of FORTH for the RCX.

- **lejos.sourceforge.net**—The home page for leJOS, a small Java runtime that allows the RCX to be programmed using Java.

Afterword

I hope you have enjoyed building the various robots presented in this book. More important than the robots themselves, however, are the techniques used in their construction and programming. Armed with the knowledge of gear ratios and feedback systems, you are now ready to let your imagination roam and to build some truly unique creations.

The next steps depend entirely on your own preferences. For more advanced programming, you can move from RCX Code to NQC, or even from NQC to alternative firmware such as brickOS. From a mechanical perspective, consider investing in some of the LEGO Technic sets. Besides providing a wealth of new parts, the models themselves usually demonstrate some interesting design techniques. Although the larger sets are rather expensive, some of them are true marvels of LEGO design.

For inspiration, turn to the real world. I got the idea for Vending Machine while using a cash card to buy a candy bar, and Bumpbot was inspired by bumper cars in an amusement park. Even nature can provide ideas—some bugs scurrying around served as the impetus for Bugbot.

Whatever creations you decide to build, never hesitate to experiment and try new ideas. LEGO is remarkably easy to put together and take apart. Take advantage of this by trying out different combinations of pieces or unusual constructions. Staring at a pile of LEGO parts while trying to imagine the optimal design for a robot is usually quite unproductive. Instead, throw something together as quickly as possible, then continue to refine it. All of the robots in this book went through several iterations before I felt they were ready for presentation.

Last of all, remember that MINDSTORMS is a toy. Have fun with it.

Index